The Christmas

Almanac

The Christmas Almanac

Edited by
Natasha Tabori Fried
and Lena Tabori

Designed by
Timothy Shaner
and Christopher Measom

welcome
BOOKS

Published in 2003, 2009 by Welcome Books®
An imprint of Welcome Enterprises, Inc.
6 West 18 Street, New York, NY 10011
(212) 989-3200; Fax (212) 989-3205
www.welcomebooks.com

Publisher: Lena Tabori
Project Director: Natasha Tabori Fried
Designed by: Timothy Shaner and Christopher Measom
Original text by: Monique Peterson, Ellen Leach
Editorial assistants: Lawrence Chesler, Robyn Curtis, Nicholas
    Liu, Gavin O'Connor, Frank Rehor, Marta A. Sparago;
    Recipes by Natasha Tabori Fried and Lena Tabori;
    Caribbean Black Cake recipe by: Lynette Philadelphia;
    Finnish Christmas Coffee Bread recipe by: Aili Bertocci;
    New Zealand Pavlova recipe by: Charlotte Simcock; Italian
    Stufoli recipe by: Frank Rehor

Copyright © 2003 Welcome Enterprises
Revised and updated, 2009

ISBN 978-1-59962-069-5

Pg. 18: "Christmas Trees: A Christmas Circular Letter" from
The Poetry of Robert Frost, edited by Edward Connery
Lathem. © 1916, © 1944 by Robert Frost. © 1969 by Henry Holt
and Company. Reprinted by permission of Henry Holt & Co.,
LLC. *Pg. 28:* The Literary Trustees of Walter de la Mare and
the Society of Authors as their representative. *Pg. 40: Frosty
the Snowman* by Steve Nelson and Jack Rollins © 1950 Hill and
Range Songs, Inc. © Renewed, assigned to Chappell & Co. All
rights reserved. Used by permission. *Pg. 123:* "A Miserable,
Merry Christmas" from *The Autobiography of Lincoln Steffens*,
by Lincoln Steffens © 1931 by Harcourt Inc. and renewed 1959
by Peter Steffens. Reprinted by permission of the publisher.
Pg. 158: Santa Claus Is Coming To Town by J. Fred Coots and
Haven Gillespie © 1934, renewed 1962 by Leo Feist Inc. and
Haven Gillespie Music. Used by permission of The Songwriters
Guild of America. All rights reserved. *Pg. 177:* The Society of
Authors as the Literary Representative of the Estate of John
Masefield. *Pg. 164:* "The Boy Who Laughed at Santa Claus" ©
1942 by Ogden Nash, renewed. Reprinted by permission of
Curtis Brown, Ltd. *Pg. 208:* from "Flight into Egypt" © 1944 &
renewed 1972 by W. H. Auden, from *W. H. Auden: The Collected
Poems* by W. H. Auden. Used by permission of Random House,
Inc. *Pg. 226:* "A Carol for Children" © 1936 by Ogden Nash,
renewed. Reprinted by permission of Curtis Brown, Ltd.

Art Credits: *Pg. 21:* R.F.; *Pg. 23:* Marion Miller; *Pg. 24:*
Lawrence Chesler; *Pg. 26:* Jessie Wilcox Smith; *Pgs. 30, 56, 114,
118, 156, 167, 236:* Ellen H. Clapsaddle; *Pg. 41:* F. Newton
Shepard; *Pgs. 46–47:* I.W.; *Pgs. 49, 63:* Mary C. Low; *Pg. 55:*
Mariam Story Hurford; *Pg. 61:* Melozzo da Forli; *Pg. 64:*
Tenggren; *Pg. 66:* E. Kubem; *Pg. 73:* G. H. Mitchell; *Pgs. 82–83:*
Maxfield Parrish; *Pg. 86:* Pauli Ebner; *Pgs. 93, 95:* Francis
Brundage; *Pg. 98:* Henry Stahlhut; *Pg. 132:* McClelland
Barclay; *Pg. 142:* Ernest Townsend; *Pg. 157:* Rosa C. Petherick;
Pg. 164: H. KaulBach; *Pgs. 174–175:* Torre Bevasro; *Pg. 184:*
Gertrude A. Kay; *Pgs. 188–189:* D.M. Payne; *Pg. 192:* W.
Hagelberg; *Pg. 232:* P. Ebner.

Library of Congress Cataloging-in-Publication Data on file.

Printed in China

FIRST EDITION

10 9 8 7 6 5 4 3 2

Contents

Contents

Contents

Deck the Halls
Trees, Trimming & Tinsel

The Fir Tree

Hans Christian Andersen

ut in the forest stood a pretty little Fir Tree. It had a good place; it could have sunlight, air there was in plenty, and all around grew many larger comrades—pines as well as firs. But the little Fir Tree wished ardently to become greater. It did not care for the warm sun and the fresh air; it took no notice of the peasant children, who went about talking together, when they had come out to look for strawberries and raspberries. Often they came with a whole potful, or had strung berries on a straw; then they would sit down by the little Fir Tree and say, "How pretty and small that one is!" and the Fir Tree did not like to hear that at all.

Next year he had grown a great joint, and the following year he was longer still, for in fir trees one can always tell by the number of rings they have how many years they have been growing.

"Oh, if I were only as great a tree as the others!" sighed the little Fir, "then I would spread my branches far around and look out from my crown into the wide world. The birds would then build nests in my boughs, and when the wind blew I could nod just as grandly as the others yonder."

He took no pleasure in the sunshine, in the birds, and in the red clouds that went sailing over him morning and evening.

When it was winter, the snow lay all around, white and sparkling, a hare would often come jumping along, and spring right over the little Fir Tree. Oh! this made him so angry. But two winters went by, and when the third came the little Tree had grown so tall that the hare was obliged to run around it.

"Oh! to grow, to grow, and become old; that's the only fine thing in the world," thought the Tree.

> The first Christmas tree to be decorated was in Strasbourg, Germany in 1605. Before long, Christmas trees were common throughout Scandinavia, Russia, and Europe.

In the autumn woodcutters always came and felled a few of the largest trees; that was done this year too, and the little Fir Tree, that was now quite well grown, shuddered with fear, for the great stately trees fell to the ground with a crash, and their branches were cut off, so that the trees looked quite naked, long, and slender—they could hardly be recognized. But then they were laid upon wagons, and horses dragged them away out of the wood. Where were they going? What destiny awaited them?

In the spring when the Swallows and the Stork came, the Tree asked them, "Do you know where they were taken? Did you not meet them?"

The Swallows knew nothing about it, but the Stork looked thoughtful, nodded his head, and said:

"Yes, I think so. I met many new ships when I flew out of Egypt; on the ships were stately masts; I fancy these were the trees. They smelled like fir. I can assure you they're stately—very stately."

"Oh that I were only big enough to go over the sea! What kind of thing is this sea, and how does it look?"

"It would take too long to explain all that," said the Stork, and he went away.

"Rejoice in thy youth," said the Sunbeams; "rejoice in thy fresh growth, and in the young life that is within thee."

And the wind kissed the Tree, and the dew wept tears upon it; but the Fir Tree did not understand about that.

When Christmas time approached, quite young trees were felled, sometimes trees which were neither so old nor so large as this Fir Tree, that never rested, but always wanted to go away.

These young trees, which were always the most beautiful, kept all their branches; they were put upon wagons, and the horses dragged them away out of the wood.

"Where are they all going?" asked the Fir Tree. "They are not greater than I—indeed, one of them was much smaller. Why do they keep all their branches? Whither are they taken?"

"We know that! We know that!" chirped the Sparrows. "Yonder in the town we looked in at the windows. We know where they go. Oh! they are dressed up in the greatest pomp and splendor that can be imagined. We have looked in at the windows, and have perceived that they are planted in the middle of a warm room, and adorned with the most beautiful things—gilt apples, honey cakes, playthings, and many hundreds of candles."

"And then?" asked the Fir Tree, and trembled through all its branches. "And then? What happens then?"

"Why, we have not seen anything more. But it is incomparable."

"Perhaps I may be destined to tread this glorious path one day!" cried the Fir Tree, rejoicingly. "That is even better than traveling across the sea. How painfully I long for it! If it were only Christmas now! Now I am great and grown up, like the rest who were led away last year. Oh, if I were only on the carriage! If I were only in the warm room, among all the pomp and splendor! And then? Yes, then something even better will come, something far more charming, or else why should they adorn me so? There must be something grander, something greater still to come; but what? Oh! I'm suffering. I'm longing! I don't know myself what is the matter with me!"

"Rejoice in us," said the Air and Sunshine. "Rejoice in thy fresh youth here in the woodland."

But the Fir Tree did not rejoice at all, but it grew and grew; winter and summer it stood there, green, dark green. The people who saw it said, "That's a handsome tree!" and at Christmas time it was felled before any of the others. The ax cut deep into its marrow, and the tree fell to the ground with a sigh; it felt pain, a sensation of faintness, and could not think at all of happiness, for it was sad at parting from its home, from the place where it had grown up; it knew that it should never again see the dear old companions, the little bushes and flowers all around—perhaps not even the birds. The parting was not at all agreeable.

The Tree only came to itself when it was unloaded in a yard, with other trees, and heard a man say:

"This one is famous; we want only this one!"

Now two servants came in gay liveries, and carried the Fir Tree into a large, beautiful salon. All around the walls hung pictures, and by the great stove stood large Chinese vases with lions on the covers; there were rocking-chairs, silken sofas, great tables covered with picture-books, and toys worth a hundred times a hundred dollars, at least the children said so. And the Fir Tree was put into a great tub filled with sand; but no one could see that it was a tub, for it was hung round with green cloth, and stood on a large, many-colored carpet. Oh, how the Tree trembled! What was to happen now? The servants, and the young ladies also, decked it out. On one branch they hung little nets, cut out of colored paper; every net was filled with sweetmeats; golden apples and walnuts hung down, as if they grew there, and more than a hundred little candles, red, white, and blue, were fastened to the different boughs. Dolls that looked exactly like real people—the Tree had never seen such before—swung among the foliage, and high on the summit of the Tree was fixed a tinsel star. It was splendid, particularly splendid.

"This evening," said all, "this evening it will shine."

"Oh," thought the Tree, "that it were evening already! Oh, that the lights may soon be lit up! When may that be done? Will the sparrows fly against the panes? Shall I grow fast here, and stand adorned in summer and winter?"

> *At Christmas play and make good cheer, for Christmas comes but once a year.*
> —THOMAS TUSSER

Yes, he did not guess badly. But he had a complete backache from mere longing, and backache is just as bad for a tree as a headache for a person.

At last the candles were lighted. What a brilliance, what a splendor! The Tree trembled so in all its branches that one of the candles set fire to a green twig, and it was scorched.

"Heaven preserve us!" cried the young ladies; and they hastily put the fire out.

Now the Tree might not even tremble. Oh, that was terrible! It was so afraid of setting fire to some of its ornaments, and it was quite bewildered with all the brilliance. And now the folding doors were thrown wide open, and a number of children rushed in as if they would have overturned the whole Tree; the older people followed more deliberately. The little ones stood quite silent, but only for a minute; then they shouted till the room rang; they danced gleefully round the Tree, and one present after another was plucked from it.

"What are they about?" thought the Tree. "What's going to be done?"

And the candles burned down to the twigs, and as they burned down they were extinguished, and then the children received permission to plunder the Tree. Oh! they rushed in upon it, so that every branch cracked again: if it had not been fastened by the top and by the golden star to the ceiling, it would have fallen down.

The children danced about with their pretty toys. No one looked at the Tree except one old

A single acre of living Christmas trees generates enough oxygen to meet the daily requirement for eighteen humans. Approximately one million acres of U.S. soil are designated for Christmas tree farms.

man, who came up and peeped among the branches, but only to see if a fig or an apple had not been forgotten.

"A story! A story!" shouted the children; and they drew a little fat man toward the tree; and he sat down just beneath it—"for then we shall be in the green wood," said he, "and the tree may have the advantage of listening to my tale. But I can only tell one. Will you hear the story of Ivede-Avede, or of Klumpey-Dumpey, who fell downstairs, and still was raised up to honor and married the Princess?"

"Ivede-Avede!" cried some, "Klumpey-Dumpey!" cried others, and there was a great crying and shouting. Only the Fir Tree was quite silent, and thought, "Shall I not be in it? Shall I have nothing to do in it?" But he had been in the evening's amusement, and had done what was required of him.

And the fat man told about Klumpey-Dumpey who fell downstairs and yet was raised to honor and married a Princess. And the children clapped their hands and cried, "Tell another! Tell another!" and they wanted to hear about Ivede-Avede; but they only got the story of Klumpey-Dumpey. The Fir Tree stood quite silent and thoughtful; never had the birds in the wood told such a story as that. Klumpey-Dumpey fell downstairs, and yet came to honor and married a Princess!

"Yes, so it happens in the world!" thought the Fir Tree, and believed it must be true, because that was such a nice man who told it.

"Well, who can know? Perhaps I shall fall downstairs, too, and marry a Princess!" And it looked forward with pleasure to being adorned again, the next evening, with candles and toys, gold and fruit. "Tomorrow I shall not tremble," it thought.

"I shall rejoice in all my splendor. Tomorrow I shall hear the story of Klumpey-Dumpey again, and perhaps that of Ivede-Avede, too."

And the Tree stood all night quiet and thoughtful.

In the morning the servants and the chambermaid came in.

"Now my splendor will begin afresh," thought the Tree. But they dragged him out of the room, and upstairs to the garret, and here they put him in a dark corner where no daylight shone.

"What's the meaning of this?" thought the Tree. "What am I to do here? What is to happen?"

And he leaned against the wall, and thought, and thought. And he had time enough, for days and nights went by, and nobody came up; and when at length some one came, it was only to put some great boxes in a corner. Now the Tree stood quite hidden away, and the supposition is that it was quite forgotten.

"Now it's winter outside," thought the Tree. "The earth is hard and covered with snow, and people cannot plant me; therefore I suppose I'm to be sheltered here until Spring comes. How considerate that is! How good people are! If it were only not so dark here, and so terribly solitary!—not even a little hare? That was pretty out there in the wood, when the snow lay thick and the hare sprang past; yes, even when he jumped over me; but then I did not like it. It is terribly lonely up here!"

"Piep! piep!" said a little Mouse, and crept forward, and then came another little one. They smelled at the Fir Tree, and then slipped among the branches.

"It's horribly cold," said the two little Mice, "or else it would be comfortable here. Don't you think so, old Fir Tree?"

"I'm not old at all," said the Fir Tree. "There are many much older than I."

"Where do you come from?" asked the Mice. "And what do you know?" They were dreadfully inquisitive. "Tell us about the most beautiful spot on earth. Have you been there? Have you been in the storeroom, where cheeses lie on the shelves, and hams hang from the ceiling, where one dances on tallow candles, and goes in thin and comes out fat?"

"I don't know that," replied the Tree; "but I know the wood, where the sun shines and the birds sing."

And then it told all about its youth.

And the little Mice had never heard anything of the kind; and they listened and said:

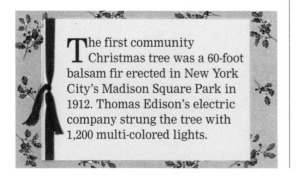

The first community Christmas tree was a 60-foot balsam fir erected in New York City's Madison Square Park in 1912. Thomas Edison's electric company strung the tree with 1,200 multi-colored lights.

"What a number of things you have seen! How happy you must have been!"

"I" replied the Fir Tree; and it thought about what it had told. "Yes, those were really quite happy times." But then he told of the Christmas Eve, when he had been hung with sweetmeats and candles.

"Oh!" said the little Mice, "how happy you have been, you old Fir Tree!"

"I'm not old at all," said the Tree. "I only came out of the wood this winter. I'm only rather backward in my growth."

"What splendid stories you can tell!" said the little Mice.

And the next night they came with four other little Mice, to hear what the Tree had to relate; and the more it said, the more clearly did it remember everything, and thought, "Those were quite merry days! But they may come again. Klumpey-Dumpey fell downstairs, and yet he married a Princess. Perhaps I shall marry a Princess, too!" And the Fir Tree thought of a pretty little Birch Tree that grew out in the forest; for the Fir Tree, that Birch was a real Princess.

"Who's Klumpey-Dumpey?" asked the little Mice.

And then the Fir Tree told the whole story. It could remember every single word; and the little Mice were ready to leap to the very top of the Tree with pleasure. Next night a great many more Mice came, and on Sunday two Rats even appeared; but these thought the story was not pretty, and the little Mice were sorry for that, for now they also did not like it so much as before.

"Do you know only one story?" asked the Rats.

"Only that one," replied the Tree. "I heard that on the happiest evening of my life; I did not think then how happy I was."

"That's a very miserable story. Don't you know any about bacon and tallow candles—a storeroom story?"

"No," said the Tree.

"Then we'd rather not hear you," said the Rats.

And they went back to their own people. The little Mice at last stayed away also; and then the Tree sighed and said:

"It was very nice when they sat round me, the merry little Mice, and listened when I spoke to them. Now that's past too. But I shall remember to be pleased when they take me out."

But when did that happen? Why, it was one morning that people came and rummaged in the garret; the boxes were put away, and the tree brought out; they certainly threw him rather roughly on the floor, but a servant dragged him away at once to the stairs, where the daylight shone.

"Now life is beginning again!" thought the Tree.

It felt the fresh air and the first sunbeam, and now it was out in the courtyard. Everything passed so quickly that the Tree quite forgot to look at itself, there was so much to look at all round. The courtyard was close to a garden, and here everything was blooming; the roses hung fresh over the paling, the linden trees were in blossom, and the swallows cried, "Quinze-wit! quinze-wit! my husband's come!" But it was not the Fir Tree they meant.

"Now I shall live!" said the Tree, rejoicingly, and spread its branches far out; but, alas! they were all withered and yellow; and it lay in the corner among nettles and weeds. The tinsel star was still upon it, and shone in the bright sunshine.

In the courtyard a couple of the merry children were playing who had danced round the tree at Christmas time, and had rejoiced over it. One of the youngest ran up and tore off the golden star.

"Look what is sticking to the ugly old fir tree!" said the child, and he trod upon the branches till they cracked again under his boots.

And the Tree looked at all the blooming flowers and the splendor of the garden, and then looked at itself, and wished it had remained in the dark corner of the garret; it thought of its fresh youth in the wood, of the merry Christmas Eve, and of the little Mice which had listened so pleasantly to the story of Klumpey-Dumpey.

"Past! past!" said the old Tree. "Had I but rejoiced when I could have done so! Past! past!"

And the servant came and chopped the Tree into little pieces; a whole bundle lay there; it blazed brightly under the great brewing copper, and it sighed deeply, and each sigh was like a little shot; and the children who were at play there ran up and seated themselves at the fire, looked into it, and cried "Puff! puff!" But at each explosion, which was a deep sigh, the Tree thought of

a summer day in the woods, or of a winter night there, when the stars beamed; he thought of Christmas Eve and of Klumpey-Dumpey, the only story he had ever heard or knew how to tell; and then the Tree was burned.

The boys played in the garden, and the youngest had on his breast a golden star, which the Tree had worn on its happiest evening. Now that was past, and the Tree's life was past, and the story is past too: past! past!—and that's the way with all stories.

CHRISTMAS TREES:
A CHRISTMAS CIRCULAR LETTER

Robert Frost

The city had withdrawn into itself
And left at last the country to the country;
When between whirls of snow not come to lie
And whirls of foliage not yet laid, there drove
A stranger to our yard, who looked the city,
Yet did in country fashion in that there
He sat and waited till he drew us out,
A-buttoning coats, to ask him who he was.
He proved to be the city come again
To look for something it had left behind
And could not do without and keep its Christmas.
He asked if I would sell my Christmas trees;
My woods—the young fir balsams like a place
Where houses all are churches and have spires.
I hadn't thought of them as Christmas trees.
I doubt if I was tempted for a moment
To sell them off their feet to go in cars
And leave the slope behind the house all bare,
Where the sun shines now no warmer than the moon.
I'd hate to have them know it if I was.
Yet more I'd hate to hold my trees, except
As others hold theirs or refuse for them,
Beyond the time of profitable growth—
The trial by market everything must come to.
I dallied so much with the thought of selling.
Then whether from mistaken courtesy
And fear of seeming short of speech, or whether
From hope of hearing good of what was mine,
I said, "There aren't enough to be worth while."

"I could soon tell how many they would cut,
You let me look them over."

"You could look.

But don't expect I'm going to let you have them."
Pasture they spring in, some in clumps too close
That lop each other of boughs, but not a few
Quite solitary and having equal boughs
All round and round. The latter he nodded "Yes" to,
Or paused to say beneath some lovelier one,
With a buyer's moderation, "That would do."
I thought so too, but wasn't there to say so.
We climbed the pasture on the south, crossed over,
And came down on the north.

He said, "A thousand."

"A thousand Christmas trees!—at what apiece?"

He felt some need of softening that to me:
"A thousand trees would come to thirty dollars."

Then I was certain I had never meant
To let him have them. Never show surprise!
But thirty dollars seemed so small beside
The extent of pasture I should strip, three cents
(For that was all they figured out apiece)—
Three cents so small beside the dollar friends
I should be writing to within the hour
Would pay in cities for good trees like those,
Regular vestry-trees whole Sunday Schools
Could hang enough on to pick off enough.

A thousand Christmas trees I didn't know I had!
Worth three cents more to give away than sell
As may be shown by a simple calculation.
Too bad I couldn't lay one in a letter.
I can't help wishing I could send you one,
In wishing you herewith a Merry Christmas.

The Christmas Tree's History

Before the advent of the Christmas tree as we know it, the evergreen plant had long been a symbol of life and vitality. Celebrations around the fir tree began during pagan winter solstice celebrations in the heart of the Black Forest in Germany. These pre-Christian peoples would decorate the chosen tree as a way to encourage the tree spirits to return to the forest and sprout anew in the spring.

Although the Germans are responsible for introducing the Christmas tree to other parts of the world, they were not the first to decorate evergreens at the end of the year. Ancient Romans decorated boughs of pine, holly, and ivy during Saturnalia, the year-end festival honoring the god of bounty and agriculture. In ancient Egypt, people commonly adorned their homes with green palm branches on the shortest day of the year.

By the fourteenth and fifteenth centuries, miracle plays became popular throughout Europe as ways to depict the events of creation and other Biblical stories. Mummers, as participants were known, decorated pine trees with fruit to symbolize the Tree of Life. After these plays were banned for becoming too secular with singing and dancing, people kept the tradition of decorating trees alive in their homes, stringing wafers on the branches to represent the Eucharist.

The year 1605 marks the first written records of people decorating trees in their homes in the town of Strasbourg. These early German trees were often lit with real candles, a tradition that continued for several hundred years. Then Thomas Edison's electric company manufactured the first electric tree lights, making safer "flames" available. By the 1880s, people could string as many as eighty red, white, and blue glass light bulbs on their Christmas trees.

Legend has it that the lighting of the first Christmas trees on American soil occurred during the Battle of Trenton in 1776. Defeated Hessian mercenaries, paid by the British to fight rebel American colonists, were apparently seen by George Washington's men attaching lighted candles to the branches of a pine tree. Whether or not the story is true, German soldiers were likely the ones who introduced the Christmas tree to the American colonies.

Queen Victoria's husband, Prince Albert, introduced his fatherland custom to the British royal family in 1841, by setting up the first Christmas tree in Windsor Castle. Soon homes all over England copied the tradition, following the lead of the trend-setting Victorians.

At the turn of the twentieth century, Christmas trees had become more common throughout America, especially in places where German immigrants had settled, like Pennsylvania, Wisconsin, and North Carolina. Nowadays, more than one million acres of land in the U.S. are dedicated Christmas tree farms. The multi-billion-dollar industry produces between 25 and 30 million trees each year for Christmas celebrations across the country.

HOW TO CARE FOR A CHRISTMAS TREE

After bringing your new Christmas tree back home, it's important to keep it moisturized. Make a fresh cut at a slight angle about one inch above the base. This will clear any old, clogged wood so that water can be absorbed. For a reservoir, use a large container of fresh tap water. On the first day, the tree might absorb more than a gallon, so check frequently and replace the water as needed.

The Rockefeller Center Christmas Tree

Perhaps one of the most beloved Christmas trees in the United States is the tree erected each year in New York City's Rockefeller Center. The idea for a public tree began in 1931, during the Great Depression. A 20-foot tall balsam was set up at Fifth Avenue and 50th Street, as a way to bring cheer to the city's numerous unemployed and struggling citizens. Two years later officials put up a second tree, and the tradition has been a major part of New York City's Christmas celebrations ever since.

The search for "the tree," as the famous evergreen is known, begins in the spring. Rockefeller Center executives scour the northeast by helicopter, with tips from unsolicited letters and tree spotters. The tree, which can be up to ninety feet tall, is usually chosen by July 4, after which it is fertilized, pruned, and eventually corseted before the media-event cutting in December. A new tree is planted in its place.

It takes two days to put up the scaffolding for decorators, who dress the tree with about 26,000 light bulbs, and give the tree's owners the privilege of flipping the switch.

Did You Know?

The earliest Christmas trees were smaller trees that stood on tables. The concept of the floor-ceiling tree was introduced in forest-rich America in the early 1800s. 🌲 *The National Christmas Tree Association selects the White House tree every year at their convention.* 🌲 Legend has it that Martin Luther created the first Christmas tree on a crisp winter's eve in 1510, when, while on a walk, he glimpsed the stars through the branches of a fir tree. Inspired, he cut it down, brought it inside, and adorned it with the candles representing the light from the night skies. Another legend says the first tree was in Strasbourg, Germany in 1605. 🌲 *Christmas trees take 7–10 years to mature.* 🌲 For every Christmas tree that is cut and sold in America, 2–3 trees are planted in its place. 🌲 *In Sweden and Norway, the Christmas tree is not taken down until January 13. This is called "Twentieth Day," and is the official end to the holiday season.* 🌲 In 1926, President Calvin Coolidge designated a *Sequoia gigantea* in northern California's redwood forest as "The Nation's Christmas Tree." The world's tallest living Christmas tree towers 267.4 feet and measures 107.6 feet around its trunk. 🌲 *The record for the tallest tree ever erected goes to a shopping center near Seattle, Washington. In 1950, bringers of yuletide cheer set up a 212-foot, 25-ton tree in the Northgate parking lot.* 🌲 Every Christmas, Norway presents Great Britain with a huge tree: it's set up in London's Trafalgar Square to commemorate Britain's assistance to King Haakan during World War II, when the king set up a temporary government in London during the Nazi occupation. 🌲 *Every August the National Christmas Tree Association holds a beauty pageant for the country's most ideal tree. The winning tree must have uniform branches, a straight trunk, and a 66 percent taper so that the width of the bottommost branches equals two-thirds of its total height. Of course, the winner must also have a single branch at the top for a star.*

Selecting the Perfect Tree

Order a New England Christmas

Mail-order king **L. L. Bean** ships balsam Christmas trees hand-selected and cut from Maine's fresh, cold, snowy climes. Floor-size "models" range from 5 to 6 feet, while tabletop trees reach diameters of 18 to 20 inches. The small-size trees arrive pre-decorated, in a patented frame with a foam center for easy watering. L. L. Bean also carries a reasonably priced set of four balsam window wreaths, as well as more elaborately decorated designs with over-the-door hangers. No room for a tree in your small apartment or dorm room? Try one of their lovely centerpieces. Mmmmm, balsam: *llbean.com* or (800) 221-4221.

Painless Tree Shopping

Whether your family tradition requires cutting your own or ordering on-line, you can rely on the **National Christmas Tree Association's** easy-to-use website to find a natural tree. Select the species desired (over 50 available) and location (USA, Canada, Mexico, Germany, Denmark), and plug in your zip code. Click on the Mail Order link for a lengthy list of tree farm websites that sell over the Internet. Click on Mail Order Wreaths to find plenty of farms that offer decorations—in old favorites like balsam, spruce, Douglas fir, and Scotch pine, as well as some varieties you've never heard of. Some sites allow wholesale ordering and include instructions on how to run a fundraiser at your local school or church: *christmastree.org/search.cfm*.

Trees and wreaths are available by mail order at **Daniken Tree Farm's** photo-enhanced website. Located in Greenville, Illinois, the farm was founded in 1968. Price lists for trees, wreaths, and wreath decorations are included. Shop the site for Scotch and white pine, Canaan and Fraser firs, or blue spruce: *danikentree-farm.com* or (618) 664-4067.

Barefoot Mountain Farms in Laurel Springs, North Carolina, specializes in Fraser fir trees and wreaths, both available by mail order. Browse the site to pick up pine roping, tree stands, and T-shirts: *barefootmountain.com*.

Not Looking Forward to the Annual Tree-buying Expedition?

If the thought of getting in the car one more time and hauling home a natural tree makes you weary, consider making a one-time investment in a handcrafted artificial tree made by the **Holiday Tree and Trim Company**. The branches are permanently bound to the specially wrapped trunk for a lifelike look, yet fold up for easy storage. They even have pine cones! Dozens of varieties are available at their exclusive worldwide distributor, **Christmas Depot**, including Alaskan white pine, golden pine, spruce, and fiber optic models. The Depot, which claims to be "the largest Christmas

The Business of Christmas Trees

- The top Christmas tree producing states are: Oregon, North Carolina, Michigan, Pennsylvania, Winsconsin, and Washington. Christmas trees are grown, however, in all 50 states.
- The Christmas tree industry employs 100,000 people.
- Approximately 30 million trees are harvested in an average year.
- 80 percent of all artificial Christmas trees are made in China.

superstore on the Net," also carries wreaths, poinsettias, lights, ornaments, and holiday records. Weatherproof, traditional-looking wreaths come plain, decorated, and even illuminated: *ChristmasDepot.com* or (877) 353-5263.

It's a Plan, on a Budget!

No one develops a complete decorating scheme more skillfully—or at more affordable prices—than **Kmart**. For those of us who want a simple, one-stop Christmas shopping tour, this store has managed to edit out the elaborate and the ridiculous. Find a no-nonsense and fun collection that has everything from tree skirts and stockings to wreaths of holly leaves or pine cones at Martha Stewart Holiday. Kmart also has inexpensive artificial trees (including Alaskan and Manchester pines), trim kits, stands for as little as $5, accessories, and lights from $3. To keep things straight, the website has both indoor and outdoor departments. Visit the Holiday Shop, or type "Christmas" into the search feature: *kmart.com*.

Small, Medium, and Really, Really LARGE

From 9 to 30 feet tall, **Treeforest.com** has artificial "gigantic" and "gigantic super trees"! Order from your desktop, and while you're at it, view Treeforest's huge selection of Christmas lighting. Each artificial tree you buy saves seven real trees: *treeforest.com/trees.asp* or call (866) 462-7337.

Save On Crafts has a variety of artificial trees and wreaths, including a 5-foot Alpine tree that comes pre-lit with 150 lights. Their "natural trunk" artificial Alpine trees, 2 to 5 feet tall and available singly or in groupings, are adorable, as are the 3-inch-high mini pines. Save on Crafts also sells very reasonably priced string-to-string lights, candle lamps, and floral supplies, as well as ornaments: *save-on-crafts.com*.

The National Christmas Tree

In 1856, New Hampshire native Franklin Pierce became the first president to set up a Christmas tree in the White House. Later presidents followed suit, and in 1895, Grover Cleveland upped the ante when he used the first string of electric lights to adorn the White House tree. In 1902, ardent conservationist Teddy Roosevelt needed extra persuasion to allow his children to decorate a tree. Were it not for the founder of the Yale School of Forestry, who convinced the president that thinning the tree population would benefit growth, there would have been no White House Christmas tree that year.

It wasn't until Calvin Coolidge's presidency that the first national public Christmas tree adorned the White House's south lawn. On Christmas Eve, 1923, the president lit 3,000 electric lights on the 60-foot fir tree harvested from Vermont's Green Mountains, kicking off this first annual event. Like Roosevelt, Coolidge had reservations about cutting down healthy trees for merely symbolic reasons. So, the following year, he commissioned the American Forestry Association to plant "The National Living Christmas Tree" in Sherman Square near the White House. The tree has been lit every year by the nation's top executive ever since.

Christmas Tree Botany

More than 20 tree species are grown specifically for Christmas tree crops in the United States. Evergreens can take ten years or more to grow tall enough for cultivation. Although prices vary from tree to tree, many vendors charge by height as opposed to species. Here's a sampling of what you can expect to find at the Christmas tree lot ready for decorating:

BALSAM FIR The 3/4" to 1 1/2" long dark green needles on this tree have a silvery cast. The attractive long-lasting needles are flat with blunt edges. Balsams thrive in cold climates and are readily found in Canada and the Northeastern United States.

COLORADO BLUE SPRUCE The natural symmetry of this tree, with its silvery bluish-gray needles, makes it an increasingly popular Christmas and ornamental tree. Found commonly in the higher elevations from Wyoming to Arizona, it has stiff branches that are ideal for holding heavy decorations. It has the best needle retention among spruces.

DOUGLAS FIR Not part of the true fir species, the Douglas Fir has 1" to 1½" long needles that grow in all directions from the branch. The fragrance is especially sweet when the needles are crushed. Common in the Sierra Nevadas, this species has been the number one

Christmas tree in the Pacific Northwest since the 1920s.

EASTERN RED CEDAR The conical shape and abundant supply of these trees has made them popular in the South. Their shiny, sticky, blue-green needles grow 1/8" to 1/2" long and maintain good retention.

EASTERN WHITE PINE The largest pine in the U.S., found from Michigan to Maine, sports blue-green, slender needles up to 5" long. Although less fragrant than other Christmas trees, this densely branched tree has excellent needle retention.

FRASER FIR Sometimes called the "Southern balsam," this tree's flattened needles grow up to 1" long on upward-turning branches. The rich scent, dark blue-green shade, and excellent needle retention make Frasers among the most popular Christmas trees in the country.

NOBLE FIR The long, bluish-green needles and stiff branches of the Noble fir are especially good for making wreaths and garlands. The 1" needles have mostly rounded tips and are often arranged spirally on the branches.

SCOTCH PINE This species has excellent dark green foliage, 1" to 3" long needles, and stiff branches for hanging all shapes and sizes of ornaments. Its hardiness and adaptability have made it the single most popular choice for Christmas trees across the country.

Storing Christmas Keepsakes

Try the **Container Store's** easy-to-use Artificial Tree Bag for your artificial Christmas tree. Store it with or without lights. Their Archival Ornament Storage Boxes are an ideal way to store breakables. Each box can hold 28 ornaments and has adjustable interior dividers for easy customization: *containerstore.com* ❄ **Santa's Drawers** features chest-of-drawers-style cartons, as well as boxes with removable panel organizers that keep hundreds of light strings tangle free: *ornamentbox.com.* ❄ Everyone knows that **Organize.com** is the expert in super-attractive and innovative storage units of all kinds: *organize.com* or (800) 600–9817. ❄ **Ultimate Christmas Storage** specializes in acid-free ornament, figurine, and archival supplies: *ultimatechristmas.com/cgi-bin/CATstore.pl.* ❄ The **Ornament Safe** can store up to 75 ornaments on three hangers within one attractive case: *ornamentsafe.com.*

Recycling Your Christmas Tree

Many communities have programs that will recycle your Christmas tree. Most commonly, they are turned into mulch for use in city parks and recreation areas. Ocean communities use the mulch to stabilize sand dunes. Still other communities bind trees together and sink them in reservoirs to create habitats for fish. Gardeners can recycle their own trees as well by cutting off the branches and using them to protect perennial beds in the winter. For information about recycling your tree, call your local sanitation or environmental department, or log on to *earth911.com* and enter "Christmas Tree" and your zip code in the green bar at the top of the page.

A Christmas Tree

Charles Dickens

I have been looking on, this evening, at a merry company of children assembled round that pretty German toy, a Christmas tree. The tree was planted in the middle of a great round table, and towered high above their heads. It was brilliantly lighted by a multitude of little tapers and everywhere sparkled and glittered with bright objects. There were rosy-cheeked dolls, hiding behind the green leaves; there were real watches (with movable hands, at least, and an endless capacity of being wound up) dangling from innumerable twigs; there were jolly, broad-faced little men, much more agreeable in appearance than many real men—and no wonder, for their heads came off, and showed them to be full of sugarplums; there were fiddles and drums; there were tambourines, books, workboxes, paint boxes, sweetmeat boxes, peep-show boxes, and all kinds of boxes; there were trinkets for the elder girls, far brighter than any grown-up gold and jewels . . . in short, as a pretty child, before me delightedly whispered to another pretty child, "There was everything and more."

Being now at home again, and alone, the only person in the house awake, my thoughts are drawn back, by a fascination which I do not care to resist, to my own childhood. I begin to consider, what do we all remember best upon the branches of the Christmas tree of our own young Christmas days, by which we climbed to real life?

Straight, in the middle of the room, cramped in the freedom of its growth by now encircling walls or soon-reached ceiling, a shadowy tree arises; and, looking up into the dreamy brightness of its top—for I observe in this tree the singular property that it appears to grow downward toward the earth—I look into my youngest Christmas recollection. . . .

I see a wonderful row of little lights rise smoothly out of the ground, before a vast green curtain. Now a bell rings—a magic bell, which still sounds in my ears unlike all other bells—and music plays, amid a buzz of voices, and a fragrant smell of orange peel. Anon, the magic bell commands the music to cease, and the great green curtain rolls itself up majestically, and The Play begins. . . . Out of this delight springs the toy theater—there it is, with its familiar proscenium, and ladies in feathers, in the boxes!—and all its attendant occupation with paste and glue, and gum, and water colors, in the getting up of the Miller and His Man. . . .

Among the later toys and fancies hanging there—as idle often and less pure—be the images once associated with the sweet old Waits, the softened music in the night, ever unalterable! Encircled by the social thoughts of Christmastime, still let the benignant figure of my childhood stand unchanged! In every cheerful image and suggestion that the season brings, may the bright star that rested above the poor roof be the star of all the Christian world! A moment's pause, O vanishing tree, of which the lower branches are dark to me as yet, and let me look once more! I know there are blank spaces on thy branches, where eyes that I have loved have looked and smiled; from which they are departed. If age be hiding for me in the unseen portion of thy downward growth, O may I, with a gray head, turn a child's heart to that figure yet, and a child's trustfulness and confidence!

Now, the tree is decorated with bright merriment, and song, and dance, and cheerfulness. And they are welcome be they ever held, beneath the branches of the Christmas tree, which cast no gloomy shadow.

MISTLETOE

Walter de la Mare

Sitting under the mistletoe
(Pale-green, fairy mistletoe),
One last candle burning low,
All the sleepy dancers gone,
Just one candle burning on,
Shadows lurking everywhere:
Some one came, and kissed me there.

Tired I was; my head would go
Nodding under the mistletoe
(Pale-green, fairy mistletoe),
No footsteps came, no voice, but only,
Just as I sat there, sleepy, lonely,
Stooped in the still and shadowy air
Lips unseen—and kissed me there.

Let the bright red berries glow,
Everywhere in goodly show.
—GERMAN CAROL

Christmas Plants & Flowers

The sights and smells of evergreen plants around the hearth at Christmastime are seasonal reminders of all things everlasting, of new life at the darkest time of year, of colors that are unmistakable symbols of this festive holiday. Here's a sampling of some of the best-loved Christmas bloomers:

AMARYLLIS   This perennial South American bulb generally produces two to four trumpet-like flowers each winter. The vibrant red blossoms can be up to six inches across and bloom for several weeks. Red is most commonly seen at Christmas, although hybrids come in pink, white, and other various colors.

CHRISTMAS CACTUS   This flowering succulent hangs from trees in the rainforests of Brazil. It has segmented stems that drape downward resembling crab legs. As days get shorter, toward the winter equinox, pink, white, or fuchsia buds appear—just in time for Christmas.

CHRISTMAS PEPPER   The chili peppers on this plant are shaped like Christmas bulbs and are just as colorful. Berries begin to appear in the fall and start out green. Over the course of the next few months they change colors from creamy white to yellow to purple, and finally, to orange and red by Christmastime.

HOLLY   Ancient Druids considered this plant sacred, and brought branches indoors during the winter to give shelter to the spirits they believed inhabited the magical plant. Ancient Romans, too, decorated their homes with the evergreen during Saturnalia. For Christians, the holly berries have come to symbolize the blood of Christ, the spiked leaves the crown of thorns, and the white flowers, purity.

IVY Called the "Christ-thorn" in Denmark, ivy has long been a symbol of Christmas and winter solstice celebrations. Its clinging abilities make it a natural metaphor for ever-lasting love and fidelity. Because it bears fruit in the winter, along with holly and evergreen, ivy was an integral part of the ancient Roman festival of Saturnalia that took place at the end of the year.

MISTLETOE In the Victorian language of flowers, this greenery means "give me a kiss." Each time a gentleman kissed a lady under the mistletoe, he would have to pick a berry. Once the berries had been all plucked, there would be no more kisses to give out and everyone involved would prosper. The tradition took root across the Atlantic as well. By the 1870s and 1880s, steamboat loads of mistletoe arrived in New York harbor at Christmastime from England and France.

POINSETTIAS The brilliant deciduous-leaved shrub is called the "Flower of the Holy Night" in Mexico. According to legend, a poor boy had no gift to leave on the altar for Jesus on Christmas Eve. He stayed outside the church and prayed by the window. There, where he had knelt, arose a poinsettia with its flaming red star shaped flower.

SPICE BERRY Also called Coral Berry and Ardisia, this festive bush has dark green, shiny leaves on top and clusters of berries that start out green, then turn a bright red. The fruit lasts until the plant's next flowering, allowing the Christmas colors to remain vibrant for sev-eral months before the next wave of tiny, star-shaped flowers blossom.

We bring in the holly, the ivy, the pine,
The spruce and the hemlock together we twine;
With evergreen branches our walls we array
For the keeping of Christmas, our high holiday.
—ENGLISH CAROL

Did You Know?

Mango and banana trees are Christmas sym-bols in India, where Christians often deco-rate their houses with mango leaves for the holidays. In some regions, small oil-burning lamps made of clay line the edges of flat roofs and the tops of walls.

The first patents for Christmas tree stands in America were issued in 1876, but it wasn't until 1899 that the stands could hold water.

During the Middle Ages, the Christian church forbade the hanging of mistletoe as a pagan tradition. Instead they pro-posed using holly, explain-ing that the red berries symbolize drops of Christ's blood, and the jagged leaves stand for his crown of thorns.

The poinsettia was named for the first U.S. ambassador to Mexico, botanist Joel Roberts Poinsett, who introduced it into the United States in 1829.

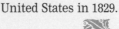

The first electric Christmas tree lights were sold by General Electric in 1903.

According to early English tradition, a woman who stands under the mistletoe and is not kissed, will not be married during the coming year.

Buying Flowers

In addition to their usual selection of every kind of floral arrangement imaginable, **1-800-flowers** offers a romantic winter floral arrangement of red roses, wax flowers, and ruscus in a lovely red glass mosaic vase. Their website: *1800flowers.com.*

Need same-day delivery? **Flowers Across America** puts you in touch with preferred local florists providing rush service. Search by occasion and click on Christmas: *flowersacrossamerica.com.*

6Florist.com offers Christmas flowers on-line, advertising that their Christmas flowers have been delivered "throughout the world, from Singapore to Sao Paulo, Los Angeles to London, New York to New Brunswick, Miami to Melbourne:" *6florist.com.*

The World Flowers handles national and international shipping of elegant bouquets as well as other holiday gifts that vary by country: *theworldflowers.com* or (954) 414-0703.

Lovers of the exotic will appreciate **SendOrchids.com**'s beautiful purple *phalaenopsis* orchid in a pot at Christmas. Other tropical arrangements include anthuriums and ginger from **SendFlowers.com**; and remember, African violets are traditional Christmas plants, too. And the extraordinary arrangements at **City Blossoms** in New York have to be seen to be believed: *cityblossoms.com.*

Florist Express guarantees same-day delivery, or set up a date in advance. Choose from their attractive collection of bouquets with a cuddly stuffed animal for that special someone, or send one of their potted beauties like the Exotic Bromeliad or the Potted Cyclamen. They even have various gift baskets: *floristexpress.net* or 888-444-1922.

The photo gallery at **David Beahme Designs** is a treat for the senses. Featured in such publications as *Town and Country, InStyle,* and *Modern Bride*, this upscale New York floral studio draws upon experience in theater, event design, and television. Buy a simple arrangement or go over the top: *dbdny.com.*

Ingela's Floral Design, event specialists in the San Francisco area, makes centerpieces and bouquets that are works of fine art: *ingelasdesign.com*. And the Dallas region's **Cebolla** florists carries a number of tasteful winter arrangements, ranging in size from "Petite" to "Grand" (this *is* Texas), each one made fresh: *cebollafineflowers.com*

When selecting a plant yourself, make sure it is clean, free of parasites, and at the start of its blooming season when you buy it (otherwise, the blooms will be over by Christmas). Shop early and care for it yourself for a few days to make sure it is healthy before giving it as a gift. Do not transport the plant in cold temperatures without first sealing it inside double garbage bags, with plenty of warm air trapped inside as insulation. Freezing air is a shock to delicate plants.

The Holly and the Ivy

1.

The hol - ly and _ the i - vy, Now both _ are full _ well grown, _ Of all the trees that are in the wood, The hol - ly bears the crown. _ O the ris - ing of the sun, The run - ning of _ the deer, _ The play - ing of the mer - ry or - gan, Sweet sing - ing in _ the choir, _ Sweet sing - ing in the choir. _

2. The holly bears a blossom
   As white as lily flow'r,
   And Mary bore sweet Jesus Christ,
   To be our sweet Saviour:

   Chorus

3. The holly bears a berry
   As red as any blood,
   And Mary bore sweet Jesus Christ,
   To do poor sinners good:

   Chorus

4. The holly bears a prickle,
   As sharp as any thorn,
   And Mary bore sweet Jesus Christ
   On Christmas day in the morn:

A Trimmer's Primer

Glass and Ceramic Ornaments

Lighted **Department 56** ceramic houses to tuck under the tree are much in demand, as are **Christopher Radko**'s brilliant glass ornaments and **Old World** styles imported from Germany and Poland. Order complete collections at **Bronner's**: *bronners.com*, the **Christmas Loft**: *ChristmasLoft.com*, and many other Web locations.

A brilliant and unique selection of glass ornaments—appealing to lighthouse enthusiasts or anyone who loves the ocean—is available at **Lighthouse Depot**: *lighthousedepot.com*. Handcrafted in the Polish tradition, these are sure to become collector's items. A few other collectible lines to look for are Snowbabies, Seraphim, and Fontanini Nativities: *christmases-past.com, bronners.com,* and *ChristmasLoft.com,* **David Frykman**: *davidfrykmanoriginals.com,* and **Williamsburg Marketplace**: *williamsburgmarketplace.com,* a treasure trove of keepsakes.

Pottery Barn carries clear, etched hanging globes, and wreaths and garland made of tiny glass beads. While you're there, check out the tree skirts and stockings, beaded-ball string lights, stocking holders and other holiday accessories: *potterybarn.com*.

"Make ornaments that look like blown glass using acrylic paints!" advertises **Save On Crafts** of their boxed sets of clear glass orna-

> *In German fairytales, snow is said to be feathers shaken from the Queen of Winter's mattress.*

> *Among the other boughs gilded apples and walnuts were suspended, looking as though they had grown there.*
> —HANS CHRISTIAN ANDERSEN

ment balls. Purists might leave them plain, to magnify the surrounding light. Either way, these glass balls are an incredible bargain, at about $6 per dozen and (50 percent off after Christmas). Iridescent balls also are available: *save-on-crafts.com*. Speaking of old-fashioned Victorian silver "reflector balls"— the ones with red and green finials and knobs — *old-world-christmas.com* has the best on the Web.

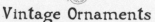

Vintage Ornaments

Gifts Galore has a limited supply of "made in occupied Japan" Shiny Brite collectible glass Christmas tree ornaments that were made between 1945 and 1952 and never reached the public. Each original package contains a dozen ornaments. Click on Collectibles: *giftsgalore.com*. For more vintage ornaments, visit **AR's Scavenger Hunt** and type Christmas Ornament into their search feature. Up pops a list with photos: Look for English trumpets, carousel animals, and various other brilliant hand-painted glass designs: *arsh.com*. Collecting Christmas ornaments is so popular that there are clubs and publications just for that purpose. Searching for **Hallmark** collectibles connections? Log on at *yulelog.com/yulelinks.htm*.

Origami on a Shoestring

For low-cost, eye-popping paper animal sculptures that make spectacular ornaments at Christmastime, order from **All Things Origami**. For a few dollars, you can turn an evergreen bough into a home for your favorite brightly colored critter, and—*presto!*—you have

a centerpiece. The site also sells true origami models (folding time: 10 minutes to $2\frac{1}{2}$ hours) of butterflies, grasshoppers, antelope, frogs, turtles, peacocks, swans, and countless other extraordinary-looking creatures. Teens who've outgrown their stuffed animals (and some of us never do) can spend hours at this site. Consult the photo gallery and diagrams for help and links to other origami sites: *all-things-origami.com.*

Elegantly Unbreakable

Do you have a two-year-old, or a kitten who loves to climb? Cover the tree with **Save On Crafts'** bright silk poinsettia blooms for a spectacular statement. This site is a treasure: *save-on-crafts.com.* The **National Wildlife Federation** will plant a tree when you purchase a pewter wreath tree ornament; this increases wildlife habitat, preventing soil erosion and cleaning the air: *nwf.org/shopping.* **Pottery Barn's** metal ornaments are monogrammable, while **The Wood Wagon's** German ornaments' beautifully detailed designs (tops, angels, trees, Santas, and a myriad of others) range from

$4.50 to $35.00: *thewoodenwagon.com.* **Bronner's** in Michigan claims to be the largest Christmas store in the world, with over 50,000 items for both commercial and home use. Bronner's many affordable, personalized ornaments crafted of wood, ceramic, or clay dough, make perfect family keepsakes: *bronners.com/personalizedornaments.html.* Not to be outdone by anyone, the **Christmas Loft** has a plethora of good-looking nonbreakable ornaments, among them the "Baby's 1st Christmas" series and boxed sets of durable Itty Bitty plastic crystals, Itty Bitty resin figures that look like iced cookies, and the 12 Days of Christmas: *ChristmasLoft.com.* And **Hallmark's** keepsake ornaments are hot! Buy at numerous website vendors, or become a member at the official site: *hallmark.com.*

Good Enough to Eat?

Check out **Seasonal Reflections'** candy cane ornament in all its variations: plain or in bundles, candy cane icicles, peppermint candies, ribbon candy, and more: *seasonalreflections.com*

According to German folklore, the first tinsel was magically transformed from spider webs.

The snow turned all to pearl, the dark trees strung with pearls, the sky beginning to flow with such a radiance as never was on land or sea. And the stillness everywhere...
—GLADYS HASTY CARROLL

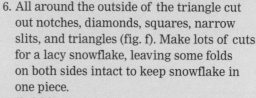

Paper Snowflakes

No two snowflakes are alike! Decorate a tree or window with your own unique paper creation.

Plain white paper, scissors, waxed paper, iron

1. Cut paper into a square with sides no smaller than 5".
2. Fold a square in half diagonally to form a triangle (fig. a).
3. Fold the triangle in half (fig. b).
4. Fold the triangle into thirds (fig. c), one side toward the front, the other to the back (fig. d).
5. Trim the extra paper off the bottom of the triangle (fig. e).

6. All around the outside of the triangle cut out notches, diamonds, squares, narrow slits, and triangles (fig. f). Make lots of cuts for a lacy snowflake, leaving some folds on both sides intact to keep snowflake in one piece.
7. Unfold your triangle to reveal a six-sided snowflake!
8. Sandwich your snowflake between a piece of paper and a piece of waxed paper. Lay another sheet of paper on top of the waxed paper, and iron on low heat to melt the wax onto your snowflake and make it stiff.
9. Peel off the waxed paper right away, while it is still warm.

Try making snowflakes out of tissue paper, silver foil wrapping paper, doilies, waxed paper, or construction paper.

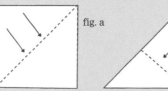

fig. a   fig. b

fig. c   fig. d   fig. e   fig. f

HOLLY SONG
William Shakespeare

Blow blow thou winter winde,
Thou art not so unkinde,
    As man's ingratitude
Thy tooth is not so keene,
Because thou art not seene,
    Although thy breath be rude.
Heigh ho, sing heigh ho, unto
    the greene holly.
Most friendship, is fayning; most
    Loving, meere folly;
Then heigh ho, the holly.
This Life is most jolly.

Freize, freize, thou bitter skie
Thou dost not bight so nigh
    As benefitts forgot;
Though thou the waters warpe,
Thy sting is not so sharpe,
    As friend remembered not,
Heigh ho, sing heigh ho, unto
    the greene holly,
Most friendship, is faying; most
    Loving, meere folly;
Then heigh ho, the holly,
This Life is most jolly.

Safe and Secure

Looking for electric candoliers? These candle lamps add class to your windows or mantel. **The Christmas Loft** has a lovely model with a snowman couple cozied up to the candle. Their regular solid brass candle lamp sells for six dollars and has an on-off sensor: *ChristmasLoft.com*. **Save On Crafts** sells battery-operated candle lamps at an ultra-discounted price: *save-on-crafts.com*

Christmas by Candlelight

With scents like Pumpkin Pie, Candy Cane, Mulled Wine, Cinnamon, Gingerbread, and dozens of others to choose from, how can you go wrong? **Illuminations** sends out seasonal catalogs, each one comprising an assortment of pillars, jars, goblets, home accents and other delights—or choose exactly what you want anytime from their online catalog. Illuminations offers special shapes such as stars, sleighs, and trees on their holiday products page: *illuminations.com*.

For those of us who adore the scent of vanilla, there's a heavenly place on the Web, called **Vanilla Candles.** Buy votives, tealights, and pillars in plain vanilla, French vanilla, antique lace, and others: *vanilla-candles.net*.

The Wax Wizard specializes in personalized, carved, handmade candles. All sizes and types are available: tapers, tea lights, floating poinsettias, and "faux food" candles, as well as pine cones, snowflakes, mistletoe, angels, and the like in a variety of scents and colors, including metallics. The Wizard can incorporate a favorite poem or Bible verse into your design, even adding silk fabrics. The sheen of the wax they use gives the candles a blown-glass quality. With eight pages of Christmas candles, the online catalog is sure to have something you like. Check out the hand-carved angels, the metallic ornament ball candles, and the candy cane pillars: *waxwizard.net/intro.html*.

There's nothing like a Scandinavian Christmas: advent candles, angel chimes—these essential holiday accessories and more are available at **Gundy of Scandinavia**. The Julelys angel chime candles also fit in green Christmas tree candleholders: *gundyofscandinavia.com*.

Deck The Halls

1.

Deck the halls with boughs of hol - ly, Fa la la la la la la la la.

'Tis the sea - son to be jol - ly, Fa la la la la la la la la.

Don we now our gay ap - par - el, Fa la la la la la la la la.

Troll the an - cient Yule-tide car - ol, Fa la la la la la la la la.

Angel Ornaments

This tiny, shimmering angel is covered in a whirl of sequins and can stand on her own or balance on the branches of a Christmas tree. Here's how to make her:

Half-circle of felt with a 3" radius, fabric glue, 2 metallic pipe cleaners, 1/2 yard of sequin trim, 25mm bead

1. Overlap the corners of the felt about 1½" to form a cone with a tiny opening at the point. Glue the corners together.
2. Bend a pipe cleaner and stick both ends into the bead's hole, leaving a loop on top for the angel's halo. Slide the ends down through the opening at the point of the cone, so that the bead rests on the point. Twist the ends underneath the felt to secure the bead.
3. Glue sequin trim to the bottom hem of the cone and spiral it around the cone all the way up to the point.
4. Bend the second pipe cleaner into two wings and glue them to the back of the angel, just below the bead head.

Light Shopping

Whether your entry in the block's decorating extravaganza is sublime, traditional, or downright ridiculous, you can't win the contest without an army of lights. • You can bend **Hammacher Schlemmer's** 9-foot indoor-outdoor lighted ribbon into whatever form you desire. Also available, an indoor-style ribbon with radiant white lights for the banister: *hammacher.com* or (800) 321-1484. • **Christmas Lights Etc** carries Net Lights—strings of bulbs with a twist: They are nets that spread out to fit any shape tree. *Christmaslightsetc.com* or (866) 962-7382 • Find traditional novelty figurine lights plus elegant strings of rice-paper shapes lit from within, at **PartyLights.com**. • **Treeforest.com** has an incredible array of holiday decorations at rock-bottom prices, from old-fashioned to trendy. "Lights in motion," candy canes, snowflakes and icicles, super brights, flexible ropes, garlands, and animated 3-D outdoor light sculptures and inflatables are just the beginning!

Cranberry & Popcorn Strings

This is a great activity for a cold winter's night, or to keep the kids busy at a Christmas party. The strings should be assembled shortly before you are ready to use them and must be disposed of after the holiday season.

Several bags of fresh cranberries, rinsed and dried, 10–12 cups of popcorn, large sewing needle, strong thread

1. Pop a bucket of popcorn according to directions. Do not add salt or butter! After making the popcorn, let it sit for a few hours until it becomes hard. This will make it easier to thread through later.
2. Start with a large piece of popcorn by passing the needle through it and tying a knot at one end of the thread.
3. You can alternate evenly between cranberries and popcorn for the length of the string, make your own pattern, or string some strands of entirely cranberries or entirely popcorn. Tie off the other end when you are done.
4. Hang your cranberry and popcorn strings on the Christmas tree or around the house for a festive decoration.

Orange Clove Balls

There is nothing that smells more like Christmas than an Orange Clove ball, hung in a window, doorway, in a bathroom before a party, or even on your tree. And making them couldn't be easier. If you make them over Thanksgiving, they'll be ready at least two weeks before Christmas!

Box of cloves, oranges, ribbon

1. Take a fresh orange and stick the fruit with cloves. You can cover the entire orange with them—leaving about $1/4 - 1/2$" between each clove—or you can make your own designs: stripes, polka dots or patterns.
2. When you are done, leave the orange in a bowl in a dry place to dry out in the open air. Then refrigerate it.
3. After a few weeks, the orange will start to shrivel up. When this happens, tie a ribbon around the ball or hook an ornament hanger through its top and hang it up where you like!

Making popcorn strings is a tradition unique to America.

Wreath Resources

Wreaths Galore, offering over 250 different wreaths to choose from, doesn't restrict itself to the normal holiday fare. Square hydrangea wreaths, egg and nest wreaths, and elaborate butterfly concoctions nestle next to wreaths of artichoke and lavender. Prelit wreaths add an instant festive cheer, while the floral arrangements give a hint of romance to the season. Pumpkins, juniper berries, wild roses and lavender are among the materials used, with new options added seasonally. From a simple wreath of delicate Queen Anne's Lace to robust boxwood garlands, Wreaths Galore has something to fit any design: *wreathsgalore.com* or 866-571-4348.

Pine cone wreaths can be hung or used as centerpieces throughout the year. **Wreaths by Gwen** makes elaborate wreaths that are crafted of cones, pods, and nuts, and are sealed in clear enamel: *wreathsbygwen.com*.

Montana's **Flower Barn** handcrafts wreaths from a mixture of local materials like noble fir, white pine, boxwood, pine cones, nigelia, white larkspur, cedar roses, and salal. Coming from the Bitterroot Valley of Montana, the wreaths feature rustic local elements of pheasant feathers, berries, pine cones, and even a horseshoe or two. Flower Barn also offers floral arrangements to complement their wreaths, including a charming sled full of red and white carnations. They make a wonderful holiday gift for anyone: *flowerbarn1.com* or 866-641-6868.

Ridgewood Designs celebrates the holiday season with a huge selection of high-quality candle rings, centerpieces and wreaths. Kids will love the hanging stocking door decoration and the tiny tabletop berry trees. The apple and berry wreath looks good enough to eat; or fall in love with their wreath of red pear and leaves. To order and join the mailing list: *creativedecorations.com*.

Among **Pottery Barn**'s offerings are faux bay leaf wreaths and garlands interwoven with feathers and pinecones. At season's end, just place them back in the box for next year: *potterybarn.com*.

Tide Mill Organic Farm crafts wreaths of local ingredients ranging from balsam fir and white pine to seashells, pine cones, and elegant ribbons. Available yearly in November and December, the handmade wreaths are the perfect accent to any door or wall. Their kissing ball wreath and balsam centerpieces are darling, too. *tidemillorganicfarm.com* or call (207) 733-2551.

The holly's up, the house is all bright;

The tree is ready, the candles alight:

Rejoice and be glad, all children tonight!

—P. Cornelius

Wreath Making 101

For centuries, people have decorated their homes with garlands and wreaths of evergreen, ivy, and holly during the winter season. With a few simple materials, you can create a basic frame and then adorn it as simply or extravagantly as you like. Whether you make one for yourself or as a gift for someone else, a holiday wreath can be a festive table centerpiece with a candle in the middle, or be an offering of Christmas cheer that hangs on a door or wall.

Heavy and light grade wire, glue, semi-gloss spray or lacquer, evergreen branches, holly, ivy, pine cones, dried flowers, ribbons, nuts, berries, mistletoe, moss, small ornaments, bay leaves, eucalyptus leaves and seedpods, candy canes, cinnamon sticks, and similar decorative elements

To make the frame:
Bend wire coat hangers or a similar grade wire into a circular frame about a foot in diameter. Alternatively, you can create a circular frame out of braided willow switches. Allow three to four weeks for the branches to dry so that the frame is sturdy enough to hold additional foliage and decorations.

For an evergreen wreath:
Arrange branches such as cedar, fir, spruce, pine, and balsam around the frame. Use additional wire to secure the boughs in place.

For a pinecone wreath:
Secure large pinecones to the frame with wire. Cluster small and medium pinecones around the larger ones and glue them in place.

Once you have your basic wreath, decorate it as you like, holding things in place with additional wire, glue, or ribbon. For a shiny wreath, spray nuts, berries, and pinecones with lacquer or semi-gloss spray.

Mark Carr, a Catskills woodsman, gets credit for setting up the nation's first Christmas tree lot. In 1851, he hauled two ox-sleds loaded with balsam firs from his farm to a section of sidewalk in New York City's Washington Market that he rented for a silver dollar. He sold out almost immediately. Carr returned the next season and had to pay $100 to set up his tree lot, but he still cleaned up. The Christmas tree business had begun. By the 1890s, more than 200,000 Catskills Christmas trees lit up homes for the holidays each season.

Frosty The Snowman

Steve Nelson and Jack Rollins

1.

Fros - ty the Snow Man was a jol - ly, hap - py soul, __ With a

corn cob pipe and a but-ton nose, __ and two eyes made out of coal.

Fros - ty the Snow Man is a fair - y tale they say, ___ He was

made of snow, but the chil-dren know __ how he came to life one day. There

must have been some ma - gic in that old silk hat they found. For

when they placed it on his head, he be - gan to dance a - round. Oh,

Fros - ty the Snow Man was a - live as he could be, ___ and the

chil-dren say he could laugh and play __ just the same as you and me.

2. Frosty the snow man knew
   The sun was hot that day,
   So he said, "Let's run and
   we'll have some fun
   now before I melt away."
   Down to the village
   with a broomstick in his hand,
   Running here and there all
   around the square, sayin',
   "Catch me if you can."
   He led them down the streets of town
   Right to the traffic cop.

And he only paused a moment when
He heard him holler "stop!"

Chorus

3. For Frosty the snow man
   had to hurry on his way,
   But he waved goodbye sayin',
   "Don't you cry,
   I'll be back again some day."

Chorus

The Snow Image: A Childish Miracle

Nathaniel Hawthorne

Yes, Violet,—yes, my little Peony," said their kind mother, "you may go out and play in the new snow."

Accordingly, the good lady bundled up her darlings in woolen jackets and wadded sacks, and put comforters round their necks, and a pair of striped gaiters on each little pair of legs, and worsted mittens on their hands, and gave them a kiss apiece, by way of a spell to keep away Jack Frost. Forth sallied the two children, with a hop-skip-and-jump, that carried them at once into the very heart of a huge snow-drift, whence Violet emerged like a snow-bunting, while little Peony floundered out with his round face in full bloom. Then what a merry time had they! To look at them, frolicking in the wintry garden, you would have thought that the dark and pitiless storm had been sent for no other purpose but to provide a new plaything for Violet and Peony; and that they themselves had been created, as the snow-birds were, to take delight only in the tempest, and in the white mantle which it spread over the earth.

At last, when they had frosted one another all over with handfuls of snow, Violet, after laughing heartily at little Peony's figure, was struck with a new idea.

"You look exactly like a snow-image, Peony," said she, "if your cheeks were not so red. And that puts me in mind! Let us make an image out of snow,—an image of a little girl,—and it shall be our sister, and shall run about and play with us all winter long. Won't it be nice?"

"Oh yes!" cried Peony, as plainly as he could speak, for he was but a little boy. "That will be nice! And mamma shall see it! . . ."

And forthwith the children began this great business of making a snow-image that should run about . . .

"Peony, Peony!" cried Violet to her brother, who had gone to another part of the garden, "bring me some of that fresh snow, Peony, from the very farthest corner, where we have not been trampling. I want it to shape our little snow-sister's bosom with. You know that part must be quite pure, just as it came out of the sky!"

"Here it is, Violet!" answered Peony, in his bluff tone,—but a very sweet tone, too,—as he came floundering through the half-trodden drifts. "Here is the snow for her little bosom. O Violet, how beau-ti-ful she begins to look!"

"Yes," said Violet, thoughtfully and quietly; "our snow-sister does look very lovely. I did not quite know, Peony, that we could make such a sweet little girl as this. . . ."

"Peony, Peony!" cried Violet; for her brother was again at the other side of the garden. "Bring me those light wreaths of snow that have rested on the lower branches of the pear-tree. You can clamber on the snowdrift, Peony, and reach them easily. I must have them to make some ringlets for our snow-sister's head!"

"Here they are, Violet!" answered the little boy. "Take care you do not break them. Well done! Well done! How pretty!"

"Does she not look sweetly?" said Violet, with a very satisfied tone; "and now we must have some little shining bits of ice, to make the brightness of her eyes. She is not finished yet. Mamma will see how very beautiful she is; but papa will say, 'Tush! nonsense!—come in out of the cold!' . . ."

"What a nice playmate she will be for us, all winter long!" said Violet. "I hope papa will not be afraid of her giving us a cold! Sha'n't you love her dearly, Peony? . . ."

There was a minute or two of silence; for Peony, whose short legs were never weary, had gone on a pilgrimage again to the other side of the garden. All of a sudden, Violet cried out, loudly and joyfully,—"Look here, Peony! Come quickly! A light has been shining on her cheek out of that rose-colored cloud! and the color does not go away! Is not that beautiful!"

"Yes; it is beau-ti-ful," answered Peony, pronouncing the three syllables with deliberate accuracy. "O Violet, only look at her hair! It is all like gold!"

"Oh certainly," said Violet, with tranquillity, as if it were very much a matter of course. "That color, you know, comes from the golden clouds, that we see up there in the sky. She is almost finished now. But her lips must be made very red,—redder than her cheeks. Perhaps, Peony, it will make them red if we both kiss them!"

Accordingly, the mother heard two smart little smacks, as if both her children were kissing the snow-image on its frozen mouth. But, as this did not seem to make the lips quite red enough, Violet next proposed that the snow-child should be invited to kiss Peony's scarlet cheek.

"Come, 'ittle snow-sister, kiss me!" cried Peony.

"There! she has kissed you," added Violet, "and now her lips are very red. And she blushed a little, too!"

"Oh, what a cold kiss!" cried Peony.

Just then, there came a breeze of the pure west-wind, sweeping through the garden and rattling the parlor-windows. It sounded so wintry cold, that the mother was about to tap on the window-pane with her thimbled finger, to summon the two children in, when they both cried out to her with one voice. The tone was not a tone of surprise, although they were evidently a good deal excited; it appeared rather as if they were very much rejoiced at some event that had now happened, but which they had been looking for, and had reckoned upon all along.

"Mamma! mamma! We have finished our little snow-sister, and she is running about the garden with us!..."

"Dear mamma!" cried Violet, "pray look out and see what a sweet playmate we have!"

The mother, being thus entreated, could no longer delay to look forth from the window. The sun was now gone out of the sky, leaving, however, a rich inheritance of his brightness among those purple and golden clouds which make the sunsets of winter so magnificent. But there was not the slightest gleam or dazzle, either on the window or on the snow; so that the good lady could look all over the garden, and see everything and everybody in it. And what do you think she saw there? Violet and Peony, of course, her own two darling children. Ah, but whom or what did she see besides? Why, if you will believe me, there was a small figure of a girl, dressed all in white, with rose-tinged cheeks and ringlets of golden hue, playing about the garden with the two children! . . .

"Violet my darling, what is this child's name?" asked she. "Does she live near us?"

"Why, dearest mamma," answered Violet, laughing to think that her mother did not comprehend so very plain an affair, "this is our little snow-sister whom we have just been making!"

"Yes, dear mamma," cried Peony, running to his mother, and looking up simply into her face. "This is our snow-image! Is it not a nice 'ittle child?"

HOW TO BUILD SNOW MEN AND SNOW WOMEN

The best time to make a snow creation is when the temperature is in the mid-thirties and the snow is not too dry or slushy. Put on some waterproof gloves, and find out where your imagination will take you!

How To Make A Snow Woman

Pack snow into a cone shape and then push a stick into the top. Pack snow around the wood to make her head. Use holly berries for her face, vines or tinsel for hair, pinecones or evergreens to decorate her gown. Add a few drops of red food coloring to a spray bottle of water and spritz to give your snow girl rosy cheeks.

How To Make A Traditional Snow Man

Pack two or three handfuls of snow together tightly into as round a ball as possible. Roll the ball around on the snow in every which direction. Be sure to roll it in every direction to keep it round. The ball will begin to grow, and you will need more hands to roll it into a large ball. Make a slightly smaller ball for the body and the smallest ball for the head. Flatten the tops of the bottom and body balls slightly before stacking the next ball on top. If balls are too heavy to lift, use a wide board for a ramp and roll them up. Pack handfuls of snow into the joints between balls to stabilize and smooth out the snowman a bit. Add branches for arms, and add stones, coal, vegetables, or berries for eyes, nose, and mouth. Dress him up with an old hat, scarf, broom and pipe.

How to Make Snow Animals or Fantasy Shapes

Use sticks or PVC pipe and some duct tape to form the basic shape, and push the form deep into the snow so that it stands by itself. Then, starting at the bottom, pack on the snow, layer by layer, until it looks the way you imagined. If it's really cold, and there's no possibility of the snow melting, you can drape your snow creatures in twinkling lights!

Hark! The Herald Angels Sing!

Holiday Music, Festivities & Events

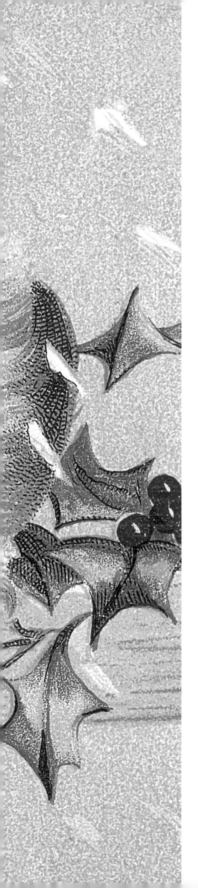

The Birds'
Christmas Carol

Kate Douglas Wiggin

I t was very early Christmas morning, and in the stillness of the dawn, with the soft snow falling on the housetops, a little child was born in the Bird household.

They had intended to name the baby Lucy, if it were a girl; but they had not expected her on Christmas morning, and a real Christmas baby was not to be lightly named—the whole family agreed in that.

They were consulting about it in the nursery. Mr. Bird said that he had assisted in naming the three boys, and that he should leave this matter entirely to Mrs. Bird; Donald wanted the child called "Dorothy," after a pretty, curly-haired girl who sat next to him in school; Paul chose "Luella," for Luella was the nurse who had been with him during his whole babyhood, up to the time of his first trousers, and the name suggested all sorts of comfortable things. Uncle Jack said that the first girl should always be named for her mother, no matter how hideous the name happened to be.

Grandma said that she would prefer not to take any part in the discussion, and everybody suddenly remembered that Mrs. Bird had thought of naming the baby Lucy, for Grandma herself; and, while it would be indelicate for her to favor that name, it would be against human nature for her to suggest any other, under the circumstances.

Hugh, the "hitherto baby," if that is a possible term, sat in one corner and said nothing, but felt, in some mysterious way, that his nose was out of joint; for there was a newer baby now, a possibility he had never taken into consideration; and the "first girl," too,—a still higher development of treason, which made him actually green with jealousy.

But it was too profound a subject to be settled then and there, on the spot; besides, Mamma had not been asked, and everybody felt it rather absurd, after all, to forestall a decree that was certain to be absolutely wise, just, and perfect.

The reason that the subject had been brought up at all so early in the day lay in the fact that Mrs. Bird never allowed her babies to go overnight unnamed. She was a person of so great decision of character that she would have blushed at such a thing; she said that to let blessed babies go dangling and dawdling about without names, for months and months,

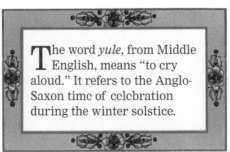

The word *yule*, from Middle English, means "to cry aloud." It refers to the Anglo-Saxon time of celebration during the winter solstice.

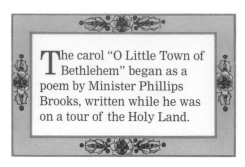

The carol "O Little Town of Bethlehem" began as a poem by Minister Phillips Brooks, written while he was on a tour of the Holy Land.

was enough to ruin them for life. She also said that if one could not make up one's mind in twenty-four hours it was a sign that—But I will not repeat the rest, as it might prejudice you against the most charming woman in the world.

So Donald took his new velocipede and went out to ride up and down the stone pavement and notch the shins of innocent people as they passed by, while Paul spun his musical top on the front steps.

But Hugh refused to leave the scene of action. He seated himself on the top stair in the hall, banged his head against the railing a few times, just by way of uncorking the vials of his wrath, and then subsided into gloomy silence, waiting to declare war if more "first girl babies" were thrust upon a family already surfeited with that unnecessary article.

Meanwhile dear Mrs. Bird lay in her room, weak, but safe and happy, with her sweet girl baby by her side and the heaven of motherhood opening again before her. Nurse was making gruel in the kitchen, and the room was dim and quiet. There was a cheerful open fire in the grate, but though the shutters were closed, the side windows that looked out on the Church of Our Saviour, next door, were a little open.

Suddenly a sound of music poured out into the bright air and drifted into the chamber. It was the boy choir singing Christmas anthems. Higher and higher rose the clear, fresh voices, full of hope and cheer, as children's voices always are. Fuller and fuller grew the burst of melody as one glad strain fell upon another in joyful harmony:—

"Carol, brothers, carol,
  Carol joyfully,
  Carol the good tidings,
  Carol merrily!
And pray a gladsome Christmas
  For all your fellow-men:
Carol, brothers, carol,
  Christmas Day again."

One verse followed another, always with the same sweet refrain:—

"And pray a gladsome Christmas
  For all your fellow-men:
Carol, brothers, carol,
  Christmas Day again."

Mrs. Bird thought, as the music floated in upon her gentle sleep, that she had slipped into heaven with her new baby, and that the angels

were bidding them welcome. But the tiny bundle by her side stirred a little, and though it was scarcely more than the ruffling of a feather, she awoke; for the mother-ear is so close to the heart that it can hear the faintest whisper of a child.

She opened her eyes and drew the baby closer. It looked like a rose dipped in milk, she thought, this pink and white blossom of girlhood, or like a pink cherub, with its halo of pale yellow hair, finer than floss silk.

> "Carol, brothers, carol,
> Carol joyfully,
> Carol the good tidings,
> Carol merrily!"

The voices were brimming over with joy.

"Why, my baby," whispered Mrs. Bird in soft surprise, "I had forgotten what day it was. You are a little Christmas child, and we will name you 'Carol'—mother's Christmas Carol!"

"What!" said Mr. Bird, coming in softly and closing the door behind him.

"Why, Donald, don't you think 'Carol' is a sweet name for a Christmas baby? It came to me just a moment ago in the singing, as I was lying here half asleep and half awake."

"I think it is a charming name, dear heart, and sounds just like you, and I hope that, being a girl, this baby has some chance of being as lovely as her mother;"—at which speech from the baby's papa Mrs. Bird, though she was as weak and tired as she could be, blushed with happiness.

And so Carol came by her name.

Of course, it was thought foolish by many people, though Uncle Jack declared laughingly that it was very strange if a whole family of Birds could not be indulged in a single Carol; and Grandma, who adored the child, thought the name much more appropriate than Lucy, but was glad that people would probably think it short for Caroline.

Perhaps because she was born in holiday time, Carol was a very happy baby. Of course, she was too tiny to understand the joy of Christmas-tide, but people say there is everything in a good beginning, and she may have breathed in unconsciously the fragrance of evergreens and holiday dinners; while the peals of sleigh-bells and the laughter of happy children may have fallen upon her baby ears and wakened in them a glad surprise at the merry world she had come to live in.

Her cheeks and lips were as red as hollyberries; her hair was for all the world the color of a Christmas candle-flame; her eyes were bright as stars; her laugh like a chime of Christmas-bells, and her tiny hands forever outstretched in giving.

Such a generous little creature you never saw! A spoonful of bread and milk had always to be taken by Mamma or nurse before Carol could enjoy her supper; whatever bit of cake or sweetmeat found its way into her pretty fingers was straightway broken in half to be shared with Donald, Paul, or Hugh; and when they made believe nibble the morsel with affected enjoyment, she would clap her hands and crow with delight.

"Why does she do it?" asked Donald thoughtfully. "None of us boys ever did."

"I hardly know," said Mamma, catching her darling to her heart, "except that she is a little Christmas child, and so she has a tiny share of the blessedest birthday the world ever knew!"

CHRISTMAS BELLS

Henry Wadsworth Longfellow

I heard the bells on Christmas Day
Their old, familiar carols play,
And wild and sweet
The words repeat
Of peace on earth, good-will to men!

O Little Town of Bethlehem

O Lit - tle Town of Beth - le - hem, How
still we __ see thee lie; A - bove thy deep and
dream - less sleep The si - lent __ stars go by; Yet
in thy dark streets shi - neth The ev - er - last - ing
light; The hopes and fears of all the years Are
met in thee to - - - night.

2. For Christ is born of Mary,
And gathered all above,
While mortals sleep, the angels keep
Their watch of wond'ring love.
O morning stars, together
Proclaim the holy birth!
And praises sing to God the King,
And peace to men on earth!

3. How silently, how silently,
The wondrous gift is giv'n!
So God imparts to human hearts
The blessing of his heav'n.

No ear may hear His coming,
but in this world of sin,
Where meek souls will receive Him still,
The dear Christ enters in.

4. O Holy child of Bethlehem!
Descent to us, we pray;
Cast out our sin, and enter in;
Be born in us today.
We hear the Christmas angels
The great glad tidings tell;
O come to us abide with us,
Our Lord Emmanuel.

O Come, All Ye Faithful

1.

O Come, All Ye Faith-ful, Joy-ful and tri-umph-ant, O
come ye, O come ye to Beth - - le hem.
Come and be - hold Him, Born the King of An - gels. O
come, let us a - dore Him, O come, let us a - dore Him, O
come, let us a - dore Him, Christ, the Lord.

2. Sing, choirs of angels, sing in exultation,
O sing, all ye citizens of heav'n above!
Glory to God, all Glory in the highest;

Chorus

3. Yea, Lord, we greet Thee, born this happy morning,
Jesus, to Thee be all glory giv'n;
Word of the Father, Now in flesh appearing;

Chorus

For Whom the Bell Tolls

Though the one-and-a-half-room North Trinity Evangelical Lutheran Church in Walsh County, North Dakota, closed for services in 1953, local inhabitants of Scandinavian-American descent keep tradition alive by ringing the bell each Christmas Eve. And this is a bell-ringing program with long-distance benefits: The bell-ringers call former church members who've moved away to let them listen to the chimes over the phone. If any recipients are out, the bell-ringers record the comforting peals on the person's answering machine.

North Trinity, one of many small white clapboard structures to still dot the open prairie, is a member of an endangered species. Of these picturesque meeting places—most from the late nineteenth century—some have been destroyed; but now there is a movement afoot to save them. North Dakota's state historical society has joined with Preservation North Dakota and the National Trust for Historic Preservation in a project titled Prairie Churches of North Dakota. In 2001, the churches made the National Trust's list of America's 11 Most Endangered Historic Places.

THE BELLS *by Edgar Allan Poe*

Hear the sledges with the bells—
 Silver bells!
What a world of merriment their
 melody foretells!
How they tinkle, tinkle, tinkle,
 In the icy air of night!
While the stars, that oversprinkle
All the heavens, seem to twinkle
 With a crystalline delight
Keeping time, time, time,
 In a sort of Runic rhyme.
To the tintinnabulation that so musically wells
From the bells, bells, bells, bells,
 Bells, bells, bells—
From the jingling and the tinkling of the bells.

Fa, la, la, la, la . . .

Some say the first Christmas carol ever sung was sung by a host of heavenly angels the night that the baby Jesus was born. Shepherds heard their words, "Glory to God in the highest!" as chronicled by the third Gospel writer, St. Luke. Others give the credit to St. Francis of Assisi for the first Christmas carol when in 1223, he sang about the nativity during Midnight Mass at the church in Greccio. Carols became an important way to convey the nativity story to those who couldn't read, as roaming actors and singers did during miracle plays in medieval France.

The tradition of caroling spread throughout Europe, reaching a zenith in the eighteenth and nineteenth centuries, when most of the classic Christmas carols we know today were written. Many carols started out as poems and were later set to music, conveying winter traditions and pre-Christian customs as well as biblical themes. In Victorian England, carolers roamed the streets in groups, going "a wassailing" before their friends and neighbors in exchange for food or gifts.

Caroling didn't take off in the United States until after the Civil War. In 1911, the Children's Aid Society organized bands of carolers to spread good cheer in exchange for donations toward needy causes. By 1928, community caroling had come to more than 2,000 cities across the U.S.

Silver Bells, Silver Bells,
It's Christmastime in the city.
—RAY EVANS

Best Choirs & Christmas Concerts

In its 500-year-history, the **Vienna Boys' Choir** has proven the perfect training ground for some of the world's finest musicians. Franz Joseph Haydn, Franz Schubert, and Antonio Salieri, had connections to the group. Every Sunday the choir sings Mass in Vienna's Hofburg Chapel, continuing a tradition unbroken since 1498. Two of its four groups are usually away on tour for three-month-stints; they have visited the U. S. more than 50 times since 1932. Every year the boys, aged 10 to 14, wrap up the tour with a concert at Carnegie Hall: *wsk.at*.

Christmas just isn't Christmas without the pure, energetic sound of the **Boys Choir of Harlem.** These "Children of the Sun" have undertaken some serious seasonal touring, including a 1999 trip to Israel and a 2001–2002 tour of the great cities of the Southeast that ended with a Christmas extravaganza at Lincoln Center for the Performing Arts in New York City. The choir has performed all over the world for over 150,000 people annually. Check Ticketmaster to find where they are and when: *ticketmaster.com*. There's a **Girls Choir of Harlem**, too: *boyschoirofharlem.org*.

World reknown as an outstanding choral ensemble in the Anglican tradition, New York's **Saint Thomas Choir** has appeared at Westminster Abbey, Saint Paul's Cathedral in London and the Aldeburgh and King's Lynn Festivals in England, and has sung with the New York Philharmonic and the Cleveland, Pittsburgh, American, and other symphony orchestras at Lincoln Center and Carnegie Hall. The group gave an internationally televised premiere performance of Andrew Lloyd Webber's *Requiem* with Placido Domingo at Saint Thomas Cathedral. The choir's concerts and services are often broadcast nationally and abroad, and they have recorded both their own repertory of fifteenth-century to current music as well as songs with Judy Collins and other popular artists. Their annual concert series includes the mid-December performance of Handel's *Messiah*—an event beloved by many New Yorkers: *saintthomaschurch.org*.

Try New York's **Annual Christmas Tuba Concert** at the Rockefeller Center Rink, where several hundred tuba players blow favorite seasonal tunes: (212) 332-7654. *Oom-pah*. Tickets sell out fast for the Baroque Christmas events that take place in December at the **Cathedral of St. John the Divine**, the largest cathedral in the world. Series events include a performance of *The Messiah*: *earlymusicny.org* or (212) 280-0330. Other New York singing attractions include the St. Cecilia Chorus and the New York City Men's Chorus, who make appearances at the South Street Seaport. The century-old men's and boys' **Choir of Westminster Cathedral** is considered one of the finest in the world. In 1998, the choir won Gramaphone's Record of the Year, an astonishing feat for a religious-music group. The choir performs throughout Europe; the Christmas Eve midnight Mass at the cathedral

is broadcast by BBC radio. A CD is also available for sale: *westminstercathedral.org.uk*.

As her fans know, **Charlotte Church** hails from Llandaff, Cardiff, Wales—an area said to be a hotbed of world-class singing voices—where she studied at the **Llandaff Cathedral School**. The School, in existence since about the ninth century, is the only remaining Anglican choir school in Wales. The Llandaff Cathredral Choral Society supplements the beautiful Cathedral Choir for large-scale concerts: *llandaffcathedral.org.uk*. Their CD is available from their store. Charlotte's schedule of appearances, as well as her second Christmas CD, can be found at *charlottechurch.com*.

The Grammy–award-winning **Mormon Tabernacle Choir**, based in Salt Lake City, comprises more than 300 members. The choir gives two free concerts per week in addition to special broadcast appearances and a Christmas concert at the Tabernacle in mid-December: *mormontabernaclechoir.org* or (866) 537-8457.

Washington is endowed with more fine choruses than perhaps any other city in the country. Usher in the season with bagpipers and sing-a-longs at **Washington National Cathedral's Open House**. Perhaps the best program, however, is the Cathedral's **Joy of Christmas**,

which has showcased such groups as the Cathedral Choral Society, Potomac School Concert Chorus, and the Washington Symphonic Brass: (202) 537-6200.

The **Christmas Candlelight Concerts** of the Master Chorale of Washington, held at **Kennedy Center Concert Hall**, promise not to disappoint. And the Choral Arts Society, Washington Chorus, and some exceptional school choirs all give holiday concerts at Kennedy Center: *kennedy-center.org* or (800) 444-1324.

The **Washington Ballet** gives its annual performance of *The Nutcracker* in mid-to-late December at Warner Theatre: (202) 362-3606.

The **Atlanta Symphony Orchestra Gospel Choir** presents their popular concert Gospel Christmas in early December: *atlantasymphony.org/calendar.aspx*

San Franciso's 17-member, conductorless **New Century Chamber Orchestra** offers its annual Christmas concert series at several venues in the Bay area. The innovative group's loyal patrons can now purchase subscription tickets through City Box Office at (415) 392-4400. For more information: *ncco.org* or (415) 357-1111.

In New Orleans, St. Louis Cathedral presents its prestigious **Cathedral Christmas Concerts**—featuring local choirs and New Orleans artists performing carols and gospel

In 1884 the first electrically illuminated public tree appeared at a celebration for children in the First Reformed Episcopal Church in New York.

favorites for 23 straight days in one of the country's most historic venues: (504) 525-9585.

New Orleans is truly "music-rich," especially during the holidays. Don't miss caroling in **Jackson Square**, a 60-year-old tradition. Everyone is invited to join in the fun: *patioplanters.org* or 504-524-8432. You can also hear choirs on a two-hour Mississippi steamboat cruise: *steamboatnatchez.com* or (800)-233-BOAT. Don't miss the **French Market Holiday Marching Bands**: *frenchmarket.org* or (504) 522-2621.

The **Louisiana Philharmonic Orchestra** presents holiday concerts at various locations with family favorites, including Tchaikovsky's *Nutcracker Suite*, Herbert's *March of the Toys*, Handel's *Messiah*, and many others. Or enjoy the Orchestra's special annual holiday concert full of Christmas favorites: *lpomusic.com* or (504) 523-6530.

Each year, the **Music Heals Foundation** in the Los Angeles area heads up a number of children's interactive concerts, Christmas toy drives, courses for kids, and other events: (424) 354-0590.

Merry, Merry Music
The Best Holiday CDs of All Time

Angel's Glory—Kathleen Battle & Christopher Parkening

The Beach Boy's Christmas Album—Beach Boys

Christmas Carols & Sacred Songs—Boys Choir of Harlem

The Christmas Song—Nat King Cole

Season's Greetings—Perry Como

White Christmas—Bing Crosby

Ella Wishes You a Swinging Christmas—Ella Fitzgerald

The Messiah (George Frideric Handel)—performed by the Mormon Tabernacle Choir

Aaron Neville's Soulful Christmas—Aaron Neville

Elvis's Christmas Album—Elvis Presley

A Christmas Gift for You from Phil Spector—Phil Spector

A Jolly Christmas from Frank Sinatra—Frank Sinatra

Nutcracker: The Complete Ballet (Pytor Illych Tchaikovsky)—Valery Gergiev, Kirov Orchestra and Choir

Four Seasons (Antonio Vivaldi)—Conductor: Seiji Ozawa, Performer: Joseph Silverstein, Telarc, Boston Symphony Orchestra

Just for Kids. . .

Christmas with the Chipmunks—Chipmunks

Christmas for Kids—Nat King Cole

Little Drummer Boy and Other Children's Favorites—The Countdown Kids

Christmas Together—John Denver & the Muppets

Rudolph the Red-Nosed Reindeer—Burl Ives

Kidz Bop Christmas—Kidz Bop Kids

Raffi's Christmas Album—Raffi

A Sesame Street Christmas—Sesame Street

Merry Christmas with the Smurfs—Smurfs

Tiny Tim's Christmas Album—Tiny Tim

First Christmas Record for Children—Various Artists

Here Comes Santa Claus—Various Artists

School's Out Christmas—Various Artists

Wiggly Wiggly Christmas—The Wiggles

Willie, take your little drum,
With your whistle, Robin, come!
When we hear the fife and drum
Christmas should be frolicsome.

—BURGUNDIAN CAROL

Angels We Have Heard On High

1.

An-gels we have heard on high, sweet-ly sing-ing o'er the plain,

And the moun-tains in re-ply, Ech-o-ing their joy-ous strain.

Glo - - - - - - - - - - - - - - - - ri-a in ex-cel-sis

De - o, Glo - - - - - - - - - - - - - - - - - ri-a

in ex-cel-sis De - - - - o! _

2. Shepherds, why this jubilee?
Why your joyful strains prolong?
What the gladsome tidings be
Which inspire your heav'nly song?

Chorus

3. Come to Bethlehem and see
Him whose birth the angels sing;
Come adore on bended knee
Christ, the Lord, the new-born King.

Chorus

4. See Him in a manger laid,
Whom the choir of angels praise;
Holy Spirit, lend thine aid,
While our hearts in love we raise.

Chorus

Holiday Services

Baltimore

In 1634, two Jesuit priests arrived in the American Colonies aboard the *Ark* and the *Dove*. On March 25 they held the first Roman Catholic Mass in what was to become the United States, on Saint Clement's Island in the Chesapeake Bay. Thus Baltimore became the first diocese in the country. **Baltimore's** stately **Cathedral of Mary Our Queen** stands in tribute to this early beginning. It offers a full schedule of lessons and services December 24–25, and has a choir school: *cathedralofmary.org*.

Bethlehem

Christmas is celebrated on three different dates in **Bethlehem**. December 25 for Westerners, January 7 for the Russian Orthodox Church, and January 19 for the Armenian Church. A 14-pointed silver star marks the spot where it is believed Christ was born in a manger, at the site of the Church of the Nativity, a place that attracts thousands of pilgrims. The Christmas Eve service, sung in Latin, starts at Shepherds' Field and then moves on to the church, which has room for only a few hundred people.

Boston

Trinity Church Boston's Christmas worship schedule offers two candlelight carol services, a Christmas Eve pageant, two additional Christmas Eve services, and a Christmas Day service. Music is provided by the Trinity Choir, Parish Choir, Cantebury Singers, and Children's Choirs: *trinityboston.org* or (617) 536-0944. Other memorable Boston-area church services include afternoon and evening Christmas Eve celebrations at **King's Chapel** (pageant; lessons and carols), the **Arlington Street Church** (Boston Gay Men's Chorus), and the **Emmanuel Church** (Emmanuel Music).

Lititz

At joyful Christmas services in Pennsylvania, the congregation must be served *liebesmahl* (buns) and coffee in the time it takes to sing three hymns. The Christmas Eve service at the **Moravian Church** in Lititz, Lancaster County—"Pennsylvania Dutch Country"—was first held in 1759. It's a touching service, with a trombone choir, baroque music, and ancient chorales; beautiful Moravian stars hanging everywhere; and a lit candle passed to each attendee. Find a complete listing of area parishes and phone numbers, at *padutch.com/churches.html*. Folks who have the desire to rid themselves of the trappings of a commercial Christmas entirely can get a taste of the simpler life in Old Salem, North Carolina. Each mid-December, visitors celebrate Christmas all day with Moravian brass bands, refreshments, candlelight tours, and other authentic Moravian Christmas activities.

London

Christmas Eve services in London: Lessons and carols in the afternoon at the legendary **Westminster Abbey**. Later in the evening the world-famous Abbey Choir sings the First Eucharist. **St Martins-in-the-Fields** at Trafalgar Square also holds a well-attended midnight mass with spectacular music (not a carol service), as does **Holy Trinity**.

New York

St. Thomas Church in New York has a world-renowned men's and boys' choir that not only records and gives special concerts, but provides pageantry throughout the full schedule of Christmas Eve and Christmas Day services at the Episcopal church's Fifth Avenue location: *saintthomaschurch.org* or (212) 757-7013. New York's Episcopal **Cathedral of St. John the Divine** offers an unsurpassed atmosphere for music, worship, and quiet contemplation. Hear the Cathedral Choir, the Cathedral Singers, and the Ensemble for Early Music as they perform during regular liturgical services and special events: *stjohndivine.org* or (212) 316-7540. The **Seamen's Church** in lower Manhattan holds services in Norwegian, the mother tongue of many of its early members: (212) 349-9090. The midnight mass at the gothic-style **St. Patrick's Cathedral** is so popular you need advance tickets: *oldcathedral.org* or (212) 226-8075.

New Orleans

Celebrate with the traditional midnight mass at **St. Louis Cathedral** in New Orleans. Christmas Eve vigil masses and Christmas carols with the St. Louis Cathedral

Rumor has it candy canes were invented in the 17th century by a German choir master, who wanted to still fidgety children during Christmas services.

Boychoir are also held earlier in the day. On Christmas Day masses are held: (504) 525-9585.

Paris

One of Europe's oldest religious centers, the **Cathedral of Notre-Dame** occupies the Ile-de-la-Cité. With six masses a day, the cathedral offers no shortage of holiday services and concerts. International masses are celebrated on the Eve; there is a vigil with the Choir of Notre-Dame and a midnight nativity mass. Christmas Day brings five services plus a musical recital. The best resources are probably *discoverfrance.net* and *parisvoice.com*.

Rome

Entrée to **Vatican** services in Rome is so coveted that you need to request permission—in person—well ahead of your visit. At midnight on the 24th, the Vatican holds its *Santa Messa della Notte di Natale* ("Christmas Night Religious Service"). On Christmas Day it holds the Benedizione *Urbi et Orbi* ("Blessing to the Town and to the World"). Visit *vatican.va/liturgical_year/liturgico_en/christmas.html* or *travour.com/christmas-celebrations/*

Washington, D.C.

The Cathedral Choral Society became the resident symphonic chorus of **Washington National Cathedral** in 1941, participating in the festive Christmas services held at the facility December 24–25. Its Christmas Day service has been televised for more than 50 years: *cathedral.org/cathedral* or (202) 537-6200.

Silent Night

1.

Si - lent Night, ho - - ly night,

all is calm, all is bright

'round yon vir - gin moth - er and child.

Ho - ly in - fant so ten - der and mild,

sleep in heav - en - ly peace.

sleep in heav - en - ly peace.

2. Silent night! Holy night!
Shepherds quake at the sight!
Glories stream from Heaven afar,
Heav'nly hosts sing Alleluia,
Christ, the Saviour, is born!
Christ, the Saviour, is born!

3. Silent night! Holy night!
Son of God, love's pure light,
Radiant beams from Thy holy face,
With the dawn of redeeming grace,
Jesus, Lord, at Thy birth,
Jesus, Lord, at Thy birth.

Fabulous Festivities

London

Somerset House Ice Rink, on London's Strand, opens from late November through January, and has a café for people-watching. Flaming torches and a 40-foot Christmas tree imported from Sweden illuminate the rink at night. Want to be sure the money you spend on gifts goes to ethical companies? London's annual **Without Cruelty Fayre**, held in early December, offers a broad range of cruelty-free products. Take in the **Covent Garden Market Great Christmas Pudding Race**, and see celebrities make fools of themselves navigating an obstacle course while balancing a tray of Christmas pudding. **Somerset House** presents an 18th-century Christmas weekend of recipe demos, chocolate tasting, lantern making, and caroling by the skating rink: *somerset-house.org.uk*. **The Royal Albert Hall Christmas Spectacular** gets help from the Rhapsodettes and the Santa Symphony Orchestra in addition to a featured musician: *royalalberthall.com*. **The Royal Philharmonic Christmas Concert** is totally family-oriented, with renditions of all the old favorite Christmas pop tunes and a presentation of a children's story. The **Royal Festival Hall** presents its share of Christmas classics, too, including the **Hospitals' Choir Christmas Carol Concert**: *southbankcentre.co.uk*. A favorite among Londoners is the annual **BBC Christmas Carol Concert**, held at a different location every year. The concert features traditional carols, readings, and special presentations: *bbc.co.uk*. **St. John's**, at Smith Square, is a beautiful church that manages to book some world-renowned talent for Christmas: *sjss.org.uk* for details of this season's offerings.

Melbourne

December 25 in Australia often means temperatures near 100 degrees! Santa traditionally arrives with his white beard—not on a sled pulled by reindeer—but on water-skis and wearing a red bathing suit! Every year on Christmas Eve in Melbourne, thousands of people gather under the stars for the **Carols by Candlelight** festival. The view of the Southern Cross is spectacular: *visionaustralia.org.au/events/carols*

Mexico City

On December 12, pilgrims from all over the country converge for religious services at **La Villa de Guadalupe**, the legendary sanctuary just north of this city of 20 million. Then, the real partying—**la navidád**—kicks off with the fiesta for the **Virgin de la Soledad**, the patron saint of Oaxaca, from December 16 to 18. Held at a different church each night from December 16 to 24, the **posada**, a reenactment of Joseph and Mary's journey, is considered a highlight of the festivities, as is the **Noche de los Rábanos** ("Night of the Radishes") on December 23. At this unusual celebration, vendors fill the Zócalo (town center) with booths featuring rather bizarre exhibits of giant Mexican radishes carved into figures and scenes—often with a religious or humorous edge. The **Nochebuena processions** usher in Christmas Eve with a humongous display of fireworks, dancing, piñatas, and decorated floats. The evening culminates in the late-night **Misa de Gallo** ("Rooster's Mass"). Call the Mexican Government Tourism Office at (800) 446-3942 for more information.

New Orleans

You guessed it: New Orleans and Christmas make a splendid combination. Don't miss the **Celebration in the Oaks**, one of **New Orleans'** most beloved traditions. Consisting of a stroll underneath beautifully-lit oak trees, among the attractions are a miniature train and a gallery of trees decorated with handmade ornaments by local students from over 200 schools: *neworleanscitypark.com/calendar.html*. If historic places are your passion, take the **Candlelight Tour of Historic Homes and Landmarks** in the French Quarter—all done up for Christmas: *christmasneworleans.com* or (504) 522-5730 for advance tickets. For carolers, there's free **Caroling in Washington Square**: (504) 945-8014; **Caroling on the River** aboard the steamboat Natchez: *steamboatnatchez.com* or (800) 233-BOAT; and **Caroling Under the Stars** at Jazzland Theme Park, a free, hugely popular, community sing-a-long event. Witness the outdoor lighting of the **Menorah** at Congregation Temple Sinai and join with the Youth Choir in singing **Chanukah** songs: *templesinaino.org* or (504) 861-3693.

The historic St. Louis Cathedral hosts both a concert series and a popular **Christmas Eve Mass** (see Christmas Concerts). Other traditions include **Christmas Eve Cruises**, where bonfires line the shore to guide Papa Noel (River Road Tour: *bigeasy.com* or 504-529-4567;

Creole Queen or Cajun Queen: *neworleanspaddlewheels.com* or (800)-445-4109; Steamboat Natchez: *steamboat-natchez.com* or (800)-233-BOAT; the **French Market parade**, and the **Louisiana Living History Project** in Jackson Square every afternoon throughout December; not to mention ongoing **Merriment on Magazine Street** and the Creole dining tradition of **Reveillon** at area restaurants. Consult *christmasneworleans.com* for more.

New York

Christmas wouldn't be Christmas in the Big Apple without these three components: **Macy's Thanksgiving Day Parade**, Radio City Music Hall, and Rockefeller Center. The world's largest department store has been putting on the world-famous parade since 1924. The whole extravaganza begins Thanksgiving morning at 9 A.M., moves down Central Park West from 77th Street, and then takes Broadway to 34th Street, where it turns at Herald Square and ends up on 7th Avenue. Find your viewing spot early along Broadway to get a good look at Santa, Snoopy, and the whole gang. For a behind-the-scenes thrill Thanksgiving Eve, attend the big helium balloon inflation, 3–10 P.M., on Central Park West. Call the parade hotline at (212) 494-4495. Macy's Christmas windows are so enchanting that people wait in line on the sidewalk to view them.

Probably every little girl has dreamed of what it would be like to be a high-kicking Rockette at Radio City Music Hall. The **Radio City Christmas Spectacular**, which runs from November to early January, is synonymous with "family entertainment." Hurry! For tickets log on to *radiocity.com/eventcalendar* or call (212) 307-7171.

The Tree, with a capital "T," is the Big Kahuna of Christmas trees. **Rockefeller Center**'s elegant plaza is its home, right above the sunken skating rink, where it's lit the first Wednesday evening after Thanksgiving. Most likely, it's a Norway spruce—from somebody's yard! People from all over the U. S. write in, offering their tree in the hopes that it will be THE ONE. The manager of the Rockefeller Center gardens scours the countryside summer and winter—using a helicopter when needed—looking for the perfect specimen. Genetically speaking, only about one in a million has the right stuff, according to the official website. Want more Rockefeller tree trivia? Log on at "The Tree," *rockefellercenter.com*. Then get a good look at the conifer while you work on that double Salchow in the Rockefeller Center Ice Rink. The entire Rockefeller Center complex, a richly detailed, one-of-a-kind global marketplace, stretches from 47th to 51st Streets and from Fifth to Seventh Avenues. Have lunch or dinner with a view of the skaters and the gorgeous gold statue of Prometheus. At night, the plaza is aglow with larger-than-life horn-blowing Christmas angels—another Christmas tradition New Yorkers never tire of. Take a bus down Fifth Avenue and get off at 50th Street—you can't miss them!

Paris

Paris at Christmastime is magical—even delightfully gaudy. Enjoy the Christmas windows along the Boulevard Haussmann—which rival New York's—against a romantic backdrop of eighteenth- and nineteenth-century architecture. Rumor has it that the City of Light's best lights are found on the **Rue Montorgueil**. Soak up the atmosphere at the annual **Christmas marchés** (markets) at the Place de la Bourse, Place de la Nation, Place Bastille, Bercy Village, and Place Maurice-Chevallier in Ménilmontant, and the pedestrian mall adjacent to the Centre Pompidou. Also not to be missed is the **Noël la Paix Dans le Monde**, with its 200 crèches from around the world, at the Paroisse Saint-Joseph Artisan. Paris seems to be the capital of crèches: The big one, **La Crèche de l'Espérance**, is on display at Notre Dame Cathedral, of course. Yet another giant crèche makes its home on the square in front of the Hôtel de Ville.

Some of the city's best musical concerts occur in the churches during the **Festival d'Art Sacré**, held in November and December (and they're free!). Midnight mass at Notre Dame is by invitation only, but is broadcast live on French TV. For further details of cultural events, consult *metropoleparis.com*.

Santa Fe

Just as popular here as in Mexico, the **posada** is an important part of local holiday tradition. Santa Fe's **Las Posadas** begins at the Palace of the Governors, winds around the Plaza and is open to everyone. By the end of the procession, dozens of people will have joined the Mary and Joseph characters as they search for a place to spend the night.

Pueblos near Santa Fe present Native American animal dances throughout the winter, especially on Christmas and the days that follow. Some pueblos to visit: Jemez, Taos, Picuris, Nambe, San Juan, Santa Clara, and San Ildefonso: (505) 852-4265. Visitors can be invited to dine briefly with tribal members at the Pojoaque Pueblo on December 12 every year: (505) 455-3549. For more Christmas events in Santa Fe log on to *santafe.org*.

Seattle

Similar to New Orleans, the Northwest has its own version of heralding Papa Noel with bonfires and river cruising. In fact, Seattle runs its **Argosy Christmas Ship™ Festival** for 23 straight nights. The parade features a lead ship and an entire flotilla of smaller boats broadcasting the music of onboard choirs and carolers to landlubbers attending the enormous bonfire rituals on shore. Kids love the contests and visits from Santa aboard ship; the entire family can enjoy a three-course meal. Visit *argosy-cruises.com*.

Jingle Bells

2. Day or two ago
   I thought I'd take a ride,
   Soon Miss Fanny Bright
   Was seated at my side.
   The horse was lean and lank,
   Misfortune seem'd his lot,
   He got into a drifted bank,
   And we, we got upsot!

   Chorus

3. Now the ground is white,
   Go it while you're young!
   Take the girls tonight,
   And sing this sleighing song.
   Just get a bobtail'd bay,
   Twoforty for his speed,
   Then hitch him to an open sleigh
   And crack! You'll take the lead.

   Chorus

Joy To The World

1.

Joy To The World! The Lord is come; Let
earth re - ceive her King. _____ Let
ev - 'ry ____ heart ____ pre - pare ____ Him ____ room, _____ And ____
heav'n and na - ture ____ sing, And ____ heav'n and na - ture ____ sing, And ____
heav'n ____ and heav'n _____ and na - ture sing.

2. Joy to the world! The Saviour reigns;
   Let men their songs employ;
   While fields and floods, rocks, hills and plains
   Repeat the sounding joy,
   Repeat the sounding joy,
   Repeat, repeat the sounding joy.

3. He rules the world with truth and grace,
   And makes the nations prove
   The glories of His righteousness,
   And wonders of His love,
   And wonders of His love,
   And wonders, and wonders of
   His Love.

The Best Ice-Skating Rinks

Open from October to April each year, **New York's Rockefeller Center Ice Rink** beloved skating spot provides relaxing urban outdoor recreation to over a quarter million, and free entertainment for anyone who wants to hang out and watch. The skating surface has the capacity for 150 skaters at one time. With the plaza all decked out for the holidays, skating here is a wondrous experience. Skating periods can start as early as 8 A.M. and end as late as midnight: (212) 332-7654. New York also boasts two **Wollman Rink**s—the Central Park one, and its less-crowded but lovely sister rink in Brooklyn's beautiful Prospect Park.

Paris' Hotel de Ville Skating Rink (City Hall) is open late most nights in the winter season. Closes in March. Smaller rinks also are open at the Place de Stalingrad and in front of the Gare Montparnasse. Skates are available for rent.

Eight members of the **Colorado Springs World Arena Ice Hall**'s famous Broadmoor Skating Club have medaled at the Olympics; the club boasts 200 national medalists. This is one of a handful of prestige rinks where folks can learn free-style figure skating, good sportsmanship, and maybe even launch a career. Public skating sessions are held Saturday through Wednesday. Very low cost eight-lesson learn-to-skate packages are available, as are pick-up hockey games and plenty of other programs. Visit *worldarena.com* or (719) 477-2150 to get acquainted.

In the shivery winter in **Minneapolis/St. Paul**, Minnesota ice sports are a great way to stay warm and amused. And the Twin Cities are blessed with a "chain of lakes," which seem to attract a large number of tall, blond people on skates who seem immune to the cold—descendants of Scandinavian immigrants who

were drawn to Minnesota's climate. There are, in all, 24 skating venues in the region. The **Depot Rink** in downtown Minneapolis (*depotrink.com*), with its metal trusswork overhead and soaring expanses of glass, manages to bring the outdoors in while making skaters forget the below-zero chill outside. Visit the **Starlight Ice Dance Club** at *geocities.com/starlighticedance* for schedules of area rinks.

At **Vail, Colorado's Adventure Ridge**, they do mean adventure—amid Rocky Mountain scenery. Take the gondola to the Ridge; after 2 P.M., it's free. The rink is open 12:30–10 P.M. daily through mid-April. Skating is free. Skate rental is $8/hour. For details, call (970) 479-2271.

The **Boston Common** is the oldest public park in the United States. With 16,000 square feet of ice, its **Frog Pond** is one of the city's favorite outdoor attractions. Lessons, rentals, and snacks are offered. Open every day from 10 A.M. Phone (617) 635-2121.

Does **Los Angeles'** summery atmosphere have you in the mood for some winter sports action? Head for the home of ice hockey's Mighty Ducks. Two skating surfaces at **AnaheimICE** in **Anaheim**, California—NHL and Olympic-size—assure that participants get all the room they need to free-style it, figure skate, practice their slap shot, or play broomball (hockey in your shoes!). The pro shop carries a full line of the best skating and hockey gear available. A birthday or Christmas party for your child may include food, cake, and even an ice skating instructor. Take a virtual tour of this state-of-the-art facility at *anaheimice.com*.

They were all laughing together, as hand in hand they flew along the canal, never thinking whether the ice would bear them or not, for in Holland ice is generally an all-winter affair. It settles itself upon the water in a determined kind of way, and so far from growing thin and uncertain every time the sun is a little severe upon it, it gathers its forces day by day and flashes defiance to every beam.

—*Hans Brinker* or *the Silver Skates*
by Mary Mapes Dodge

Hark! The Herald Angels Sing

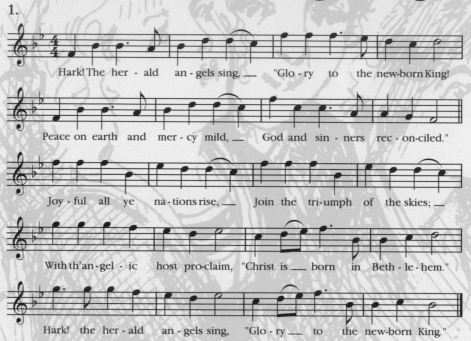

1.

Hark! The her-ald an-gels sing, __ "Glo-ry to the new-born King!

Peace on earth and mer-cy mild, __ God and sin-ners rec-on-ciled."

Joy-ful all ye na-tions rise, __ Join the tri-umph of the skies; __

With th'an-gel-ic host pro-claim, "Christ is __ born in Beth-le-hem."

Hark! the her-ald an-gels sing, "Glo-ry __ to the new-born King."

2. Christ, by highest heaven adored;
Christ, the everlasting Lord;
Come, Desire of Nations, come,
Fix in us thy humble home.
Veiled in flesh the Godhead see;
Hail th'Incarnate Deity,
Pleased as man with man to dwell;
Jesus, our Emmanuel

Chorus

3. Hail, the heave'n born Prince of Peace!
Hail, the Sun of Righteousness!
Light and life to all He brings,
Ris'n with healing in His wing;
Mild He lays His glory by,
Born that man no more may die,
Born to raise the sons of earth,
Born to give them second birth;

Chorus

The First Noel

1. The First Noel the angels did say
Was to certain poor shepherds in fields as they lay,
In fields where they lay keeping their sheep,
On a cold winter's night that was so deep.
Noel, Noel, Noel, Noel.
Born is the King of Israel.

2. They looked up and saw a star
Shining in the East beyond them far,
And to the earth it gave great light,
And so it continued both day and night.

Chorus

3. This star drew nigh to the Northwest,
O'er Bethlehem it took its rest,
And there it did both stop and stay,
Right over the place where Jesus lay.

Chorus

4. Then entered in those wisemen three,
Full rev'rently upon their knee,
And offered there in His presence,
Their gold and myrrh and frankincense.

Chorus

Winter Gardens

Visit the annual **International Ice Carving Competition** held at the **Crystal Gardens** in **Ottawa, Ontario**. Held every winter, the sculptures make a beautiful winter garden until they melt. Winterlude, or Bal de Neige, features four ice carving competitions. Sculptures range from delicate angels to grinning snowmen— made of ice, of course: *canadascapital.gc.ca*. Another ice sculpture garden to visit, if you can brave the cold, is the **Ice Art Championship** in **Fairbanks, Alaska**. Finished ice sculptures can weigh up to 20 tons and are often 20 feet tall: *icealaska.com*. The **Harbin** snow and ice parks in **Russia** are also a treat for the eyes. Lit nightly, the ice glows in red, green, amber, and other colors to show off the grandeur and remarkable detail of the giant sculptures.

A spectacular Cesar Pelli winter garden is located at the **World Financial Center** in **New York**. Flanked by an amphitheater of steps leading to upscale boutiques, it was reopened after being severely damaged in the September 11 attacks. Lunchtime choral concerts are enjoyed by many New Yorkers, who relax under its towering palm trees.

Western contemporary winter gardens trace their roots to England, the birthplace of the Victorian conservatory and Joseph Paxton's

famous Crystal Palace. Best-loved current examples are the **Princess of Wales Conservatory** at the Royal Botanic Gardens, **Kew Gardens** *(kew.org)*, and the Winter Gardens at **Blackpool**. The latter is actually part of a huge 1800s seaside resort complex that includes Winter Gardens Opera House, Winter Gardens Pavilion, Winter Gardens Spanish Hall, and the North Pier *(wintergardensblackpool.co.uk)*.

Perhaps the largest and most well known winter garden in the Midwest is Chicago's **Garfield Park Conservatory**, encompassing nearly two acres of plants and "Jurassic Park–size" palms under its sprawling glass roof. Included is a 5,000-square-foot kids' exhibit, featuring a giant two-story plant model that has a slide for a stem! The conservatory is free: *garfield-conservatory.org*.

The **Fuqua Conservatory** at the **Atlanta** Botanical Garden is special because of it contents: over 2,000 orchids: *atlantabotanicalgarden.org*.

After you've finished with the rides at Busch Gardens in **Tampa Bay**, Florida, visit the **Tropical Gardens** and the **Bird Gardens**, with over 350 different exotic flowers and flamingos: *buschgardens.com*.

Open since 1915, the **Como Park Conservatory** in **St. Paul** is the largest Victorian–style glass conservatory in the Minneapolis area. Explore the Palm Dome, North Garden, and Sunken Garden, where flower shows, afternoon teas, and other events abound: *comozooconservatory*.org

The **Gardens Collaborative** boasts 33 public garden attractions in the **Philadelphia** area, which has the largest concentration of public

gardens in the United States. The region hosts the nation's foremost horticultural garden, **Longwood Gardens** (sometimes called **du Pont Gardens**), near Kennett Square, Pennsylvania. It has over four acres of heated greenhouses, with the area around the East Conservatory decked out beautifully for Christmas. Visit the Orangery, Ballroom, Exhibition Hall, Organ Chamber (with pipe organ and organ museum), and 16 other indoor garden spaces. Longwood is home to 11,000 types of plants and 800 annual horticultural and performing arts events, including flower shows, educational programs, concerts, organ and carillon recitals, theatrical presentations, and fireworks: *longwoodgardens.org*.

Phipps Conservatory, a gift to the City of **Pittsburgh** from industrialist Henry Phipps, sports an elaborate H. H. Richardson entrance, as well as silvered domes and soaring glass vaults serving a full schedule of cultural events. When it opened, in 1893, it was the largest winter garden in the United States: *phipps.conservatory.org*.

The **Bolz Conservatory** at the Olbrich Botanical Gardens—another renowned institution—is a 50-foot-high glass pyramid located in **Madison, Wisconsin**. Its computerized climatic control system, with 220 misting nozzles, is linked to a weather station that regulates heat, shade, and humidity. The environment mimics the rain forest, and includes fish, geckos, frogs, toads, insects, and free-flying, hand-raised birds: *olbrich.org/gardens/conservatory.cfm*

Ski Spots

Western New York's Allegheny Mountains have some of the nicest verticals in the region, and may be one of the best-kept secrets of the East. Ellicottville, a charming village that is the Southern tier's answer to Woodstock, is minutes from **Holiday Valley** and **HoliMont** ski resorts. Sit on a wooden deck in the sun and sip hot chocolate or something stronger at one of Holiday's lodges, or tackle that very challenging headwall. There's something for every level of skier or boarder, the locals are super-friendly, and the local ski races here allow you to get up close and personal with some top-notch skiers. The nighttime skiing is great, too. Family-oriented HoliMont also features miles of quiet, softly wooded cross-country trails, as well as skating and sledding: *ellicottvilleny.com*.

Lake Placid's Whiteface Mountain in the Adirondacks offers challenging conditions and the highest vertical in the East. Alpine championships, extensive children's and adult programs, Little Whiteface, shuttle bus to accom-

Oh the weather outside is frightful,
But the fire is so delightful,
And since we've no place to go
Let it snow, let it snow, let it snow!

—SAMMY CAHN

modations, and plenty of room for everyone: *whiteface.com*.

If a **New England** holiday ski vacation is what you have in mind, try the old favorites for the best downhill: **Killington**, **Stowe**, and **Sugarbush** in Vermont; **Waterville Valley** in New Hampshire; **Sugarloaf** in Maine. With 205 trails and 12 quad lifts, Killington's facilities and ski-and-stay packages give you what you're looking for, along with snowshoeing, sleigh rides, cross-country, skating, and evening entertainment. Stowe and Sugarbush have large helpings of intermediate-level alpine, weekend getaways, and ski and snowboard schools. Waterville Valley emphasizes its Snowsports School. Sugarloaf has a huge network of well-groomed Nordic trails. Visit *skiing.alpinezone.com* for links to all.

With generally less vertical—around 500 feet—the sleepy **Pocono Mountains** offer a pleasant, relaxing getaway. Ski **Big Boulder-Jack Frost**, **Mountain Manor**, **Shawnee Mountain**, **Alpine Mountain**, and others. You can even go snow tubing. Lots of packages are available at *skipocono.com*.

You wouldn't think so, but **Granite Peak**'s 700-foot vertical drop is located in—yes—the heart of **Wisconsin**. The slope was cited for best deals in the region, with superb skiing and snowboarding on 77 runs—and a new chalet: *skigranitepeak.com*.

Heart set on the **Rockies**? **Aspen/Snowmass** is an old chestnut with a new generation of fans—snowboarders. For one ticket, you can ski or ride Aspen Mountain (Ajax), Snowmass, Buttermilk, and Aspen Highlands via free shuttle, all within a 12-mile radius. **Vail**, Colorado is the largest, most famous resort in the U.S., attracting the wealthy to its slopes and upscale

shops. Head to its famous back bowls for some of the best deep-powder skiing to be found anywhere. Vail's snowboarding school has 800 instructors. **Steamboat Springs**, Colorado, another classic, was the first to offer a Kids' Ski Free program: Children 12 and under can ski free on a parent's five-day or longer lift ticket. **Alta**, Utah, is the place to find uncrowded slopes, challenging, open-bowl terrain, and the coveted fresh powder that comes down nowhere else the way it does there. It's only for skiers, who say there's no place on earth like it. **Jackson Hole**, Wyoming is legendary for its backcountry atmosphere and awe-inspiring views. **Big Mountain**'s 3,000 skiable and boardable acres makes it one of Montana's largest, and it boasts a complete alpine village for vacationers as well. No review of skiing on the Continental Divide would be complete without mentioning **Banff**, Canada, not far from the stunning city of **Calgary**, Alberta. Banff Sunshine Village is a family-oriented resort, while Banff Mount Norquay's slopes are 44 percent advanced: *skiingtherockies.com*.

Comprising six **High Sierra** peaks, **Squaw Valley**, California, hosted the 1960 Winter Olympics. (Granite Chief is an awesome 9,000 feet high.) No lift lines here. Though the resort is classified 70 percent beginner to intermediate, "vast areas have been left in their pristine state for a true wilderness experience and some of the best advanced skiing anywhere," says

Ski Resorts Guide. California's **Mammoth Mountain** is truly mammoth and boasts a super-long ski season: *skiresorts-guide.com/statemap.cfm/CA.* For the **Lake Tahoe** bound, **Heavenly Ski Resort** resides on the south shore, straddling California and Nevada with 4,800 acres and 29 lifts: *skiresortsguide.com/statemap.cfm/NV.*

Are your downhill skills advanced enough to try **helicopter skiing**? Link up with *heliskiguide.com.*

Nordic-style adventurers looking for a natural outdoor high should check out the **Cross-Country** Ski Areas Association, with listings from New England, the Mid-Atlantic, Midwest, Mountain, and Far West regions, Canada, and France. The most popular attractions include Smuggler's Notch, Stowe, Sugarloaf, the American Birkebeiner Ski Foundation, Lutsen Resort, Sundance Nordic Center, Jackson Hole, Aspen, Royal Gorge XC Resort, and Yosemite. Many are near alpine skiing: *xcski.org/resorts_search.php*

With some 50 million copies sold, Irving Berlin's "White Christmas," recorded in 1942 by Bing Crosby, is still the best-selling single in history.

Christmas Movies

The Best Christmas Movies of All Time

The Bishop's Wife (1948)
A Charlie Brown Christmas (1965)
A Christmas Carol (1951)
Christmas in Connecticut (1945)
Dr Suess: How the Grinch Stole Christmas! (1966)
Frosty the Snowman (1969)
Home Alone (1990)
It's a Wonderful Life (1946)
The Little Drummer Boy (1968)
Little Lord Fauntleroy (1936)
The Little Princess (1939)
Mickey's Christmas Carol (1983)
The Miracle on 34th Street (1947)
The Muppet Christmas Carol (1992)
National Lampoon's Christmas Vacation (1989)
The Nightmare Before Christmas (1993)
Olive, the Other Reindeer (1999)
Rudolph, the Red-Nosed Reindeer (1964)
The Santa Clause (1994)
White Christmas (1954)

Go Tell It On The Mountain

1.

When I was a seek-er, I sought both night and day. I
asked the Lord to help me, And he showed me the way.

Chorus

Go tell it on the moun-tain, O-ver the hills and ev-'ry-where; —
Go tell it on the moun-tain, that Je-sus Christ is born!

2. He made me a watchman
Upon a city wall,
And if I am a Christian,
I am the least of all.

Chorus

These days sledding is just for fun, but once upon a time sleds were the only way for folks to travel and transport goods over snow and icy roads during the winter months.

Bring Us Some Figgy Pudding

The Christmas Feast

M · P

Champagne, Sparkling Wines, and Wine

Find the perfect champagne for your menu, learn its history, and find out when it's considered appropriate at the official website of **Champagne** wines: *champagne.fr*.

Established in 1743 by Claude Moët in Epernay, France, **Moët & Chandon** was favored by the Emperor Napoleon. The largest house in the Champagne region produces over 20 million bottles a year. Brut Imperial is the world's best selling non-vintage champagne; Moët & Chandon's best champagne, Dom Pérignon, is considered among the finest in the world. Moët & Chandon Bottles start at $50: *moet.com*.

Established by Perrier Nicolas-Marie Perrier in 1811, **Perrier-Jouët** is a fine, balanced champagne known for its art nouveau, "Belle Époque" flowery designed bottle. Bottles range from approximately $50.00–$150.00: *perrier-jouet.com*.

Pierre Taittinger dates back to 1734, when it was established by Jacques Fourneaux. In 1931, it was bought by Pierre Taittinger and his family still owns and runs it. Chardonnay is the main grape in its light and delicate champagne. Bottles range from $40.00–$200.00: *taittinger.com*, or call +(33) 03 26 85 45 35.

Founded by Etienne Bouvet in 1851, **Bouvet-Ladubay** produces its sparkling Saumur in the heart of the Loire Valley. This champagne is light, dry, and refreshing. Since 1974, it has been a subsidiary of Taittinger. Bottles range from $11.00–$20.00: *bouvet-ladubay.fr*.

Founded in 1829 and still run by the Bollinger family, **Bollinger** still ferments its champagnes in oak barrels and ages it well. The result is bold and complex—James Bond's champagne of choice. Bottles start at $50: *bollinger.fr*.

Joseph Perrier was established in 1825 in Châlons-sur-Marne. Its Cuvée Royale, Brut is aged 3–4 years and has a full, round body. Bottles range from approximately $14.00–$150.00: *joseph-perrier.com*.

Louis Roederer, established in 1982 in Anderson Valley, California, produces sparkling wine by combining their own vineyard grapes (Pinot Noir and Chardonnay) in the traditional *méthode champenoise*. They produce three wines: Anderson Valley Brut, Brut Rosé, and Tête de Cuvée, L'Ermitage: *roederer-estate.com*, or call (510) 286-2000.

Located in Spokane, Washington, **Mountain Dome** specializes in sparkling wine made in the traditional *méthode champenoise* style that's fermented in French oak barrels. Mountain Dome currently offers four unique sparkling wines: a Brut, A Brut Rosé, a Non Vintage Brut and a Tete Cuvée. Bottles range from from $12.00–$27.00: *mountaindome.com*, or call (509) 928-BRUT.

> Dear Lord, I've been asked, nay commanded, to thank thee for the Christmas turkey before us— a turkey which was no doubt a lively, intelligent bird—a social being capable of actual affection nuzzling its young with almost human-like compassion. Anyway, it's dead and we're gonna eat it. Please give our respects to its family.
>
> —BERKE BREATHED

📦

Established in 1882 in Sonoma's Russian River Valley, **Korbel** produces a California champagne that's very dry, fermented right in the bottle *à la méthode champenoise*. Korbel has been the exclusive sparkling wine served at the last six presidential inaugurations. Bottles range from $10.00–$35.00: *korbel.com/store*, or call (707) 824-7000.

📦

Litchfield County, Connecticut's **Hopkins Vineyard** has made wine for over 25 years, winning national and international medals. Their semi-sweet and sparkling wines range from $12.00–$41.00: *hopkinsvineyard.com*, or call (860) 868-7954.

📦

America's oldest winery, in the village of Washingtonville, New York, is the **Brotherhood Winery** which lists 24 premium New York State wines and sparkling wines including Chardonnay, White Zinfandel, Seyval Blanc, Chelois, Cabernet Sauvignon, Merlot, and Pinot Noir. Listed on the New York State Register of Historical Places, it offers on-line ordering and personalized wine labels: *brotherhoodwinery.net*, or call (845) 496-3661.

📦

Robert Mondavi founded his winery in 1966 in California's Napa Valley. Mondavi's progressive wine making techniques—cold fermentation, stainless steel tanks, and environmental friendly packaging—produce a variety of the valley's best wines: *robertmondavi.com*, or call (888) 766-6328.

📦

Uncorked Glens Falls specializes in wines from over 100 New York State wineries, and includes links to calendar events, recipes, and articles: *nywinecork.com*.

📦

A1champagne.com directs you to various links and sites, with categories such as Champagne, Champagne gift, Wine online,

Wine rating, Fine Wine, and Wine Book: *a1champagne.com*.

📦

1-800-4Champagne will deliver champagne nationwide today or tomorrow. Specializing in Champagne gift sets (bottle or case), it will include gift-wrapping and a message: *18004champagne.com*, or call (800) 424-2672

📦

On-line since 1994, **wine.com** will deliver any of 2,500 wines to your doorstep anywhere in the U.S. Search by region, type, winery, rating or packs: *wine.com*.

📦

Wine-searcher.com is excellent resource for locating and pricing wines with some 9,000 stores listed and over 1,000,000 wines: *wine-searcher.com*.

📦

NapaCabs.com specializes in "Fine wines and more" (especially Cabernet Sauvignon) at a discount. Search by winery, by *Wine Spectator's* listings, or by price, with free shipping and 12-pack specials: *NapaCabs.com*.

Christmas Cookies

Contact **Adriana's Italian Almond Cookies** for freshly baked gourmet almond, fig, and pistachio cookies: *cookiesfromitaly.com*.

Delightful Deliveries offers cookie and candy bouquets, to send anywhere. *delightfuldeliveries.com,* or call (800) 597-4489

Maurice Lenell sends Christmas cookie collections in special themed boxes. *ecomallbiz.com/lenell*, or call (800) 323-1760.

Now, here's the "real thing": imported Hungarian and European Christmas goodies, like *beigli* (walnut and poppyseed cookies), *pfeffernüsse* (gingerbread cookies), *gesztenyepüré* (chestnut puree), poppyseed *kipfli*, and *magyar szaloncukor* (Hungarian Christmas bon bons in assorted flavors) shipped from **Otto's Hungarian Import Store & Deli**:

hungariandeli.com, or call (818) 845-0433.

For the gourmet cookie lover, **Williams Sonoma** always has a good selection: *williamssonoma.com*, or call (877) 812-6235.

Cookie Dough

For delicious ready-made cookie dough in many flavors, try **David's Cookies**: *davidscookies.com*, or call (800) 500-2800; or log on to *doughtogo.com*, or call (800) 220-2339; and **Dancing Deer Baking Company**: *dancingdeer.com* or call (888) 699-DEER. Then scoop and bake!

Kosher-certified frozen cookie dough is available from **Fatboy's Outrageous Cookie Dough**: *outrageouscookiedough.com* and from **Chip-N-Dough**: *chipndough-fundraisers.com*, or call (866) 368-4448.

Of course domestic goddess **Martha Stewart** offers a classic selection of cookie cutters and decorations, along with her own easy-to-make cookie dough: *marthastewart.com* or call (800) 357-7060.

Cookie Cutters & Decorations

The Cookie Cutter has hundreds of cookie-cutter designs, including seasonal and theme sets: *cookiecutter.com*, or call (866) 756-6543.

Cooking.com has some great stars and animal designs on their attractive website: *cooking.com* or call (800) 663-8810.

Kitchenetc.com sells a good selection of cookie cutters and other baking essentials: *kitchenetc.com*, or call (800) 571-6316.

For an extensive selection of cookie cutters and decorations, **Confectionery House** is the place to visit. Online orders are preferable: *confectioneryhouse.com*, or call (518) 279-3179.

Can't find the cookie cutter you want? Try the "make your own cookie cutter" kit from **Sugar Craft:** *sugarcraft.com* or call (513) 896-7089.

Gingerbread Houses and Kits

Order gingerbread houses, carousels, and trains, pre-assembled or in kits, from **Candyland Crafts**: *candylandcrafts.com.*

Order a giant gingerbread chalet from **Bed Bath & Beyond**: *bedbathandbeyond.com* or a house kit from **Amazon**: *amazon.com*

Enchanted Gingerbread will make personalized houses for you, with the recipient's name written right over the door. There's also room for a tea candle inside (included) which, when, lit, will infuse your home with the holiday scent of gingerbread: *enchantedgingerbread.com,* or call (615) 228-9421.

Cookies were invented in Holland, where they were called *koekjes* (test cakes). These small portions of cake batter were used to test oven temperature before the full-size cakes were baked.

Mail-Order Christmas Dinner and International Delicacies

DelightfulDeliveries.com, (800) 597-4489 is a gourmet meal and gift basket superstore; mouth-watering pictures of their cheese baskets can be seen on their site. *gourmetstation.com,* (888)-944-9794 offers four-course gourmet dinners in Parisian, Tuscan and fusion menus, a New Orleans Cajun feast, and catered dinner parties. *scottishgourmethampers.co.uk* (+44 1667 451051) features Scottish gourmet Christmas hampers and everything needed for an intimate Scottish dinner, mailed from the Highlands. *chefshop.com* promises "Gourmet ingredients for the professional and home chef." *allfreshseafood.com* has wonderful whole fish—striped bass, sardines, red snapper, and trout—gourmet recipes and next-day delivery. *homebistro.com/delivery* (800) 628-5588 offers Christmas dinner and other holiday meals delivered nationwide in 48 hours. *gourmetdinnerservice.com.au* +61 (02) 9905 0266 will send an Australian Christmas picnic to that warm-climate family. *britsinthestates.com* is a British super mall, with links to dozens of online delivery sites.

The Best Hot Chocolate

Café Angelina: Open in Paris since 1903, this establishment serves its famously thick hot chocolate made the purists' way—from melted chocolate bars—and served with whipped cream.

Earthtones Coffee House: Located in Webster, New York, it publishes its own catalog and menu, featuring Mayan and Mexican-style drinks—on the Web: *earthtonescoffee.com.*

MarieBelle's Fine Treats and Chocolates: Artist and caterer Maribel Lieberman created this now world-famous, spicy, Aztec–style concoction in four flavors, just waiting for hot milk. Refrigerate it and it turns into a thick, luscious pudding. Contains no cocoa powder. Relax and enjoy it at her SoHo boutique, or order on-line—it's available from a variety of retailers: *mariebelle.com*

Dean and DeLuca: Sells Bensdorp fine cocoa. Refuel in your local Dean and DeLuca coffee bar, or order online for that Christmas party: *deandeluca.com.*

Schakolad Chocolate Factory: This franchiser, which handcrafts chocolate products on the premises of each of its thirty locations, is ready to take on Godiva. The stores have chocolate coffee bars featuring Schako Latte™ —real, not powdered, hot chocolate: *schakolad.com.*

Godiva Chocolatier: After your skate at Rockefeller Center, stop by one of the Center's two upscale Godiva Retail Boutiques for some gourmet hot cocoa—milk or dark chocolate. Godiva has sixteen boutiques in New York City alone: *Godiva.com.*

Starbucks: It's hard not to stumble upon a location of this ubiquitous chain. There's a reason for the company's success: The products, service, and atmosphere are good! Their menu offers premium cocoa blended with hot milk, and some interesting coffee and cocoa combos: *starbucks.com.*

Mother Fool's Coffee House in Madison, Wisconsin: a unique and quirky enterprise ensconced in one of America's best-loved towns. In addition to the organic "Alterra Coffee" and hot chocolate, the cafe advertises wireless DSL, Mother Fool's travel mugs, and art on the walls. Do we smell a cult following? *motherfools.com.*

> Gingerbread cookies were made famous in the 1600s by the Lebkuchler of Nuremberg, a guild of master bakers, who baked the favored treats for annual gingerbread fairs.

Gingerbread Cookies

7 cups white flour
3 teaspoons baking soda
4 teaspoons ground cinnamon
2 teaspoons ground cloves
4 teaspoons ground ginger
1 cup white sugar
1 cup brown sugar
1 cup butter (2 sticks), at room temperature
1 cup dark corn syrup
1¼ cups heavy cream

1. In a bowl, mix together the flour, baking soda, and spices.
2. Cream the sugar and butter in a separate bowl. Stir in the corn syrup and heavy cream. Slowly add the dry ingredients and blend well.
3. Flour your hands and toss the dough quickly on a floured surface. Roll into a ball, then divide that into 3 balls. Cover each in waxed paper. Put them in the refrigerator to chill for at least 2 hours.
4. Preheat the oven to 350°F and line baking sheets with parchment paper.
5. Turn the dough out on a lightly floured surface, one ball at a time, and roll out. You can roll the dough pretty thin for crisp cookies. You can also roll the dough directly onto waxed paper.
6. Cut with cookie cutters. Use a spatula to move the shapes onto cookie sheets. You can decorate the cookies with colored sprinkles or sugar crystals before baking.
7. Bake for approximately 15–20 minutes. When cookies are beginning to brown, remove them from the oven and slide the parchment off the baking sheet. When the cookies have cooled a bit, slide them off the parchment. Cool the cookie sheet before using it again.

24 to 48 cookies
depending on size and thickness.

Cranberry Walnut Bread

Great for breakfast Christmas morning, or as an afternoon snack.

4 cups white flour
1 tablespoon baking powder
1 teaspoon baking soda
¾ teaspoon cinnamon
1⅓ cup packed brown sugar
½ cup granulated sugar
½ cup butter (1 stick), melted
1 tablespoon grated orange rind
1½ cups orange juice
2 eggs
2 cups fresh cranberries, chopped
1 cup dried cranberries, chopped
1 cup walnuts, chopped

1. Preheat oven to 350°F. Butter and flour two 9" x 5" bread pans.
2. Combine all dry ingredients. In a separate bowl, combine butter, sugar, orange rind, juice and eggs. Slowly beat in dry ingredients. Add nuts and cranberries.
3. Divide batter evenly between two pans. Bake for 55–60 minutes or until fork inserted into the center comes out clean.
4. Cool in pan for at least ten minutes, then turn out.

Sugar Cookies

1 cup butter (2 sticks), at room temperature
1 cup sugar
2 eggs
1 teaspoon vanilla extract
3 cups flour
Grated zest of 2 oranges

1. Cream the butter and sugar. Beat in the eggs and add the vanilla and orange zest. Add the flour and mix well. Refrigerate for at least 2 hours.
2. Preheat the oven to 375°F and line baking sheets with parchment paper.
3. Roll the dough out on a lightly floured surface (marble or wood) and cut with a cookie cutter. Transfer the cookies with a spatula to cookie sheets. Bake for approximately 10 minutes.
4. When the cookies are beginning to brown, remove them from the oven and slide the parchment off the baking sheet. Wait until they are completely cool before icing (see recipe opposite). Ice with knife or icing bags and, if desired, sprinkle with colored sugars or other decorations before icing hardens.

Makes 36 to 60 cookies
depending on size and thickness.

The country's largest Christmas confection on record is a candy elephant, made in 1878.

Of course there were sweets. It was the marshmallows that squelched. Hardboileds, toffee, fudge and all sorts, crunches, cracknels, humbugs, glaciers, and marzipan and butter-welsh for the Welsh.

—DYLAN THOMAS

Snow Icing

1 pound confectioner's sugar
3 egg whites
1 tablespoon white vinegar
1 teaspoon vanilla
Assorted food coloring

1. Place the confectioner's sugar in a mixing bowl.
2. In a separate bowl, beat the egg whites lightly with a fork. Add them to the sugar and beat with an electric mixer on the lowest speed for 1 minute. Add vanilla. Add vinegar and beat for 2 more minutes at high speed, or until the mixture is stiff and glossy, as for stiff meringue.
3. Separate the mixture into small bowls and tint with different colors. Ice immediately or refrigerate in airtight container to keep icing from hardening before use.

Apple Crumb Pie

Frozen pie crust
1 cup sugar
2 tablespoons ground cinnamon
1 teaspoon ground nutmeg
$1/8$ teaspoon salt
Juice from one lemon
6 apples, peeled, cored, and sliced thin
$3/4$ cup flour
$1/2$ cup brown sugar
$1/2$ cup butter (1 stick), softened
Pinch of salt

1. Preheat oven to 425°F.
2. In a bowl, combine sugar, one tablespoon cinnamon, $1/2$ teaspoon nutmeg, $1/8$ teaspoon salt, and lemon juice. Add apples and toss.
3. Fill pie crust with apple mixture, mounding it slightly.
4. In a clean bowl, combine flour, brown sugar, butter, pinch of salt and remaining cinnamon and nutmeg, and crumble together with your fingers. Sprinkle over apple mixture.
5. Bake 30–40 minutes or until golden brown.

Marshmallow Snowmen

Sweet, fluffy, and plump, these marshmallow snowmen bring winter fun into the kitchen.

3 packets unflavored gelatin
2 cups white sugar
Pinch of salt
2 cups water
2 teaspoons vanilla
2 teaspoons baking powder
2 cups confectioner's sugar
Shredded coconut
Toothpicks
Melted chocolate (optional)

1. Mix gelatin, sugar, salt, and water in saucepan and simmer for 10 minutes. Let cool.
2. Add the vanilla, baking powder, and icing sugar. Beat until thick.
3. Spread mixture into a buttered 9" x 11" pan and refrigerate for 3 hours.
4. Cut out four $1^1/2$" and four 2" circles. Roll circles in coconut.
5. Attach each small circle to a larger circle with a toothpick. Add dots of melted chocolate for eyes, noses, and buttons.

Makes 8 snowmen.

Roast Turkey with Giblet Gravy

1 large bag (14 ounces) Pepperidge Farm
    Country Style or Herb Seasoned Stuffing
1/4 cup Italian parsley, minced
2 onions, minced
2 sticks celery, chopped
1 cup chopped walnuts or chestnuts
1 Turkey, approximately 14 pounds
1 stick (4 ounces) of butter
2 lemons
5 cups chicken stock
1 tablespoon white flour
1 teaspoon cornstarch

1. Preheat oven to 450°F.
2. Prepare stuffing following package instructions and add parsley, onions, celery, and nuts.
3. Remove gizzard, livers, neck, and anything else in the turkey cavity. Wash and dry.
4. Rub inside and out with lemons.
5. Slice stick of butter into thin slices and place all over outside of turkey. Stuff turkey.
6. Put turkey into turkey pan and pour the chicken stock around it.
7. Put into oven and leave for 20 minutes.
8. Turn heat down to 375°F and baste every 15 minutes for just under five hours (around 20 minutes per pound). If it is getting too brown, cover loosely with tin foil wrap.
9. Remove turkey and let rest for 20 minutes.
10. Remove as much fat as possible from the remaining liquid in the pan. Pour 1/2 cup out of the pan and mix with the flour and the cornstarch. When smooth, return to pan and stir until thickened.
11. Remove stuffing from turkey. Carve turkey and serve.

Serves 12 plus leftovers.

It is estimated that 400,000 people become sick each year from eating spoiled Christmas leftovers.

Maple Syrup Sweet Potatoes

4 sweet potatoes (or yams), peeled and quartered
4 tablespoons heavy cream
8 tablespoons maple syrup
4 tablespoons butter
Nutmeg, cinnamon, salt, freshly
    ground pepper to taste

1. Place potatoes in lightly salted cold water and cover.
2. Bring to a boil and then continue boiling lightly approximately 20 minutes.
3. Drain.
4. Mash the potatoes.
5. Place pot with mashed potatoes over medium heat and stirring with a wooden spoon, gradually pour in the cream, butter, and finally the maple syrup. Mix until potatoes are smooth and creamy.
6. Add seasonings to taste.

Serves 6–8.

Classic Cranberry Sauce

4 cups fresh cranberries
2 cups sugar
1 cup water

1. Combine ingredients in a pot over low heat and cover. Cook for about 15 minutes or until cranberries have burst.
2. Cool completely before serving.

Danish Deep Dish Apple Pie

6–7 cups white flour
2 cups white sugar, additional $^1/_2$ cup
3 teaspoons baking powder
3 sticks (12 ounces) butter
scant teaspoon salt
4 eggs
Grated zest of 6 lemons
12 apples (sliced and stored in the juice from
    the four lemons and the $^1/_2$ cup sugar)

1. Cream the butter and the sugar. Add the lemon rind.
2. Mix all the dry ingredients together and add those slowly to the butter, sugar, and lemon rind.
3. Line the deep dish pan with this using about half the dough. Add apples and more dough. Layering generously.
4. Bake for approximately 50 minutes—or until golden brown—at 375°F.

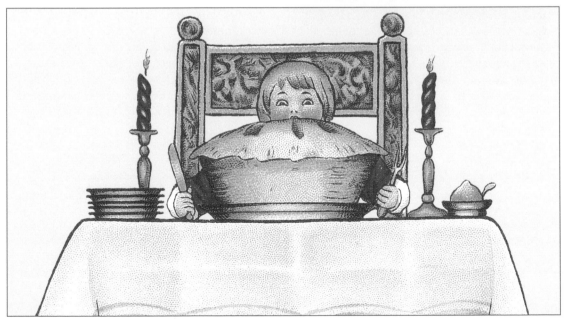

Caribbean Black Cake

This cake is made especially at Christmas, for weddings and other special occasions; it is known as Black Cake because traditionally, burnt sugar/caramel is used to give the color.

3 pounds mixed fruits: 1 pound currants, 1¹/₂ pounds raisins, and ¹/₂ pound prunes, pitted
¹/₂ pound mixed citrus peel
6 tablespoons rum—more if needed
1¹/₂ cups sherry—more if needed
2 cups burnt sugar or caramel (you will need 1 pound white or brown sugar, plus several tablespoons sherry, stout, or water)
1 pound all-purpose flour
2 teaspoons ground cinnamon
1 teaspoon grated nutmeg
1 pound (4 sticks) butter
1 pound dark brown sugar
12 eggs beaten
1 tablespoon olive oil (optional)
1¹/₂ teaspoon vanilla extract—more if needed

1. Wash and grind or process fruits until finely chopped. Place in a jar or bowl with rum and sherry and set aside for 2 weeks to 3 months—the longer it is left the better the flavor will be. Stir occasionally and add more rum & sherry to keep moist. If in a hurry, simmer the fruits in the sherry for about 15 minutes and leave overnight.
2. Preheat the oven to 325°F. Grease and line two 8-inch round cake pans with foil or wax paper.
3. Put 2 cups white or brown sugar on a pot on low heat. When all the grains of the sugar have melted into dark brown syrup, take it off the burner. Use a low heat—a high flame will cause the liquid to bubble erratically. Before sugar is completely cooled add just enough liquid—water, sherry or stout—to completely dissolve the sugar. Set aside.
4. Combine flour, cinnamon, and nutmeg. Set aside.
5. Cream the butter and sugar together and beat in the eggs until the mixture is smooth and creamy.
6. Add the fruit mixture, then gradually stir in the flour mixture and add vanilla extract. Add olive oil (optional). Mix well, adding burned sugar until the desired color is achieved. Be sure to taste as you add to avoid bitterness. Mixture should fall off back of the spoon but should not be too runny.
7. Spoon the mixture into the prepared pans and bake for 30 minutes, then reduce heat to 225°F. The cakes are finished when a wooden toothpick inserted comes out clean. Remove cakes from oven, and while still hot sprinkle with rum and/sherry as desired. Leave in pan overnight. Wrap the cakes in wax paper to keep them moist.

Figgy Facts

Thought to be the forerunner of modern Christmas puddings, *frumenty* was a spiced Celtic porridge. Legend had it that the harvest god Dagda whipped up a porridge made from all the good things of the Earth. Today's flaming Christmas pudding dates back to 1670.

By the beginning of the 19th century, the original Celtic porridge—which was made with plums—had become a pudding, and the plums had been replaced with raisins.

A plum pudding can also be called a Christmas pudding or a Figgy pudding. Normally made without figs, the term "fig" means raisin—at least in Cornwall, England.

Traditionally, a plum pudding should have a button, a ring and a coin baked into it. Whoever got the button would remain a bachelor or spinster, while the ring foretold marriage, and the coin wealth.

Christmas pudding promises good luck: Make a wish while mixing it up, but remember, it can come true only if you stir in a clockwise direction.

Figgy Pudding

1 cup finely chopped beef suet
$^1/_2$ cup white sugar
$^1/_2$ cup brown sugar
3 egg yolks
1 cup milk
4 tablespoons rum or brandy
1 apple, peeled, cored and finely sliced
$^1/_2$ pound dried figs, ground or finely chopped
$^1/_4$ pound raisins
$^1/_4$ pound back currants
Grated peel of 1 lemon
Grated peel of 1 orange
1 cup chopped almonds and walnuts
$^1/_2$ teaspoon ground cinnamon
$^1/_4$ teaspoon ground cloves
$^1/_4$ teaspoon ground ginger
$^1/_8$ teaspoon allspice
$^1/_8$ teaspoon nutmeg
$1^1/_2$ cups bread crumbs
2 teaspoons baking powder
3 egg whites, stiffly beaten

1. Preheat oven to 325°F. Grease an oven-safe 2 quart bowl and set aside.
2. Place suet in a separate bowl and gradually add sugar, egg yolks, milk, rum or brandy, apple, figs, raisins, currants, and citrus peels. Then add nuts, spices, bread crumbs, and baking powder. Fold in egg whites.
3. Pour mixture into the prepared bowl, and place in a large, shallow pan on the middle oven rack. Half fill the shallow pan with boiling water and steam pudding for four hours, adding water as needed.
4. Serve pudding warm with custard sauce spooned on top.

Custard Sauce

2 cups half-and-half
1 egg
$^3/_4$ cup sugar
1 tablespoon water
1 tablespoon vanilla extract
1 tablespoon flour
1 tablespoon butter

1. In saucepan, scald half and half and then set aside to cool.
2. Combine egg, sugar, water, vanilla and flour and add to cooled cream. Cook custard over low heat until thickened. Remove from heat and stir in butter, mixing well.

The great fire was banked high and red in the grate, And when dinner was ended the big plum pudding would be carried in, studded with peeled almonds and springs of holly, with bluish fire running around it . . .

—James Joyce

Finnish Christmas Coffee Bread

2 packets Fleischman's Regular Dry Yeast
1 cup warm water
1 tablespoon sugar
1 large teaspoon fresh cardamom seeds
$^1/_2$ cup (1 stick) melted butter
1 teaspoon salt
1 cup + tablespoons milk
4 eggs, beaten
$^3/_4$ cup sugar
8 cups white flour
1 egg
1 cup sugar
$^1/_2$ cup cinnamon
1 cup walnuts

1. Dissolve yeast into a glass cup of warm water with 1 tablespoon of sugar. It should take about 10 minutes for the yeast to activate and bubble. If this does not occur, discard and s tart over.
2. Pulverize cardamom seeds.
3. In a large pot melt butter, 1 teaspoon salt. Then add milk and cardamom and turn off heat.
4. Preheat oven to 250°F. Turn oven off after five minutes; it will remain warm.
5. Add activated yeast to 4 beaten eggs and $^3/_4$ cups sugar.
6. Add 4 cups of white flour, spooning in each cupful so that flour is fluffy. Stir well, then add yeast mixture and stir well.
7. Cover dough with a dish towel and place in warmed oven for one hour, until surface puffs a little and has air holes.
8. Add another $3^1/_2$ cups flour, grease your hands, and knead dough for about ten minutes, until it will lift out of pot into a floured board in one big glob. Add $^1/_2$ cup flour gradually (only as needed) as you knead with the heels of your hand until dough feels soft and rubbery with a smooth, satiny finish (will still be a little sticky).
9. Put dough in a greased bowl and cover with a cloth and place back in the oven to rise. It should double in size over 2–$2^1/_2$ hours.
10. Punch down and knead for two to three minutes. Cut dough into four parts with a sharp knife, then cut each part into three pieces.
11. Dust board with flour and roll each part in oiled hands into a sausage shape. Then roll each sausage into a long strand. Roll at the center moving outward and make long strips. Line up the strips of two greased cookie sheets, six to a sheet. Braid them into two coffee breads per cookie sheet.
12. Cover breads with cloth and place back in the oven and let rise for about one and a half hours or until loaves have doubled in size.
13. Wisk an egg in a bowl and set aside. In another bowl mix 1 cup sugar with cinnamon. In a third bowl chop walnuts. When loaves have risen remove from oven and pre-heat to 375°F. Brush loaves with egg and then sprinkle liberally with cinnamon sugar and nuts.
14. Bake for 15–20 minutes, repositioning baking sheets as necessary to keep bottoms from burning. Loaves should be lightly browned.

Makes 4 braided loaves.

Bûche de Noël

WHIPPED CREAM FILLING:
2 cups heavy cream
1/4 cup confectioners' sugar
1 teaspoon vanilla extract

CAKE:
6 egg yolks
1/2 cup sugar
1/3 cup unsweetened cocoa powder
1 1/2 teaspoons vanilla
1/8 teaspoon salt
6 egg whites
1/4 cup white sugar
Confectioner's sugar for dusting

1. Preheat over to 375°F. Linc a 10" x 15" jelly-roll pan with parchment paper.
2. In a large bowl whip cream, 1/2 cup confectioner's sugar, 1 teaspoon vanilla until stiff peaks form. Refrigerate.
3. In a large bowl, beat egg yolks and 1/2 cup sugar with an electric mixer until thick and pale. Add 1/3 cup cocoa, 1 1/2 teaspoon vanilla and salt.
4. In a separate bowl, beat egg whites until soft peaks form. Slowly add 1/4 cup sugar and beat until stiff peaks form. Immediately add yolk mixture. Spread batter evenly into the jelly-roll pan.
5. Bake for approximately 15 minutes, or until cake springs back when lightly touched. Remove from oven and let sit for five minutes.
6. Dust a clean kitchen towel with confectioner's sugar and turn warm cake onto to towel. Discard parchment. Roll cake up in the towel, starting at the shorter end. Set aside to cool.
7. Unroll cake and spread with whipped cream to within 1 inch of the edge. Re-roll cake with filling inside.

> The traditional ending to a French Christmas meal is the *Bûche de Noël*, a Yule log sponge cake covered with chocolate butter-cream bark.

In Greece, Christians return home from mass in the wee hours of the morning to eat Christpsomo (Christ's bread).

8. Ice sides, front, and back ends of log with chocolate icing, swirling the knife to give the appearance of bark. Garnish with holly sprigs and serve.

ICING:
2 ounces unsweetened chocolate
2 tablespoons butter
1/4 cup espresso, heated
2 cups confectioner's sugar
1 teaspoon cinnamon

1. Combine chocolate and butter in microwave or double boiler and heat until melted.
2. Remove from heat and mix wel. Add espresso, then mix in sugar and cinnamon.

Serves 12.

German Pfeffernusse Cookies

These festive holiday cookies are a staple in Germany. They make great gifts and will quickly become a family favorite. If you like them spicy, feel free to double the pepper!

$3^1/_2$ cups flour
$^3/_4$ teaspoon baking powder
$^3/_4$ teaspoon baking soda
$1^1/_2$ teaspoons ground cinnamon
$^1/_4$ teaspoon ground white pepper
$^1/_2$ teaspoon ground ginger
$^1/_4$ teaspoon ground cloves
$^1/_4$ teaspoon salt
4 tablespoons butter
$1^1/_4$ cup granulated sugar
3 large eggs
$1^1/_2$ cups confectioner's sugar for dusting

1. Mix flour, baking powder, baking soda, spices and salt. Set aside.
2. In a large bowl, combine butter and sugar. Beat in eggs one at a time. Then slowly beat in dry mixture until fully blended.
3. Roll dough into a ball and refrigerate in plastic wrap until firm (approximately half an hour). Preheat oven to 350°F. Line 2 large cookie baking sheets with parchment paper.
4. Remove dough from refrigerator and scoop tablespoon-sized scoops. Roll into balls and place on baking sheet.
5. Bake for 15 minutes until golden and slightly cracked. Cool for five minutes. Then roll each warm cookie in a bowl of confectioner's sugar to coat.

According to an old German folktale, when village children helped reunite St. Nicholas and his lost donkey, the animal magically produced Pfeffernusse for them as thanks.

Italian Stufoli

4 egg whites
1 stick butter, softened
$^1/_2$ cup sugar
3 cups flour
2–3 cups safflower oil
$^1/_2$ cup honey
3 teaspoons grated orange peel
1 tablespoon vanilla extract
Confectioner's sugar for dusting

1. Combine egg whites, butter and sugar. Work in flour gradually, adding extra if necessary to make the dough stiff.
2. Roll out the dough on a floured surface to strips about the thickness of a finger, then cut into 1-inch pieces and roll each into a little ball.
3. Heat oil in a frying pan and fry balls for 3–4 minutes or until golden brown. Drain on paper towels and build into a pyramid shape on a platter.
4. In a saucepan, combine honey and orange peel and heat, stirring constantly. When warmed, turn off the heat and mix in vanilla. Pour syrup over pyramid. Dust with confectioners' sugar.

The French traditionally serve 13 desserts to top off the last meal of Advent: one for Christ and each of the 12 disciples. In the South France, the first portion of *pain calendeau* (Christmas loaf) is given to a poor person. Brittany's best-loved main dish is buckwheat cakes and sour cream, while Alsatians prefer roast goose. Turkey is served with chestnuts in Burgundy, and oysters are the favorite Christmas fare among Parisians.

Mexican Flan

2 cups whipping cream
2 cups milk
1 1/2 teaspoons vanilla extract
1/8 teaspoon ground cinnamon
1 1/4 cups sugar
4 large eggs, lightly beaten
5 egg yolks, lightly beaten

1. Preheat oven to 350°F. Heat 3/4 cups sugar in a saucepan over medium heat. When sugar begins to dissolve stir constantly with a wooden spoon. When caramel is a golden brown, pour into mold. Swirl around so that bottom and sides are coated. Set aside.
2. In a clean saucepan, combine milk, cream, vanilla and simmer about ten minutes or until liquid is reduced by half. Stir in remaining 1/2 up sugar and dissolve. Cover and remove from heat.
3. In a bowl, combine eggs and yolks, then wisk in to warm milk mixture.
4. Pour custard into flan mold. Cover mold with foil and place in larger baking pan and fill pan with water until it reaches half the height of the mold.
5. Bake 40 minutes to an hour, or until knife in the center comes out clean. Let cool for 30 minutes at room temperature, then refrigerate overnight. Prior to serving, invert mold onto a platter. Serve cold.

New Zealand Pavlova

Traditional New Zealand Pavlova was named after Anna Pavlova, the Russian ballerina whose *bourrés* were as light as air—just like the texture of this dessert.

3 egg whites
3 tablespoons cold water
1 cup castor sugar
1 teaspoon vinegar
1 teaspoon vanilla essence
3 teaspoons corn flour

1. Pre-heat oven to 300°F.
2. Beat egg whites until stiff, add cold water and beat again. Add castor sugar very gradually (1 tablespoon at a time while beating between each addition). Slow the beater and add the vinegar, vanilla, and corn flour.
3. Place on parchment paper-covered baking sheet or greased baking sheet and bake at 300°F for 10 minutes. Then turn heat off and leave Pavlova in the oven for another 35 minutes to cook as the oven cools down.
4. Whip cream until stiff peaks form. Once Pavlova is cool, spread whipped cream over the top. Slice kiwis, strawberries (other berries are good too!), or squeeze passion fruit pulp and pour over the top of the Pavlova. Slice into wedges and serve immediately.

Christmas dinner in early England was not turkey, but the head of a pig eaten with mustard. The Christmas turkey made its first appearance on English tables in the 1500s, but didn't manage to upstage the traditional beef, goose, and boar's head served in wealthy households. The Victorian era saw the popularity of the turkey rise. The turkeys were walked to London markets wearing special boots to protect their feet from the frozen mud.

Polish Poppyseed Cake

CAKE:

4 eggs
¹/₂ cup sugar
¹/₂ cup hazelnuts, finely chopped
¹/₂ cup candied orange peel, chopped
¹/₂ cup dried cranberries, chopped
¹/₂ cup dried apricots, chopped
¹/₃ cup flour
¹/₂ cup poppy seeds

ICING:

Corn syrup
Chocolate chips

1. Preheat oven to 375°F and butter a bundt cake pan.
2. Beat eggs with an electric mixer until fluffy (about 5 minutes). Add sugar, nuts, and fruit, then flour and poppy seeds. Pour into cake pan.
3. Bake for 45 minutes or until fork inserted into the center of the cake comes out clean.
4. Allow cake to cool completely before icing.

> *Poppy seed cake, or makowiec, has been the most popular Christmas cake in Poland since Armenian merchants first introduced the exotic seed from the East.*

Scottish Shortbread

Makes a great holiday gift, since it can keep for several weeks in a sealed container, it's also great to serve to drop-in holiday guests—along with coffee or mulled cider—on a chilly afternoon.

1 cup (2 sticks) butter, softened
¹/₄ cup brown sugar
¹/₄ cup granulated sugar
2 cups flour
2 sheets of parchment paper
1 tablespoon grated lemon or orange zest

1. Preheat oven to 275°F. Place two 8" cake layer pans on top of parchment paper and trace. Then cut out circles slightly inside the lines, so that parchment will fit inside cake pans. Butter pans and line with parchment. Set aside.
2. Cream butter and sugar together. Add zest. Gradually add flour until blended completely until dough is firm but slightly sticky.
3. Divide dough in half and form each into a round ball. Press each ball into a cake pan and smooth down with a spatula until dough is evenly distributed in pan.
4. With the back edge of a knife, indent pie slices into the dough. Then make decorative patterns in dough with a fork or a wooden skewer.
5. Bake for 35–45 minutes until golden but not browned.
6. Remove from oven and allow shortbread to cool for ten minutes. Then, gently turn it out of the pan and sit right side up. While still warm, a serrated knife can be used to slide into wedges or shortbread can be left intact to be given as a gift.

Did You Know?

According to English tradition, eating mincemeat pie on each of the 12 days of Christmas ensures 12 happy months ahead (and a few not-so-happy extra pounds). The custom dates back to the 16th century.

Mince pie became a Nativity Feast tradition in England after crusaders returned from the Holy Lands and flavored the Christmas pie with new-found spices.

The egg-glazed *koulourakia* favored in the Greek Christmas traditions has long been a symbol of Christ's purity.

The liquor-preserved fruitcake was a favored Christmas treat in Victorian England, but quite an undertaking: recipes called for eggs to be beaten a full half hour!

The Christmas Eve feast in Denmark begins with almond porridge and moves on to stuffed duck, pork, red cabbage, and candied potatoes. And that's not all: The Christmas Day buffet, which can last from midday until late into the evening, features pickled herring; smoked sausages, lamb, and cheeses; shrimp, meatballs, caviar, pâté, cold roast pork, beer, and Schnapps.

The Holy Days and Fasting Days Act of 1551, still part of British law, requires that every citizen attend a Christian church service on Christmas Day, and not use any kind of vehicle to get there.

Fried fish and spinach would probably be your Christmas meal in Armenia. The meal, eaten after the Christmas Eve service, commemorates the supper eaten by Mary the evening before Christ's birth.

Hot Chocolate with Peppermint Sticks

2 cups whole milk
2 tablespoons unsweetened cocoa
2 tablespoons white sugar
1/4 teaspoon vanilla
Peppermint sticks

1. Combine milk and cocoa in a medium-size saucepan on low heat.
2. Using a handheld manual egg beater or whisk, whip the mixture as it heats until smoothly blended.
3. Hot chocolate should now be warm but not boiling. Add sugar and vanilla and continue to blend until hot.

Serve with a peppermint candy cane stirrer. Nibble the candy cane between stirring.

Candy canes began as straight white sugar-candy sticks used to decorate Christmas trees. It wasn't until the 20th century that they got their red stripes.

Mulled Apple Cider with Cinnamon Sticks

1 quart (8 cups) apple cider
Grated peel from 1/2 orange
1 teaspoon whole allspice
2 cinnamon sticks (plus extra for garnish)

1. Put the cider in a large saucepan over the lowest heat.
2. Wrap up the remaining ingredients in a big piece of cheesecloth and put it into the pot, or put them in a strainer that hooks over the pot. Simmer at the lowest heat for 4 to 5 hours.
3. Throw away the spices, pour the cider into mugs, and add a cinnamon stick.

Serves 8.

Good King Wenceslas

1.

Good King Wen - ces - las look'd out on the Feast of Steph - en,

When the snow lay 'round a - bout, Deep and crisp and e - ven.

Bright - ly shone the moon that night, Tho the frost was cru - el,

Then a poor man came in sight Gath'ring win - ter fu - el.

2. "Hither, page and stand by me,
   If thou know'st it, telling,
   Yonder peasant, who is he?
   Where and what his dwelling?"
   "Sire, he lives a good league hence
   Underneath the mountain;
   Right against the forest fence,
   By saint Agnes fountain!"

3. "Bring me flesh, and bring me wine,
   Bring me pinelogs hither;
   Thou and I will see him dine
   When we bear them hither."
   Page and monarch forth they went,
   Forth they went together;
   Thro' the rude wind's wild lament
   And the bitter weather.

4. "Sire, the night is darker now,
   And the wind blows stronger;
   Fails my heart, I know not how,
   I can go no longer."
   "Mark my footsteps, my good page.
   Tread thou in them boldly,
   Thou shalt find the winter's rage
   Freeze thy blood less coldly!"

5. In his master's steps he trod,
   Where the snow lay dinted;
   Heat was in the very sod
   Which the saint had printed;
   Therefore, Christian men, be sure,
   Wealth or rank possessing,
   Ye who now will bless the poor,
   Shall yourselves find blessing.

Party Menus & Themes

Christmas may come but once a year, but 'tis the season for holiday parties. The next time you welcome friends and family over, decide on a menu that best complements your get-together, such as a cozy sit-down dinner after a night of caroling, or a buffet of fun finger foods for an evening of parlor games. Here's our sampling of menu ideas tailored for themed gatherings:

cheese platter, apple-nut tart, wassail.

Tree Trimming Party

Before ornaments became popular, people commonly decorated their Christmas trees with decorations that could be plucked off the tree to eat.

Strings of popcorn, cranberries, and dried fruit, baked apples with cinnamon and brown sugar, candy canes, nutcracker platter with walnuts, pecans, cashews, macadamias, pistachios, almonds, filberts, and Brazil nuts, assorted chocolates, iced gingerbread men, eggnog.

Caroling Night

Serve up a Victorian favorite after a winter's eve of Christmas songs with some hot, spiced wassail and a hearty stew.

Baby spinach and pear salad with goat cheese and walnuts, chicken sausage gumbo, fig and

Cookie Decorating

Complement the mouth-watering smells of baking cookies with spiced cider and an assortment of finger-licking hot and cold appetizers.

Chicken wings with ginger-plum sauce, mini-meatballs in tomato sauce, "frosty" veggie platter—with carrots, celery, broccoli and cauliflower florets, peppers, olives, and mushrooms arranged like a snowman, tangy ranch dip, spiced cider, mulled wine.

Yuletide Parlor Games

When the focus is on merriment and game playing, set up a buffet table with cocktail plates and invite invite the nibbling to go on all evening.

Corn Relish, farfalle with pancetta, peas, and mint, cheese fondue with French bread and vegetable crudités, plum pudding, hot buttered rum.

Swedish Glogg

2 quarts port wine
$1/4$ pound raisins
$1/4$ pound whole blanched almonds
10 whole cloves
6 cinnamon sticks
1 pound mixed dried apricots, apples, and prunes
1 quart dry red wine
Aquavit to taste

1. Pour port wine into cast-iron pot with raisins and almonds. Place spices and dried fruits in strainer over pot so they are well covered by the wine.
2. Simmer on low heat for 1 hour.
3. Turn off heat, cover, and let glogg steep for one day.
4. One half-hour before serving, remove strainer and add the wine to the pot. Heat mixture over low flame until hot.
5. Fill serving glasses $1/4$ full with aquavit, then spoon in some raisins and almonds from pot, and top off with hot glogg. Serve immediately.

Serves 8 to 14.

Champagne Punch

1 quart white grape juice
1 bottle red wine
1 bottle white wine
1 pint light rum
6 ounces Grand Marnier
1 bottle Champagne
$1/2$ pound sugar
Lemon and orange slices for garnish

1. Dissolve sugar in grape juice. Place a large block of ice in a large bowl and pour grape juice and sugar mixture over it. Add wine, rum and Grand Marnier.
2. Right before serving, add champagne and garnish with fruit slices.

Makes approximately three dozen servings.

Holiday Egg Nog

6 eggs
$1^3/4$ cup superfine granulated sugar
4 cups (1 quart) half-and-half
3 teaspoons ground nutmeg
3 cups whipping cream
$1/2$ cup rum
1 cup brandy
1 cup bourbon
1 tablespoon vanilla extract

1. Separate the eggs.
2. Beat yolks with electric mixer until foamy and thickened.
3. Add 1 cup sugar and 2 teaspoons of the nutmeg and mix well.
4. Add half-and-half and blend well.
5. Beat egg whites until they have soft peaks.
6. In a separate bowl, beat the cream with $3/4$ cup sugar until thick.
7. Fold whipped egg whites and cream into the yolks and half-and-half mixture.
8. Stir in alcohol and sprinkle with remaining ground nutmeg.
9. Chill. Serve from a punchbowl with a ladle.

Egg Nog is a modern relative of wassail, a spiced year-end libation meaning "to your health" that dates back to 5th-century England.

Hot Buttered Rum

2 dashes bitters
3 ounces dark rum
1 teaspoon butter
3–4 whole cloves
Boiling water

1. Dash bitters into a mug. Add the rum and place in the butter in the mug. Pour in boiling water to fill the mug. Add cloves and stir. Allow to steep for a few minutes.
2. Remove cloves and serve.

Makes one serving.

Where to Get the Best Hot Chocolate

By the eighteenth century, hot "chocolate houses" were as popular as coffee houses. The apt description "rich and decadent" held more than one meaning: Hot chocolate, in those days, was indeed a drink for the wealthy.

Lake Champlain Chocolates: All-natural gourmet hot chocolate from Vermont. Original, mocha, raspberry, and orange flavors: *lakechamplainchocolate.com.*

Shokinag Chocolate: Hot chocolate, European style. Tiny pieces of top-quality dark and milk chocolate with a dusting of cocoa powder make a smooth, rich drink. A holiday gift chocolate lovers won't forget: *worldpantry.com.*

SeriousChai.com: Carries Big Train premium dark fat-free cocoa mix and Big Train Loco Cocoa, a blend of dark chocolate and cinnamon. Mmm: *seriouschai.com*

Ghirardelli Chocolate: Highly rated hot cocoa in four flavors: Chocolate, Double Chocolate, Chocolate Hazelnut, and White Mocha: *ghirardelli.com.*

Droste Chocolate of Holland: Top-notch processed cocoa. For true hot-cocoa addicts.

Nesquik Chocolate Hot Cocoa, with bunny-shaped marshmallows: A favorite of young hot-cocoa aficionados, it's entertaining and tastes good: *verybestkids.com.*

Swiss Miss Chocolate Sensation Hot Cocoa Mix: Less sugary; appeals to adult tastes. Made from imported Dutch cocoa, it's considered one of the best commercial chocolate mixes around. Available everywhere.

Wine

Wondering what to pour for Christmas dinner? Cabernet Sauvignon has a great, fruity taste that goes well with the cranberry sauces and dried fruit stuffings that are traditional to the season. For the best flavor, white wines should be taken from the refrigerator and decanted 10 minutes prior to serving.

The raisins were so plentiful and rare, the almonds so extremely white, the other spices so delicious, the candied fruits so caked and spotted with molten sugar as to make the coldest lookers-on feel faint.

—CHARLES DICKENS

We Wish You A Merry Christmas

We wish you a Mer-ry Christ-mas, We wish you a Mer-ry

Christ-mas, We wish you a Mer-ry Christ-mas and a

Hap - py New year! Glad ti - dings we

bring to you and your kin; Glad

ti - dings for Christ-mas and a Hap - py New Year! We

My True Love Gave to Me
Gifts of the Season

The Three Magi

Pura Belpré

Llegan de noche con gran cantela
Cuando ninguno sus pasos vela
Y al dormitoria del niño van
Y al dormitoria del niño van.

Swiftly they come in the night
As every one sleeps
And no one their footsteps watches
Then to the children's bedroom they go
Then to the children's bedroom they go

It was the fifth of January, the eve of the "Three Kings" day. The day when all Spanish children eagerly await their Christmas presents.

In the sumptuous Palace of the Orient, where the Magi Kings lived, reigned great excitement and confusion. The Royal doorman had been busy all morning answering the bell as the couriers came from the four corners of the world, bringing the royal mail. Inside the palace, the Chamberlain's voice could be heard giving orders to his hundred servants.

"Open the windows," he shouted, and a hundred men glittering in uniforms decked with gold and silver, in which the initials "M.M." (Magi Messengers) stood out, ran from one side of the spacious hall to the other, and opened wide the royal windows, letting in the cool air.

Kerchoo! Kerchoo! sneezed the Chamberlain.

"Bring my highest powdered wig," he called.

Again the hundred servants darted on, getting in each other's way, stumbling over chairs and sofas, until finally a very tall and thin one was able to free himself from the rest and bring out an immense wig, which he placed on the Chamberlain's head.

In the Royal kitchen the noise rose like a thunderous wave. Like a captain before his army, and clad in white apron and high cap, the royal chef stood. With hands folded across his voluminous stomach, he gravely directed his men. They carried out his orders with dexterity and care.

At his signal eggs were broken and beaten to soft fluffy foam, flour kneaded and almonds and nuts grated to a fine powder. From the oven and frying pans rose the smell of sweetmeats and roasts. It was evident that in the Royal Kitchen of the Three Magi, the innumerable cooks were getting ready an immense repast for a long journey.

Outside the palace in the Royal stables, the stamping and neighing of the Royal horses could be heard for miles around. Lines and lines of coaches, covered with heavy blankets, could be seen down the hall.

"There comes Carlos again," whispered a dapple grey horse to another.

"Stop your stamping, stop it this minute," called out Carlos as he opened the door.

In reply the horses raised their heads and neighed loudly.

"I know, I know," said Carlos, "but this is the eve of the "Three Kings' day, and it's the camels the Magi want and not horses."

Slowly he opened the door and led the camels to the public square. Already people were gathered there, while the stable hands brought gallons of water, baskets of scented soaps and a great number of combs and brushes.

The Royal Camels were about to receive their bath and this was a ceremony always performed in public. First the water was poured reverently over their backs. Then the stable boys divided in groups of ten and armed with soap and brushes began the scrubbing. This finished, another group would begin the combing and smoothing of the hair. Decked then with red mantles and silver reins, the three choice stable boys Carlos, Juan and Pedro led them to the door of the Royal Palace. The three magnificent looking camels of the Three Magi were the happiest camels in the entire world, for it was the 5th of January and they were to carry on their backs the three most-wished-for persons in the children's world—King Gaspar, King Melchor, and King Baltazar. But they were impatient as they stood there. Putting their three heads together they asked each other:

"Where are the Three Magi? Why do they keep us waiting?"

And well might they ask, for the Three Kings could hardly be seen at that time.

In the Grand Throne Room, behind a barricade of opened envelopes they sat laughing and nodding to each other, as they read and carefully put away millions of letters sent to them.

There were letters of all sizes and colors. Some of them were written on fine paper with gilt borders, others embellished with flowers and birds, written in clear and legible handwriting, but the majority of them, and these were the ones the Kings liked best, were written on scraps of paper, and full of dots of ink and many erasures. They all carried the same message—a plea for some particular toy and a promise to be a better boy or girl in the future.

At last, the last letter was read and carefully put away. Slowly the Three Magi rose from their beautiful thrones and left the room. The Royal doorman saw them coming and opened the door wide. Solemn in their approach, majestic in their bearing, handsomely garbed with precious stones and jewelry, and with their ermine coats about them, the Three Magi of the Orient appeared at the door ready to mount their camels.

"How beautiful and handsome they are," said Carlos to the other stable boys as they held the camels for the Magi to mount.

Large parcels of food and pastries, jugs of water and innumerable baskets full of all kinds of toys were brought out and tied tightly on the camels' backs.

They were soon off while the servants waved and wished them good luck.

On and on they went.

As they entered the desert, night fell.

"Dark and somber indeed is the night," said King Gaspar.

"Fear not," remarked King Melchor, "the star will soon appear to guide us, as it appears every year. The same star that led us twenty centuries ago to the stable at Bethlehem."

He had hardly finished talking when up above their heads appeared a strange star glittering in the dark.

"Here is the star," said King Melchor again.

"Seems to me," said King Baltazar, "that on our last journey the star always appeared much later; however I may have lost all sense of time."

They followed the course it led . . . On and on they went.

For hours they travelled.

Suddenly from behind a cloud a ray of light appeared and darkness gave way to daylight.

The sun came out and the strange star disappeared.

Slowly the Three Magi pulled up their reins.

"Alas," they exclaimed. "What is the meaning of this?"

To their great surprise after having ridden away in the night, they were standing at their very door—the door of their own castle.

"What can this mean?" said King Gaspar.

"It means," answered King Melchor, "that in the course of the evening we have come back to our starting point."

"But we followed the star," said King Baltazar in a doleful voice.

"That was no star," piped a small voice.

"Wh-who speaks?" called out King Baltazar—this time in an excited voice.

"Oh, only me," said a little black beetle coming out from one of the camel's ears.

"You!" cried King Melchor, "how do you know?"

"Tell us, little black beetle, tell us all you know," said King Gaspar.

"The star," said the little beetle, trying to raise its voice loud enough for them to hear, "was just a number of fireflies in formation to imitate a star."

"What are we to do?" moaned King Melchor. "We will never reach Spain. For the first time the children will find their shoes empty. What are we to do?"

"Shush—" said the beetle. "Look!"

Towards them running so fast his thin legs scarcely touched the ground, was coming a little grey mouse.

"Raton Perez!" exclaimed the Kings.

Making a low bow, he said: "Yes, Raton Perez—bearer of good news!"

"Speak then," said the Kings.

"My Kings," said Raton Perez, "it's all the fault of the horses. They are very jealous. While they discussed their plans with the fireflies, I chanced to be resting on a bundle of straw. Too late to follow you, I thought of a plan to undo the fireflies' work. What could be easier than to ask Father Time? It was as you know a question of time and only He could arrange it. To my great surprise, I found Father Time sound asleep over his great cloak. Not to cause him the least discomfort, lest I should awaken him, I set his clock twenty-four hours back. So now my good Magi, ride on! The children of Spain must have their toys."

As if led by an invisible hand, the three camels pricked up their ears, raised their heads and went on towards the desert. Silence descended upon the group again. Above them the blue sky and all around them the sand, hot like fire under the rays of the sun. The Magi looked at each other in silence and set their eyes on the road.

Darkness soon closed in. On and on the camels went. They could hardly see themselves in the darkness that enveloped them.

Suddenly a star appeared large and resplendent, way up in the sky. Its light shone like a silver thread on the sand. In great silence, the Three Magi raised their heads to the sky, and gazed long at the star. There was hope and faith in the three eager faces that now bent their heads to lead the camels on.

From somewhere a sound of bells was heard, faintly at first, then louder and louder.

"God be praised," said King Baltazar, "we are near the city. It's the tolling of the bells—the bells from the church tower, ringing as a reminder of the entrance at Bethlehem years ago, letting us know, as they always do, that we are close to the city gates."

Ding—Dong—Ding—Dong—

The bells chimed merrily now and the hour of twelve struck. The camels shook their heads making all their headgear tinkle. Strangely enough they picked up the tempo of the bells and almost in unison passed the opened gate into the city.

That morning under each bed, inside each shoe, beside baskets and boxes wrapped with straw and flowers the children found their gifts, unaware of the hardships the Three Magi had in keeping faith with them.

Make Your Own Christmas Cards

Homemade Christmas cards can be a festive way to add a personal touch to a traditional custom. Simply cut colored card-stock construction paper into rectangles about nine inches long by six and a half inches wide, fold them in half, and decorate. In order for your cards to meet the U.S. Postal Service requirements for a single first-class mail stamp, make sure they weigh one ounce or less.

Family Photo Cards

Color copies or printouts of family holiday picture, lace trim or colored yarn, glue, scissors

1. Glue the copy of the family photo on the front of the card.
2. Frame the picture with lace trim or yarn and glue in place.

Christmas Print Cards

Styrofoam food trays, ballpoint pen or dull pencil, water-based paint, such as tempura, paintbrush

1. On the bottom of a Styrofoam food tray, draw a simple holiday scene or item, such as an angel, snowman, or Christmas tree no greater than the size of your card, by press-

ing your pen or pencil gently into the Styrofoam to create an imprint.
2. Brush a layer of water-based paint on the etched Styrofoam.
3. Gently press the card on the painted area. Carefully lift off and let dry.

Ribbon Cards

Various colors of paper satin ribbon, tracing paper, scissors, pencil, glue stick

1. On tracing paper, draw simple, stencil-like designs such as holly leaves and berries, ornaments, angels, or Christmas trees.
2. Cut out the design and lightly trace the image on the front of the Christmas card with a pencil.
3. Use the tracing paper pattern to cut similar shapes of ribbon.
4. Glue the backs of the ribbon pieces and affix to the front of the card inside the pencil markings. Carefully erase any pencil marks that remain visible.

The largest freestanding Christmas card on record was created at Ireland's University College in Dublin, on December 3, 1990. As big as 4,500 regular-sized greeting cards put together, it was made from one piece of card measuring 98 feet, 0.6 inches by 27 feet, 2 inches.Once folded, the card measured 49 feet, 2 inches by 27 feet 2 inches.

A History of the Christmas Card

The birth of the Christmas card is generally attributed to Sir Henry Cole, an Englishman. In the early 1840s, this man of letters found himself in a difficult situation: he had fallen considerably behind on his seasonal correspondence. His solution turned out to be a stroke of genius: he commissioned John Calcott Horsley, an artist friend from the Royal Academy, to create a greeting card. Horsley's design portrayed a happy family feasting and toasting the holidays, alongside vignettes of people offering clothing to the poor and feeding the hungry. Although others had created and sent hand-crafted Christmas cards, Horsley's were the first to be professionally printed; Cole had a thousand of these cards lithographed. They sold at an Old Bond Street gift-book company for a shilling apiece. The decade of the 1840s saw the beginning of the penny post in Victorian England, as well as innovations in the steam press, which made mass production—and mass mailing—possible as never before.

Christmas cards in the United States didn't take off until 1875, after the German-born lithographer, Louis Prang, designed a series of Christmas cards depicting reproductions of paintings with as many as twenty colors. Prang's cards had a huge following in England as well. To find the best Christmas art, Prang held numerous contests and offered cash prizes to contemporary painters. The art on his cards often featured nature scenes, family gatherings, singing children, and cherubim. His innovations turned a Christmas tradition into a Christmas industry.

Christmas Card Etiquette

Sending Christmas cards is a wonderful way to spread holiday spirit. A greeting on the mantle decorates the yuletide hearth and serves as a cheerful reminder to all. To make sure the cards you send best reflect your thoughtfulness, keep in mind these etiquette guidelines:

- Include a personal inscription, even if the card's message is printed, and always sign your name.
- Holiday cards do not need to be limited to those who celebrate Christmas. Be aware of others' religious beliefs and how they observe the season. Send neutral "Seasons Greetings" cards, or ones appropriate for such celebrations as Hanukkah and Kwanzaa.
- If you write a card from more than one person, sign your name last. Keep your signature informal.
- When labeling envelopes, include all your recipients in the address, as in "The Crosby Family," or "Mr. and Mrs. Hall and children."
- If the recipients have different surnames, write each name separately, as in "Alex Stone and Emma Wilson."
- Take the time to address envelopes to business associates by hand.
- Always include your return address so that recipients can update their address books.
- Use first-class postage, and a holiday stamp.
- Send cards early to account for holiday mail. Allow three to six weeks for Christmas cards to international destinations. For domestic mail, any time after Thanksgiving is fine.

> A joy that's shared
> is a joy made double.
> —English Proverb

More than 3 billion Christmas cards are mailed annually in the United States.

Best Stores . . . for Infants and Toddlers

An utterly charming experience is offered by San Francisco-based **tea**™, "for little citizens of the world." Parson School of Design graduate Emily Meyer wanted to bring global culture to children's wear: her beautifully functional mandarin-influenced outfits are sold in fine boutiques across the country, including San Francisco, New York, Beverly Hills, Boston, Atlanta, Seattle, Houston, Santa Fe, and on-line: *teacollection.com* or call (866) 374-8747.

❄

Appalachian Baby Design in Maxwelton, West Virginia, creates specialty knit items hand-loomed by local craftspeople for tiny ones, and includes "home" and "holiday" categories. Visit *appalachianbaby.com* or call (304) 497-2213.

❄

At the Southern chain **Pickles & Ice Cream**, sought-after brands like Oi Oi specialty baby and diaper bags are flying off the shelves. This is the place to find a mom-to-be or new mom a special gift. Greenville: (864) 240-6010; Nashville: (615) 778-1599; Dallas: (214) 361-1898; and other locations. *picklesandicecream.com*

❄

Robertson's Seedlings, located in the Philadelphia area, has extra-special baby gifts, including layette items, special-occasion outfits for boys and girls, hand-embroidered christening gowns, sterling silver accessories, stuffed toys and dolls, and books. Visit in person, or call (215) 242-6070.

❄

On-line store **Imagine the Challenge** offers educational and developmental toys and gifts for infant to junior high school. Shop for such well-known brands as Manhattan Toys and Small World, and listen to your little one compose with the Melody Mix.

Log on to *imaginethechallenge.com* or call (888) 777-1493.

❄

The lovingly compiled **Teddy bear directory** also lists Teddy bear hospitals: *bearsbythe-sea.com/dir*.

❄

The Internet clearinghouse **BabyGenie** posts reviews for popular baby furniture, strollers, toys, supplies, and other baby products: *babygenie.com*.

❄

Hooked on Phonics says that early readers are the most dedicated. If you're interested in helping your toddler learn reading skills, review the educational products at *hop.com*.

❄

California-based **Gymboree**, which offers children's clothing, now presents a unique concept for toddlers and their parents at their Gymboree Play & Music Centers. Activities promote motor skills, socialization, and music appreciation. A series of classes makes a wonderful Christmas gift for a young family: *gymboree.com*.

❄

Quincyshop.com is a great resource for everything from Wood Rattles to Tricycles—search by toy type or age group!

❄

Baby Sacks was voted "Best of L.A." by Los Angeles magazine. For cotton prints and chenilles, visit *BabySacks.com*.

❄

The hassle-free website for **Baby Gap** posts newborn essentials, practical and stylish maternity wear, body- and swimsuits, and infant and toddler gifts: *gap.com* or visit their brick-and-mortar locations.

❄

Babies "R" Us, a division of **Toys "R" Us**, has a huge selection of toys, games, bedding, furniture, carriers, and accessories for toddlers up to age three. Check their on-line sales or specialty stores and boutiques for that unique Christmas gift: *babiesrus.com*

❄

For trendy fashions, jewelry for tots, and fine gifts: *jewelrybasket.com* and *classicchildren.com*.

❄

The Retro Baby entices you to dress your babes in "awesome old school T-shirts straight out of the 70s and 80s." From retro style to snappy sayings, this one has everything: *theretrobaby.com* or call 877-305-8551

The Norwegians once believed that witches and michievous spirits came out on Christmas Eve to steal the household's brooms and ride them. Even today, after Christmas Eve dinner and the opening of presents, Norwegians hide all the brooms in the house.

Magic Cabin Dolls has a huge selection of reasonably-priced inventive toys for kids from babyhood to pre-teen. Check out their Halloween costumes, wooden baby toys, Circle of Friends Puzzle, and the soccer set at *magiccabin.com,* or call (888)-623-3655.

Great Gifts for Everyone

Theater Tickets
Museum Membership
Desk Calendar
Sports Tickets
Photo Albums of Family or a Recent Trip
Sheets
Spa Day/Massage Gift Certificate
Dustbuster
Manicure/Pedicure Gift Certificate
Books
CDs
Classic Movie DVDs
MP3 Player
Dog-sitting Coupons
Fruit-of-the-Month-Club Membership
New Gloves
Cashmere Sweater
Chore Coupons
Address Stamp
Babysitting Coupons

Best Stores . . . for Under Tens

With a selection that includes New York City brownstones, **Manhattan Doll House** is truly a treasure. A must-visit for unusual miniature accessories, kits, ready-made constructions, and Madame Alexander dolls, this store even has electrical, tile, carpeting, and wallpaper "departments": *manhattandollhouse.com.*

From Martians to wizards, the **Warner Brothers Shop** has everything children desire. Comic book heroes await release from their plastic confines into your son or daughter's arms. Such classics as Snow Miser and Heat Miser bring out the glory of the season: *wbstore.com*

Charly & Hannah's in Miami has wooden trains, high-quality unusual toys, stuffed animals, and kids' costumes, many European. The store provides its own signature gift wrap of brown paper and stickers: (305) 441-7677.

Little Kid Stuff's Double Decker tables gets rave reviews. Its train sets, cars, tracks, and train accessories are all compatible with Brio and Thomas wooden railroad systems and accessories: *littlekidstuff.com.*

Grandrabbits Toy Shoppe, founded by a former Montessori teacher, has been a "positive social force" in the Denver area since 1977: *grtoys.com*, or (303) 443-0780.

Denver also boasts the **Denver Doll Emporium,** which buys and sells old mint-condition dolls, paper dolls, and bears: *denverdoll.com*, or (303) 733-6339.

Got a junior Yo-Yo Ma in the house, or a young violinist or violist? Family-owned **Johnson String Instrument** has everything for the string player—including fun accessories just for kids: *johnsonstring.com*, or (800) 359-9351.

For the budding musician, Philadelphia's **Eighth Street Music Center**, a wonderful music emporium, offers child-size instruments among its large selection: *8thstreet.com* or (800) 878-8882.

Under tens will appreciate the developmental toys from **Leaps and Bounds**. Parents should check out their "happy travel" solutions: *leapsandbounds.com.*

Toys "R" Us allows you to shop on-line by age, up through 11. Favorite toys include Barbie, GI Joe, Hot Wheels, and toys by Fisher-Price, Leap Frog, LEGO, and Little Tikes: *toysrus.com.*

For a conversation piece that encourages good table etiquette, try the "Manners Mat" from **Self Presentations**: *selfpresentations.com.*

For infants to 10-year-olds, Manhattan's **Calypso Enfant & Bebe** is one fabulous place: **GoCityKids** calls it the best-smelling kids' store in the city: (212) 966-3234.

GapKids has just about everything your preteen needs, from shorts to shoes and belts to boots: *gap.com.*

Europe-based **Tamara Henriques** makes colorful children's rubber Wellington, perfect for splashing in puddles and romping around the neighborhood. You can find these not-for-the-bashful boots at various locations throughout the US as well as abroad; just check the website: *tamarahenriques.com*.

FAO Schwarz is the granddaddy of all toy stores for every age, from infancy to 100. This company understands the science of play. A visit to the Fifth Avenue headquarters in New York is as good as a trip to the zoo. For lots of exclusives on funhouses, Tonka Tools, Disney dolls, Street Flyers, FAO Wild™ Cats, FAO signature duffel bags, and plenty more, visit *fao.com*.

For the budding artist on your list, check out **Crayola** for bath paints, washable markers, easels, and paints, not to mention a 96-color pack of crayons! *Crayola.com*.

The **Discovery Channel Store** has tons of projects, kits, and experiments for the little scientist, as well as a great selection of developmental toys: *shopping.discovery.com* or (800) 627-9399.

For classic children's books, check out **Books of Wonder** for everything from vintage editions to their own line of reproductions. Visit *booksofwonder.com* or call (800) 835-4315.

Got a little Anglophile? Check out the **Harrods'** website. At this London superstore, you'll find the classic red double-decker bus and Paddington Bear: *harrods.com*.

Americans spend nearly $150 billion dollars on Christmas presents each year. 75 percent wish Christmas were less materialistic.

Many U.S. retailers make up to 70 percent of their annual revenue during the month before Christmas.

Great Gifts for Kids

Zoo Membership
Cookie Dough
Ice Skating Lessons
Horseback Riding Lessons
Skateboard
Music Box
Puppy/Kitten
Cowboy Boots/Hat
College Fund Contribution
Diary
Classic Board Games: *Candyland, Monopoly, Chutes & Ladders*
Travel Games
Charm Bracelet
Stationery
Tiara
Bicycle
Computer Games
Binoculars
Telescope
Building Blocks
Puzzles
Globe
Basketball
Radio Flyer Wagon
Motorized Airplane
Puppets/Puppet Theater
Baseball and Mitt
Magic Kit
Action Figures/Barbies
Videos/DVDs
Walkie Talkies
Classic Children's Books

Best Stores . . . for Teens

Yellow Rat Bastard is a New York City favorite with teens. The store has even earned a parents' approval rating at the **GoCityKids** website of 4 stars out of 5—despite the name. Visit the store at 483 Broadway in lower Manhattan, or log on to *yellowratbastard.com*.

In business since 1908, **Paragon** has everything related to sports and recreation, and a great place for hip sporting attire, too: *paragon-sports.com*.

Old Navy's got the gear, and it draws kids in droves to its enormous stores: *oldnavy.com*.

The Gap has the essentials of style for those young at heart, great sales, and on-time deals too: *gap.com*.

Delia's has tons of hipster flair for the fashionable teen: *store.delias.com*.

At **Barnes and Noble** stores, teens can shop for CDs and books, study, and even meet over a Coke. Browse the website for deals: *barnesand-noble.com*.

Get the scoop on what your teen listens to, and links to hundreds of sites: *teenmu-sic.about.com*.

For the largest selection of music available, try the **Virgin Records Megastore**: *vir-gin.com/megastore*.

Art prints of stars like the Jonas Brothers, Miley Cyrus, Robert Pattinson, and Selena Gomez are available at *posterplanet.net*.

Visit New York City's **Chimera** on Mercer Street in SoHo for "nifty novelties of all sizes and shapes." Caters to older kids and adults, but also offers a broad selection of stuffed animals: (212)-334-4730.

Star Magic is another wildly popular browsing place, specializing in "Jetsonian" space-age gifts like lava lights, glow in the dark desk toys, telescopes and, well, you get the idea: *starmagic.com*.

For youthful, globally influenced clothing in a delightful array of textures and colors, **Anthropologie** is the hot place to get gear: *anthropologie.com*.

A Miserable, Merry Christmas

Lincoln Steffens

My father's business seems to have been one of slow but steady growth. He and his local partner, Llewelen Tozer, had no vices. They were devoted to their families and to "the store," which grew with the town, from a gambling, mining, and ranching community to one of farming, fruit-raising, and building. Immigration poured in, not gold-seekers now, but farmers, businessmen and home-builders, who settled, planted, reaped, and traded in the natural riches of the State, which prospered greatly, "making" the people who will tell you that they "made the State."

As the store made money and I was getting through the primary school, my father bought a lot uptown, at Sixteenth and K Streets, and built us a "big" house. It was off the line of the city's growth, but it was near a new grammar school for me and my sisters, who were coming along fast after me. This interested the family, not me. They were always talking about school; they had not had much of it themselves, and they thought they had missed something. My father used to write speeches, my mother verses, and their theory seems to have been that they had talents which a school would have brought to flower. They agreed, therefore, that their children's gifts should have all the schooling there was. My view, then, was that I had had a good deal of it already, and I was not interested at all. It interfered with my own business, with my own education.

And indeed I remember very little of the primary school. I learned to read, write, spell, and count, and reading was all right. I had a practical use for books, which I searched for ideas and parts to play with, characters to be, lives to live. The primary school was probably a good one, but I cannot remember learning anything except to read aloud "perfectly" from a teacher whom I adored and who was fond of me. She used to embrace me before the whole class and she favored me openly to the scandal of the other pupils, who called me "teacher's pet." Their scorn did not trouble me; I saw and I said that they envied me. I paid for her favor, however. When she married I had queer, unhappy feelings of resentment; I didn't want to meet her husband, and when I had to I wouldn't speak to him. He laughed, and she kissed me—happily for her, to me offensively. I never would see her again. Through with her, I fell in love immediately with Miss Kay, another grown young woman who wore glasses and had a fine, clear skin. I did not know her, I only saw her in the street, but once I followed her, found out

In the 1880s, Mrs. George Hearst, wife of the millionaire senator, had their entire California lawn covered in crushed ice to make a houseguest from Vermont feel more at home on Christmas morning.

where she lived, and used to pass her house, hoping to see her, and yet choking with embarrassment if I did. This fascination lasted for years; it was still a sort of super-romance to me when later I was "going with" another girl nearer my own age.

What interested me in our new neighborhood was not the school, nor the room I was to have in the house all to myself, but the stable which was built back of the house. My father let me direct the making of a stall, a little smaller than the other stalls, for my pony, and I prayed and hoped and my sister Lou believed that that meant that I would get the pony, perhaps for Christmas. I pointed out to her that there were three other stalls and no horses at all. This I said in order that she should answer it.

She could not. My father, sounded, said that some day we might have horses and a cow; meanwhile a stable added to the value of a house. "Some day" is a pain to a boy who lives in and knows only "now." My good little sisters, to comfort me, remarked that Christmas was coming, but Christmas was always coming and grown-ups were always talking about it, asking you what you wanted and then giving you what they wanted you to have. Though everybody knew what I wanted, I told them all again. My mother knew that I told God, too, every night. I wanted a pony, and to make sure that they understood, I declared that I wanted nothing else.

"Nothing but a pony?" my father asked.

"Nothing," I said.

"Not even a pair of high boots?"

That was hard. I did want boots, but I stuck to the pony. "No, not even boots."

"Nor candy? There ought to be something to fill your stocking with, and Santa Claus can't put a pony into a stocking."

That was true, and he couldn't lead a pony down the chimney either. But no. "All I want is a pony," I said. "If I can't have a pony, give me nothing, nothing."

Now I had been looking myself for the pony I wanted, going to sales stables, inquiring of horsemen, and I had seen several that would do. My father let me "try" them. I tried so many ponies that I was learning fast to sit a horse. I chose several, but my father always found some fault with them. I was in despair. When Christmas was at hand I had given up all hope of a pony, and on Christmas Eve I hung up my stocking along with my sisters', of whom, by the way, I now had three. I haven't mentioned them or their coming because, you understand, they were girls, and girls, young girls, counted for nothing in my manly life. They did not mind me either; they were so happy that Christmas Eve that I caught some of their merriment. I speculated on what I'd get; I hung up the biggest stocking I had, and we all went reluctantly to bed to wait till morning. Not to sleep; not right away. We were told that we must not only sleep promptly, we must not wake up till seven-thirty the next morning—or if we did, we must not go to the fireplace for our Christmas. Impossible.

We did sleep that night, but we woke up at six A.M. We lay in our beds and debated through the open doors whether to obey till, say, half-past six. Then we bolted. I don't know who started it, but there was a rush. We all disobeyed; we raced to disobey and get first to the fireplace in the front room downstairs. And there they were, the gifts, all sorts of wonderful things, mixed-up piles of presents; only, as I disentangled the mess, I saw that my stocking was empty; it hung limp; not a thing in it; and under and around it— nothing. My sisters had knelt down, each by her pile of gifts; they were squealing with delight, till they looked up and saw me standing there in my nightgown with nothing. They left their piles to come to me and look with me at my empty place. Nothing. They felt my stocking: nothing.

I don't remember whether I cried at that moment, but my sisters did. They ran with me back to my bed, and there we all cried till I became indignant. That helped some. I got up, dressed, and driving my sisters away, I went alone out into the yard, down to the stable, and there, all by myself, I wept. My mother came out to me by and by; she found me in my pony stall, sobbing on the floor, and she tried to comfort me. But I heard my father outside; he had come part way with her, and she was having some sort of angry quarrel with him. She tried to comfort me; besought me to come to breakfast. I could not; I wanted no comfort and no breakfast. She left me and went on into the house with sharp words for my father.

I don't know what kind of a breakfast the family had. My sisters said it was "awful." They were ashamed to enjoy their own toys. They came to me, and I was rude. I ran away from them. I went around to the front of the house, sat down on the steps, and, the crying over, I ached. I was wronged, I was hurt—I can feel now what I felt then, and I am sure that if one could see the wounds upon our hearts, there would be found still upon mine a scar from that terrible Christmas morning. And my father, the practi-

In 1945, the number-one selling toy was the Slinky. It was developed for the Navy as a way to help keep shipboard instruments steady while at sea.

cal joker, he must have been hurt, too, a little. I saw him looking out of the window. He was watching me or something for an hour or two, drawing back the curtain ever so little lest I catch him, but I saw his face, and I think I can see now the anxiety upon it, the worried impatience.

After—I don't know how long—surely an hour or two—I was brought to the climax of my agony by the sight of a man riding a pony down the street, a pony and a brand-new saddle; the most beautiful saddle I ever saw, and it was a boy's saddle; the man's feet were not in the stirrups; his legs were too long. The outfit was perfect; it was the realization of all my dreams, the answer to all my prayers. A fine new bridle, with a light curb bit. And the pony! As he drew near, I saw that the pony was really a small horse, what we called an Indian pony, a bay, with black mane and tail, and one white foot and a white star on his forehead. For such a horse as that I would have given, I could have forgiven, anything.

But the man, a disheveled fellow with a blackened eye and a fresh-cut face, came along, reading the numbers on the houses, and, as my hopes—my impossible hopes—rose, he looked at our door and passed by, he and the pony, and the saddle and the bridle. Too much. I fell upon the steps, and having wept before, I broke now into such a flood of tears that I was a floating wreck when I heard a voice.

"Say, kid," it said, "do you know a boy named Lennie Steffens?"

I looked up. It was the man on the pony, back again, at our horse block.

"Yes," I spluttered through my tears. "That's me."

"Well," he said, "then this is your horse. I've been looking all over for you and your house. Why don't you put your number where it can be seen?"

"Get down," I said, running out to him.

He went on saying something about "ought to have got here at seven o'clock; told me to bring the nag here and tie him to your post and leave him for you. But, hell, I got into a drunk—and a fight—and a hospital, and—"

"Get down," I said.

He got down, and he boosted me up to the saddle. He offered to fit the stirrups to me, but I didn't want him to. I wanted to ride.

"What's the matter with you?" he said, angrily. "What you crying for? Don't you like the horse? He's a dandy, this horse. I know him of old. He's fine at cattle; he'll drive 'em alone."

I hardly heard, I could scarcely wait, but he persisted. He adjusted the stirrups, and then, finally, off I rode, slowly, at a walk, so happy, so thrilled, that I did not know what I was doing. I did not look back at the house or the man, I rode off up the street, taking note of everything—of the reins, of the pony's long mane, of the carved leather saddle. I had never seen anything so beautiful. And mine! I was going to ride up past Miss Kay's house. But I noticed on the horn of the saddle some stains like rain-drops, so I turned and trotted home, not to the house but to the stable. There was the family, father, mother, sisters, all working for me, all happy. They had been putting in place the tools of my new business: blankets, currycomb, brush, pitchfork—everything, and there was hay in the loft.

"What did you come back so soon for?" somebody asked. "Why didn't you go on riding?"

I pointed to the stains. "I wasn't going to get my new saddle rained on," I said. And my father laughed. "It isn't raining," he said. "Those are not rain-drops."

"They are tears," my mother gasped, and she gave my father a look which sent him off to the house. Worse still, my mother offered to wipe away the tears still running out of my eyes. I gave her such a look as she had given him, and she went off after my father, drying her own tears. My sisters remained and we all unsaddled the pony, put on his halter, led him to his stall, tied and fed him. It began really to rain; so all the rest of that memorable day we curried and combed that pony. The girls plaited his mane,

forelock, and tail, while I pitchforked hay to him and curried and brushed, curried and brushed. For a change we brought him out to drink; we led him up and down, blanketed like a race-horse; we took turns at that. But the best, the most inexhaustible fun, was to clean him. When we went reluctantly to our midday Christmas dinner, we all smelt of horse, and my sisters had to wash their faces and hands. I was asked to, but I wouldn't, till my mother bade me look in the mirror. Then I washed up—quick. My face was caked with the muddy lines of tears that had coursed over my cheeks to my mouth. Having washed away that shame, I ate my dinner, and as I ate I grew hungrier and hungrier. It was my first meal that day, and as I filled up on the turkey and the stuffing, the cranberries and the pies, the fruit and the nuts—as I swelled, I could laugh. My mother said I still choked and sobbed now and then, but I laughed, too; I saw and enjoyed my sisters' presents till—I had to go out and attend to my pony, who was there, really and truly there, the promise, the beginning, of a happy double life. And—I went and looked to make sure—there was the saddle, too, and the bridle.

But that Christmas, which my father had planned so carefully, was it the best or the worst I ever knew? He often asked me that; I never could answer as a boy. I think now that it was both. It covered the whole distance from broken-hearted misery to bursting happiness—too fast. A grown-up could hardly have stood it.

"We Three Kings of Orient Are," is one of the few Christmas carols to have its words and music written by the same person: The Reverend John Henry Hopkins, Jr. in 1857.

We Three Kings of Orient Are

1.

We Three Kings Of O - ri - ent Are,

bear - ing gifts we tra - verse a - far.

Field and foun - tain, moor and moun - tain

fol - low - ing yon - der star. O, _____

star of won - der, star of night!

Star of roy - al beau - ty bright.

West - ward lead - ing, still pro - ceed - ing

guide us to the per - fect light.

2. Born a King on Bethlehem plain,
Gold I bring to crown Him again,
King forever, Ceasing never
Over us all to reign.

Chorus

3. Frankincense to offer have I,
Incense owns a Deity night:
Prayer and praising, All men raising,
Worship Him, God on high.

Chorus

4. Myrrh is mine; its bitter perfume
Breathes a life of gathering gloom;
Sorrowing, sighing, bleeding, dying,
Sealed in the stone cold tomb.

Chorus

5. Glorious now behold Him arise,
King and God, and sacrifice;
Heaven signs Alleluia:
Alleluia the earth replies.

Chorus

The Three Wise Men

(St. Matthew 2:1-14)

ow when Jesus was born in Bethlehem of Judæa in the days of Herod the king, behold, there came wise men from the east to Jerusalem.

Saying, Where is he that is born King of the Jews? for we have seen his star in the east, and are come to worship him.

When Herod the king had heard *these things*, he was troubled, and all Jerusalem with him.

And when he had gathered all the chief priests and scribes of the people together, he demanded of them where Christ should be born.

And they said unto him, In Bethlehem of Judæa: for thus it is written by the prophet,

And thou Bethlehem, *in* the land of Juda, art not the least among the princes of Juda: for out of thee shall come a Governor, that shall rule my people Israel.

Then Herod, when he had privily called the wise men, enquired of them diligently what time the star appeared.

And he sent them to Bethlehem, and said, Go and search diligently for the young child; and when ye have found *him*, bring me word again, that I may come and worship him also.

When they had heard the king, they departed; and, lo, the star, which they saw in the east, went before them, till it came and stood over where the young child was.

When they saw the star, they rejoiced with exceeding great joy.

And when they were come into the house, they saw the young child with Mary his mother, and fell down, and worshipped him: and when they had opened their treasures, they presented unto him gifts; gold, and frankincense, and myrrh.

And being warned of God in a dream that they should not return to Herod, they departed into their own country another way.

And when they were departed, behold, the angel of the Lord appeareth to Joseph in a dream, saying, Arise, and take the young child and his mother, and flee into Egypt, and be thou there until I bring thee word: for Herod will seek the young child to destroy him.

When he arose, he took the young child and his mother by night, and departed into Egypt.

> *If I could wish a wish for you, it would be for peace and happiness not only now, but for the whole year through!*
> —CATHERINE PULSIFER

Make a Story Recording as a Gift

Have a favorite childhood book you'd like to introduce to a younger sibling, or relative? Have a grandmother who loves listening to Robert Frost while she quilts, or a sister who likes to play audiobooks in the car? Consider giving poems, fairy tales, or short stories with an added bonus: your voice. On an audiotape or recordable CD make a personalized soundtrack for someone to enjoy. Complete the package with your own cover art and contents list—whether you rely on such old-fashioned methods as paper, tape, and colored markers, or hi-tech photo editors, graphics, and label makers.

Make Cider & Mulling Spices

No yuletide festivities are complete without the wonderful aromas of mulled cider, wine, or wassail. Add some spice of your own to the season by creating a blend of homemade mulling spices—great stocking stuffers! Combine six to twelve cinnamon sticks, four to six allspice berries, a dozen whole cloves, seeds from four to six cardamom pods, and two to three crushed nutmegs. Present in a canning jar tied with festive ribbons, or bundle the spices in cheesecloth, ready for mulling.

A FRIEND'S GREETING   *Edgar A. Guest*

I'd like to be the sort of friend that you have been to me;
I'd like to be the help that you've been always glad to be;
I'd like to mean as much to you each minute of the day
As you have meant, old friend of mine, to me along the way.

I'd like to do the big things and the splendid things for you,
To brush the gray from out your skies and leave them only blue;
I'd like to say the kindly things that I so oft have heard,
And feel that I could rouse your soul the way that mine you've stirred.

I'd like to give you back the joy that you have given me,
Yet that were wishing you a need I hope will never be;
I'd like to make you feel as rich as I, who travel on
Undaunted in the darkest hours with you to lean upon.

I'm wishing at this Christmas time that I could but repay
A portion of the gladness that you've strewn along my way;
And could I have one wish this year, this only would it be:
I'd like to be the sort of friend that you have been to me.

Make an Edible Miniature Christmas Tree

This is ideal for a children's room: they can lie awake at night and watch their tree twinkle in the dark. After Christmas, the tree can be kept alive indoors until spring, then planted in the garden.

Gingerbread dough according to the recipe on page 89; small cookie cutters in shapes such as stars, hearts, wreaths, stockings; colored sugars; sprinkles; a straw; colored icing; small ornament hooks; thin ribbon for hanging ornaments; mini-M&Ms; assorted soft candies: gum drops, Swedish berries, sticks of licorice; several spools of heavy-duty thread; a large needle; a string of Christmas tree lights; a small, potted Christmas tree (approximately 2–2½ feet high).

1. Roll out the gingerbread dough and cut out cookie shapes to your liking. Arrange on a baking sheet. Decorate with sprinkles/sugars (or leave plain and ice and decorate after baking). Then, using the end of the straw, poke a hole near the top of each cookie.
2. Bake cookies according to directions on page 89. Allow to cool, then ice and decorate if desired.
3. Once icing has hardened, string ribbon or ornament holders through holes. Cookies are then ready for the tree!
4. On your needle, string a double cord of thread and create candy garlands with the soft candies. Make whatever patterns you like, alternating pieces of licorice with gumdrops or arranging by color. Keep a dish of warm water on hand to rinse your needle in when it gets sticky. This will be slow going, so leave plenty of time.
5. Single, larger soft candies and even Christmas chocolates can be turned into individual ornaments by piercing them with an ornament hook—just insert the hook carefully so as not to crack or crumble the chocolate.
6. String your tree with lights and decorate!

How did Christmas become so commercialized? Many believe it all started when Macy's opened till midnight on Christmas Eve in 1867. Their first Christmas windows, in 1874, revolutionized the way we celebrate.

The Gift of the Magi

O. Henry

ne dollar and eighty-seven cents. That was all. And sixty cents of it was in pennies. Pennies saved one and two at a time by bulldozing the grocer and the vegetable man and the butcher until one's cheeks burned with the silent imputation of parsimony that such close dealing implied. Three times Della counted it. One dollar and eighty-seven cents. And the next day would be Christmas.

There was clearly nothing to do but flop down on the shabby little couch and howl. So Della did it. Which instigates the moral reflection that life is made up of sobs, sniffles, and smiles, with sniffles predominating.

While the mistress of the home is gradually subsiding from the first stage to the second, take a look at the home. A furnished flat at $8 per week. It did not exactly beggar description, but it certainly had that word on the lookout for the mendicancy squad.

In the vestibule below was a letter-box into which no letter would go, and an electric button from which no mortal finger could coax a ring. Also appertaining thereunto was a card bearing the name "Mr. James Dillingham Young."

The "Dillingham" had been flung to the breeze during a former period of prosperity when its possessor was being paid $30 per week. Now, when the income was shrunk to $20, the letters of "Dillingham" looked blurred, as though they were thinking seriously of contracting to a modest and unassuming D. But whenever Mr. James Dillingham Young came home and reached his flat above he was called "Jim" and greatly hugged by Mrs. James Dillingham Young, already introduced to you as Della. Which is all very good.

Della finished her cry and attended to her cheeks with the powder rag. She stood by the window and looked out dully at a grey cat walking a grey fence in a grey backyard. To-morrow would be Christmas Day, and she had only $1.87 with which to buy Jim a present. She had been saving every penny she could for months, with this result. Twenty dollars a week doesn't go far. Expenses had been greater than she had calculated. They always are. Only $1.87 to buy a present for Jim. Her Jim. Many a happy hour she had spent planning for something nice for him. Something fine and rare and sterling—something just a little bit near to being worthy of the honour of being owned by Jim.

There was a pier-glass between the windows of the room. Perhaps you have seen a pier-glass in an $8 flat. A very thin and very agile person may, by observing his reflection in a rapid sequence of longitudinal strips, obtain a fairly accurate conception of his looks. Della, being slender, had mastered the art.

Suddenly she whirled from the window and stood before the glass. Her eyes were shining brilliantly, but her face had lost its colour within twenty seconds. Rapidly she pulled down her hair and let it fall to its full length.

Now, there were two possessions of the James Dillingham Youngs in which they both took a mighty pride. One was Jim's gold watch that had been his father's and grandfather's. The other was Della's hair. Had the Queen of Sheba lived in the flat across the airshaft, Della would have let her hair hang out the window some day to dry just to depreciate Her Majesty's jewels and gifts. Had King Solomon been the janitor, with all his treasures piled up in the basement, Jim would have pulled out his watch every time he passed, just to see him pluck at his beard from envy.

So now Della's beautiful hair fell about her, rippling and shining like a cascade of brown waters. It reached below her knee and made itself almost a garment for her. And then she did it up again nervously and quickly. Once she faltered for a minute and stood still while a tear or two splashed on the worn red carpet.

On went her old brown jacket; on went her old brown hat. With a whirl of skirts and with the brilliant sparkle still in her eyes, she fluttered out the door and down the stairs to the street.

Where she stopped the sign read: "Mme. Sofronie. Hair Goods of All Kinds." One flight up Della ran, and collected herself, panting. Madame, large, too white, chilly, hardly looked the "Sofronie."

"Will you buy my hair?" asked Della.

"I buy hair," said Madame. "Take yer hat off and let's have a sight at the looks of it."

Down rippled the brown cascade.

"Twenty dollars," said Madame, lifting the mass with a practised hand.

"Give it to me quick," said Della.

Oh, and the next two hours tripped by on rosy wings. Forget the hashed metaphor. She was ransacking the stores for Jim's present.

She found it at last. It surely had been made for Jim and no one else. There was no other like it in any of the stores, and she had turned all of them inside out. It was a platinum fob chain simple and chaste in design, properly proclaiming its value by substance alone and not by meretricious ornamentation—as all good things should do. It was even worthy of The Watch. As soon as she saw it she knew that it must be Jim's. It was like him. Quietness and value—the description applied to both. Twenty-one dollars they took from her for it, and she hurried home with the 87 cents. With that chain on his watch Jim might be properly anxious about the time in any company. Grand as the watch was, he sometimes looked at it on the sly on account of the old leather strap that he used in place of a chain.

When Della reached home her intoxication gave way a little to prudence and reason. She got out her curling irons and lighted the gas and went to work repairing the ravages made by generosity added to love. Which is always a tremendous task, dear friends—a mammoth task.

Within forty minutes her head was covered with tiny close-lying curls that made her look wonderfully like a truant schoolboy. She looked at her reflection in the mirror long, carefully, and critically.

"If Jim doesn't kill me," she said to herself, "before he takes a second look at me, he'll say I look like a Coney Island chorus girl. But what could I do—oh! what could I do with a dollar and eighty-seven cents?"

At 7 o'clock the coffee was made and the frying-pan was on the back of the stove hot and ready to cook the chops.

Jim was never late. Della doubled the fob chain in her hand and sat on the corner of the table near the door that he always entered. Then she heard his step on the stair away down on the first flight, and she turned white for just a moment. She had a habit of saying little silent prayers about the simplest everyday things, and now she whispered: "Please God, make him think I am still pretty."

The door opened and Jim stepped in and closed it. He looked thin and very serious. Poor fellow, he was only twenty-two—and to be burdened with a family! He needed a new overcoat and he was without gloves.

Jim stopped inside the door, as immovable as a setter at the scent of quail. His eyes were fixed upon Della, and there was an expression in them that she could not read, and it terrified her. It was not anger, nor surprise, nor disapproval, nor horror, nor any of the sentiments that she had been prepared for. He simply stared at her fixedly with that peculiar expression on his face.

Della wriggled off the table and went for him.

"Jim, darling," she cried, "don't look at me that way. I had my hair cut off and sold it because I couldn't have lived through Christmas without giving you a present. It'll grow out again—you won't mind, will you? I just had to do it. My hair grows awfully fast. Say 'Merry Christmas!' Jim, and let's be happy. You don't know what a nice—what a beautiful, nice gift I've got for you."

"You've cut off your hair?" asked Jim, laboriously, as if he had not arrived at that patent fact yet even after the hardest mental labour.

"Cut it off and sold it," said Della. "Don't you like me just as well, anyhow? I'm me without my hair, ain't I?"

Jim looked about the room curiously.

"You say your hair is gone?" he said, with an air almost of idiocy.

"You needn't look for it," said Della. "It's sold, I tell you—sold and gone, too. It's Christmas Eve, boy. Be good to me, for it went for you. Maybe the hairs of my head were numbered," she went on with a sudden serious sweetness, "but nobody could ever count my love for you. Shall I put the chops on, Jim?"

Out of his trance Jim seemed quickly to wake. He enfolded his Della. For ten seconds let us regard with discreet scrutiny some inconsequential object in the other direction. Eight dollars a week or a million a year—what is the difference? A mathematician or a wit would give you the wrong answer. The magi brought valuable gifts, but that was not among them. This dark assertion will be illuminated later on.

Jim drew a package from his overcoat pocket and threw it upon the table.

"Don't make any mistake, Dell," he said, "about me. I don't think there's anything in the way of a haircut or a shave or a shampoo that could make me like my girl any less. But if you'll unwrap that package you may see why you had me going a while at first."

White fingers and nimble tore at the string and paper. And then an ecstatic scream of joy; and then, alas! a quick feminine change to hysterical tears and wails, necessitating the immediate employment of all the comforting powers of the lord of the flat.

For there lay The Combs—the set of combs, side and back, that Della had worshipped for long in a Broadway window. Beautiful combs, pure tortoise shell, with jeweled rims—just the shade to wear in the beautiful vanished hair. They were expensive combs, she knew, and her heart had simply craved and yearned over them without the least hope of possession. And now, they were hers, but the tresses that should have adorned the coveted adornments were gone.

But she hugged them to her bosom, and at length she was able to look up with dim eyes and a smile and say: "My hair grows so fast, Jim!"

And then Della leaped up like a little singed cat and cried, "Oh, oh!"

Jim had not yet seen his beautiful present. She held it out to him eagerly upon her open palm. The dull precious metal seemed to flash with a reflection of her bright and ardent spirit.

"Isn't it a dandy, Jim? I hunted all over town to find it. You'll have to look at the time a hundred times a day now. Give me your watch. I want to see how it looks on it."

Instead of obeying, Jim tumbled down on the couch and put his hands under the back of his head and smiled.

"Dell," said he, "let's put our Christmas presents away and keep 'em a while. They're too nice to use just at present. I sold the watch to get the money to buy your combs. And now suppose you put the chops on."

The magi, as you know, were wise men—wonderfully wise men who brought gifts to the Babe in the manger. They invented the art of giving Christmas presents. Being wise, their gifts were no doubt wise ones, possibly bearing the privilege of exchange in case of duplication. And here I have lamely related to you the uneventful chronicle of two foolish children in a flat who most unwisely sacrificed for each other the greatest treasures of their house. But in a last word to the wise of these days let it be said that of all who give gifts these two were the wisest. Of all who give and receive gifts, such as they are wisest. Everywhere they are wisest. They are the magi.

The Twelve Days of Christmas

On the first day of Christ-mas my true love gave to me, a

par-tridge _ in a pear tree. On the sec-ond day of Christ-mas my

true love gave to me, Two tur-tle doves and a par-tridge _ in a pear tree. On the

third day of Christ-mas my true love gave to me, Three French _ hens,
fourth day of Christ-mas my true love gave to me, Four mock-ingbirds,

1.
Two tur-tle doves and a par-tridge _ in a pear tree. On the

2.
Three French _ hens, Two tur-tle doves and a par-tridge _ in a pear tree.

On the fifth day of Christ-mas my true love gave to me,

Five gold-en rings, Four _ mock-ing birds, Three French hens,

Two _ tur-tle doves, and a par-tridge _ in a pear tree.

6. The sixth day of Christmas my true love
     sent to me
   Six geese a-laying, *(refrain)*

7. The seventh day of Christmas my true love
     sent to me
   Seven swans a-swimming, *(refrain)*

8. The eighth day of Christmas my true love
     sent to me
   Eight maids a-milking, *(refrain)*

9. The ninth day of Christmas my true love
     sent to me
   Nine ladies dancing, *(refrain)*

10. The tenth day of Christmas my true love
     sent to me
   Ten lords a-leaping, *(refrain)*

11. The eleventh day of Christmas my true love
     sent to me
   Eleven pipers piping, *(refrain)*

12. The twelfth day of Christmas my true love
     sent to me
   Twelve drummers drumming, *(refrain)*

Great Gifts for Co-Workers

Homemade Cookies in a Festive Tin
Fancy Container of Hot Chocolate Mix &
Homemade Marshmallows
Bottle of Wine
Local Coffeehouse Gift Card
Lottery Tickets
Free Breakfast
Cranberry Bread
Movie Theater Gift Certificate
Narcissus or Amaryllis Bulbs
in a Beautiful Planter
Personalized Stationery
An alternative idea: Conduct a "Secret
Santa" or "Christmas Grab Bag" (for ideas
see Gift Ideas for Large Families, pg. 144)

15 Great Gifts for Her

Perfume
Pajamas
Yoga Mat
Day-Off Coupons
Purse
Cookbooks
Heating Pad
Shoes
Yoga Classes
Massage
Diamond Earrings
Pearls
Vintage Evening Bag
Gift Certificate to Favorite Clothing Store
Collection of Vintage Teacups & Saucers

15 Great Gifts for Him

Power Tools
Martini Shakers
Dopp Kit
Aquarium
Palm Pilot
Toolbelt
Wallet
Antique Watch
Digital Camera
Money Clip
All-in-one Screwdriver
Swiss Army Knife
Custom-made Shirts
Sharper Image Gift Certificate
Season Tickets for his Favorite Team

Adult Stocking Stuffers

Metrocards ✿ Stamps ✿ Pens/Pencils
✿ Candy ✿ Gloves ✿ Nuts
✿ Bubble Bath ✿ Soap ✿ Magnets ✿ CDs
✿ Shoe Polish ✿ Socks ✿ Batteries ✿
Magazines/Subscriptions ✿ Candles ✿ Dish
Towels ✿ Luggage Tags ✿ Tree Ornaments
✿ Gift Certificate for Video/DVD Rentals ✿
Phone Card ✿ Chapstick ✿ Lotion ✿
Lottery Tickets ✿ Gift Certificate for Movie
Tickets ✿ Film ✿ Cashmere Socks ✿
Blank CDs ✿ Travel Lock ✿ Books on Tape
✿ Travel Pillow ✿ DVDs ✿
Chocolates ✿ Wine Stopper

I love the Christmas-tide, and yet,
I notice this each year I live;
I always like the gifts I get,
But how I love the gifts I give!

—BOOTH TARKINGTON

Cookie Puzzle

A fun gift or party favor for both children and adults:

*Sugar Cookie Dough (recipe page 90) or
Gingerbread Cookie Dough (recipe page 89),
oversized cookie cutters in your choice of shapes,
cookie decorations or icing, small knife,
brightly colored construction paper, pen,
gift boxes just large enough to accommodate
cookie-cutter-cookies*

1. Roll out dough and cut out cookies according to recipe directions. Transfer to a baking sheet and decorate.
2. Use the knife to carve the cookie up into bite-sized, interesting pieces.
3. Bake and set aside to cool.
4. Trace shape of cookie cutter on a piece of colored paper and cut out the shape of your cookie. You can write a message on the cut-out such as "Put me back together again and enjoy a holiday treat!" Place it in the bottom of the gift box. Top with the decorated puzzle pieces, and wrap.

Kid Stocking Stuffers

Bath Paints ✿ Rubber Duck ✿ Candy Canes
✿ Music Gift Certificate ✿ Video Game ✿
Wind-up Toy ✿ Glitter Powder ✿ Barrettes
✿ Dress-up Jewelry ✿ Disposable Underwater
Camera ✿ Removable Tattoos ✿ Deck of
Cards ✿ Stickers ✿ Harmonica ✿ Sea
Monkeys ✿ Comic Books ✿ Trading Cards
✿ Matchbox Cars ✿ Silly Putty
✿ Magnifying Glass ✿ Kaleidoscope
✿ Yo-Yo ✿ Jacks ✿ Marbles ✿ Glow-in-the-
Dark Ceiling Stars ✿ Crayons/Colored Pencils
✿ Pencil Flashlight ✿ Slinky ✿
Compass ✿ Whistles

How the Christmas Stocking Came to Be

The tradition of hanging stockings on the chimney was born in third-century Myra, a port in Asia Minor where the beloved bishop, St. Nicholas, reportedly performed numerous miracles. As the legend goes, St. Nicholas learned of three sisters who had no money for a dowry and would be forced into prostitution for survival. One night, he tossed a sack of gold through their window—enough money for the eldest sister's dowry. The next night, St. Nicholas dropped a second bag of gold, for the middle sister. But on the third night, he found the window closed, so he dropped the gold down the chimney. The coins fell into a stocking that happened to be hung by the chimney to dry. Word of the miracle soon spread, and townsfolk all over began hanging their stockings by the chimney in the hopes of catching some of St. Nicholas' benevolence.

Where to Buy Christmas Stockings

Beribboned and hand embroidered, lovely **Elizabethan Christmas** stockings are real keepsakes for family members, and feature especially nice custom designs for a new baby: *elizabethanchristmas.com* or (215) 249-9930.

Ho Ho Holiday will personalize the stockings with your name. Choose a traditional holiday pattern, or get funky with Western-style animal prints, plaids, cute sports themes, and many others, for pets and people: *HoHoHoliday.com* or (952) 898-1920.

Rather make your own stocking? **1-2-3 Stitch** offers dozens of stocking kits to choose from. Jolly Santas and hearty snowmen can be hung next to families of polar bears and traditional nativity scenes: *123stitch.com* or 800-996-1230.

Beautiful **Dimensions Christmas** stocking kits are available at Needlework Corner: *needleworkcorner.com/cdim*.

The **Christmas Loft** has all you could ever want in wool felt, velveteen, knit, and quilted stockings, including whimsical deer and moose designs, an interesting velvet reindeer, nativity and Nordic themes, nostalgic snowman and snowflakes, and a cute superhero collection. There are 25 stocking designs in all! Check out the popular snowman and Santa stocking holders, too: *christmasloft.com*.

Order personalized tartan stockings in your choice of plaid or get lovely embroidered stockings from **Merry Stockings**: *merrystockings.com*.

Cherry Lane Collection devotes an entire department to holiday gifts for the "family furs," including dog (by breed) and cat stockings: *cherrylanecollection.com* or (800) 854-5049.

The Country Mouse sells adorable personalized stocking holders for children to place on a shelf or mantelpiece: *country-mouse.com/housiloz*.

MERRY CHRISTMAS

It came without ribbons,
It came without tags,
It came without packages, boxes, or bags.
Christmas can't be bought from a store...
Maybe Christmas means a little bit more.
—DR. SEUSS

Scented Sachets

Cookies baking, spiced cider, evergreen . . . the scents conjure up memories of Christmases past and bring festive smiles on people's faces. Infuse your home with the aromas of the season by tucking scented sachets in linen drawers, or placing them in small bowls on tables or windowsills. If possible, gather fresh aromatic herbs, flowers, and seedpods to make your own potpourri, and embroider linen handkerchiefs to use for. Enliven your potpourri with a few drops of essential oils, such as lavender, tea rose, or coriander.

To your favorite aromatic blends, choose from these:

Bay leaves, pinecones, fragrant wood chips, cinnamon sticks, whole cloves, allspice berries, whole star anise, lavender, rosehips, rosebuds and petals, chamomile, lemon verbena leaves, cornflower, rosemary, eucalyptus seedpods, dried hops, dried orange and lemon peel, bayberry bark, juniper berries, hibiscus

SACHET POUCH Cut a circle of cotton or muslin about five inches in diameter. Place a small palmful of blended potpourri in the center and tie the ends with a length of ribbon.

SACHET PILLOW Embroidered handkerchiefs can make a nice sachet pillowcase. Fill with a muslin sachet pouch that you can refresh with essential oils, or replace with a new blend of potpourri. Add some snaps to the pillow, to keep its contents from spilling out:

1. Pin two handkerchiefs of equal size front to front.
2. Stitch three sides together with a basic backstitch. Leave the fourth side open and turn pillowcase right side out.
3. Sew three sets of snap fasteners onto the inner seam of the pillowcase opening.
4. Cut two pieces of muslin about two square inches less in area than the handkerchiefs.

5. Sew three sides together using a backstitch. Fill the pouch with potpourri and sew the fourth side together. Place the pillow in its case, and snap shut.

Snow Globes

Create a little magical snow world of your own! Snow globes are so easy—make several with different scenes to enjoy or give away.

Small glass jar with lid, 1 eggshell, small plastic resealable bag, rolling pin, strong waterproof glue, small plastic toys or ornaments (snowman, angel, Santa, trees, star, cabin, etc.), baby oil, glitter, pie tin

1. Wash and dry the jar inside and out.
2. Wash and dry the eggshell. Place in the plastic bag, pushing as much air as possible out of the bag before sealing it. Crush the eggshell with the rolling pin until it is as fine as sugar.
3. Glue toys to the inside of the jar lid, making sure finished scene will fit inside closed jar. Sprinkle a little bit of the eggshell over any exposed glue. Let dry.
4. Fill the jar three-fourths full with baby oil. Add the crushed eggshell and some glitter to create sparkle in your snow. Allow the snow to settle at the bottom of the jar.
5. Place the jar on a pie tin to catch any overflow of the oil.
6. Put beads of glue on the threads of the lid and carefully lower the ornaments into the oil. Screw the lid on tight.
7. Allow five minutes for the glue to set, and then give it a shake!

Options: Use different sized baby food, jam, or pickle jars. Use plastic jars if you have small children (i.e. peanut-butter jars). Try cutting up aluminum foil or shaving colored crayons for snow. Jar can also be filled with water and a bit of corn syrup or liquid dish soap.

Great Romantic Gifts

❦ Lingerie/Silk Boxers/Robe ❦ Massage Oils ❦ Tropical Vacation ❦ Framed Poem ❦ Coupon for Dinner Out ❦ Ballroom Dancing Lessons ❦ Opera Tickets ❦ Coupon for a Day Doing Whatever S/he Wants ❦ A Weekend at a Bed & Breakfast ❦ *Sonnets for the Portuguese* by Elizabeth Barrett Browning ❦

Green Gifts

Trying to make your lifestyle more eco-conscious? Plant a tree in the name of a loved one through *treepeople.com* or stuff stockings with a carbon offset with Climate Change Chocolate from *terrapass.com*. For the children in your life, try an organic stuffed animal that they'll love for years to come: *organictoybox.com*. Have a fashionable friend to please? Get a Stella McCartney handbag made from vegan materials from **Neiman Marcus.** There are a myriad of choices for those that have everything: adopt a coral reef from the **Nature Conservatory** and get a personalized certificate for the gift recipient: *nature.org*; or buy a family a goat or a trio of rabbits from **Heifer International,** where every gift comes with a card to let your loved ones know that you've honored them with a priceless gift: *heifer.org*. Looking for some green eats? Try organic wine from *ecowine.com* or environmentally responsible cheese from *cowgirlcreamery.com*. Log on to *treehugger.com/giftguide* for more ideas.

Keep a Gift List

Take a holiday planning tip from Santa and keep a Christmas gift list in your engagement calendar. Throughout the year, make note of the moments when your mother mentions she'd like to read *Anna Karenina* or when your nephew tells you about his favorite new band. By the time the holiday season rolls around, you'll have all the ideas you'll need. Not only will you be able to avoid last minute Christmas Eve shopping—you'll infuse extra thoughtfulness into your gift-giving.

Gifts in Large Families

Instead of buying gifts for every member of the family, let everyone pull one name out of a hat at Thanksgiving and be responsible for giving to that one person only. It cuts back on the crazy spending that large families can inspire, and can be a great way to get to know a more distant relative.

Another alternative: set an age limit. Only those under 18 get gifts, for instance, while the rest of the family gets to enjoy the watching the presents get opened.

Grab bags are another way to keep the gift giving in check. Put out the word ahead of time that every family member must bring just one wrapped gift worth up to an agreed-upon limit (say, $30.00). When everyone arrives, the gifts are placed in a basket: everyone picks a number out of a hat. Number one goes first, selecting an unmarked gift from the basket and opening it for all to see. Then number two goes, and so on. But the fun's only just begun. Once everyone has selected and opened a gift, number one gets to go again, and may exchange their gift for any other gift they find more desirable. Then number two goes, and so on, with a favorite gift often changing hands many times, and the highest number being the only one to have final say!

Have a tree trimming Christmas party. Invite family and friends for egg nog, Christmas cookies, mulled cider and cold cuts (or cocktails and take out Chinese), and ask each guest to bring an ornament in lieu of a gift. To make it more fun, choose a theme each year: Santa Claus, Snowmen, Glass, or a color—such as white, red, or blue.

Greeks do not give presents at Christmas, but wait until St. Basil's Day (January 1). They have their hands full fending off malicious gremlins called *kallikantzaroi*, who play troublesome pranks at Christmastime. Burn salt or an old shoe, the stench of either being enough to drive them off. Other methods include hanging a pig's jawbone by the door and keeping a large fire going so they can't sneak down the chimney. A priest might throw a tiny cross into the village water and go from house to house sprinkling holy water.

He who has not Christmas in his heart will never find it under a tree.

—Roy L. Smith

A History of Christmas Presents

The joy of Christmas gift giving is a tradition borne from heaven, first scribed by St. John in the Fourth Gospel: "For God so loved the world that he gave his only begotten son, that whosoever believeth in him should not perish, but have everlasting life." News of God's gift, the birth of "a babe, in swaddling clothes," drew angels, shepherds, and wise men into its midst. To the Christ child, three Magis presented the first Christmas gifts: gold, frankincense, and myrrh.

Nativity scenes under the Christmas tree—surrounded by mounds of presents—may serve as reminders of the first gift-exchange, but presenting gifts at the end of the year is actually a custom predating Christianity. In the Golden Age of Rome, people made presents for each other and gave gifts of fruit, vegetables, and baked goods during the winter Saturnalia festival. For ten days, all civic activities ceased, while the citizens feasted and bestowed generosity on each other, including imparting slaves with great liberties. But with the rise of Christianity, early church leaders sought to get rid of such pagan customs and practices. Luckily they were not successful.

The Christmas spirit of giving to others in need is often attributed to the legend of St. Nicholas of Myra, the forefather of the modern Santa Claus. He set the example when he

slipped dowry money through the window of three poor sisters, so they wouldn't have to face a life of hardship. Following the tradition of King Henry III, who established the custom in 1248, English monarchs have remembered the needy at Christmas by providing food to the poor. Still, the practice of exchanging gifts with family or friends was not widespread until the sixteenth and seventeenth centuries, when Christmas presents became a regular part of the holiday, especially for children.

The German town of Nuremberg had become famous for its *Christkindelsmarket*, where parents bought "Christ-bundles" for their children. On Christmas Eve, children eagerly awaited these packages filled with gingerbread, candies, toys, nuts, clothes, and the like. Not all the presents were welcome, however, for behavior played a determining role. Unruly children found lumps of coal in their shoes, or a bundle of sticks.

Victorians in England did much to establish spirited gift-giving as part of the Christmas tradition. Children would find gifts at the end of elaborately planned parlor games, or wrapped up in balls of yarn that first needed to be unraveled. With the exception of the Christmas stocking, most presents for the children would be displayed around a room, or hanging from the Christmas tree, ready to be plucked off. Gifts for adults might be packaged, but not until the 1870s did they begin to appear as elaborately decorated parcels. By the late nineteenth century, the giving of manufactured goods for Christmas gifts had fueled an industry. Holiday packages, once sealed shut with wax and straight pins, began appearing bundled in bright paper and ribbons.

Museum Catalogs

Museums are a great source for creative and unusual gifts.

The British Museum, founded in 1753, tops the list for finest-in-the-world exhibits and related gifts, including Egyptian; Asian, Greek, and Roman antiquities; prints and drawings by Michelangelo and Goya, and entertaining collections of visiting, trade, and playing cards. The museum's many shops are at your service: *britishmuseum.co.uk*.

New York's **Museum of Modern Art** has an appropriately well-designed website featuring gifts for lovers of all things beautiful. Desktop, kitchen, and tabletop items are among the favorites: *momastore.org* or (800) 851-4509.

How about a pair of Cypriot citrine earrings that look like they are from the 4th century B.C.? The **Metropolitan Museum of Art**, in New York has a myriad of gifts, many based on originals in the museum's vast collections: *metmuseum.org/store* or (800) 468-7386.

The **Chicago Museum of Contemporary Art** has an unparalleled store and bookstore that includes prints, catalogs, and limited-edition craft pieces and accessories related to the many sculptors, photographers, and other artists who have exhibited at Chicago: *mcachicago.org* or (312) 397-4000.

In Florida for the holidays? Don't miss the **Salvador Dalí Museum**, St. Petersburg, for a healthy dose of whimsy. Or try the next best thing: the website has Dalí Wear, jewelry, a home collection, and more. Fans will love the etched Disintegration watch: *salvadordalimuseum.org* or (727) 823-3767.

The **Museum of Contemporary Art**, Los Angeles departs from the subtly tasteful neutral tones of the typical museum store with a flamboyantly colorful selection of intriguing items and books at its fun, HOT website. Subject matter includes the automobile, of course: *moca.org/store* or (213) 633-5329.

Boston's **Isabella Stewart Gardner Museum**, with its collections of tapestries, furnishings, paintings, sculpture, and artifacts spanning thirty centuries, and its legendary flower-filled courtyard, is in a category all its own: *gardnermuseum.org* or (617) 278-5180.

The **Smithsonian Institution**, in Washington, DC, includes, among other facilities, the Arts and Industries Building, National Air and Space Museum, Hirshhorn Museum, National Portrait Gallery, Anacostia Museum and Center for African American History and Culture, National Postal Museum, National Museum of Natural History, and the National Zoological Park. The easy-to-shop website has clothing, home furnishings, jewelry, toys, Smithsonian treasures, and more: *smithsonianstore.com/home.asp* or (800) 322-0344.

The **Kennedy Space Center** Space Shop offers hundreds of collectibles, plus flight suits and jackets for the whole family: *thespaceshop.com* or (800) 621-9826.

Immerse yourself in the colorful history of the American West, at Topeka's world-renowned **Kansas Museum of History**. Its stores feature works by local artists and native craftspeople, books and journals, and teaching materials: *kshs.org/shop* or (785) 272-8681.

Twenty-two national science centers, zoos, and aquariums have joined with American manufacturers to fill the **Museum Tour catalog** with thought-provoking "toys and museum gifts that stimulate curiosity, provide aesthetic pleasure and enhance the joy of learning": *museumtour.com* or (800) 360-9116.

In 1901, a wealthy passenger ordered a 4-foot-wide mince pie for the baggage car crewmembers' Christmas dinner on Pennsylvania Railroad's train number 273–283, which ran between Point Pleasant, New Jersey and Jersey City.

Shiny Angel Card

With a head of metallic loops, a shiny dress, and feather wings, this dazzling angel card carries your holiday message written or printed on the back.

6" x 5" piece of mylar, tacky glue, 6 small feathers with the quills cut off, 1 metallic paper cord or colored wire, 5" x 5" x 2½" arts and crafts foil triangle, small star stickers, 6" x 5" piece of paper or card stock

1. Place a nickel-size dab of glue on the mylar, 2" down from the top at the center.
2. Place the feathers on the mylar, their quill ends in the glue, radiating out from the glue dab, three to each side. These are the angel's wings.
3. Loop the cord around two fingers several times and tie securely.
4. Glue the ends of the cord to the mylar where the feathers meet.
5. Fold the top point of the triangle under about 1", and fold the bottom up about ¼" making a hem. This will be the body of your angel.

6. Glue the triangle to the mylar with the top covering the quill ends of the feathers and the glue. Add stars to decorate her dress. With a small dab of glue in each corner, attach a 6" x 5" piece of paper or card stock, decorated with any greeting you choose, to the back of your shiny angel.

The Best Christmas Books

❄ *Swingin' and Swingin' and Gettin' Merry Like Christmas* by Maya Angelou ❄
The Christmas Train by David Baldacci ❄ *The Life and Adventures of Santa Claus* by Frank L. Baum ❄ *A Christmas Memory, One Christmas & Thanksgiving Visitor* by Truman Capote ❄ *The Gift: A Christmas Story* by R. Louis Carroll ❄ *Miracle on 34th Street* by Valentine Davies ❄ *A Christmas Carol* and *Christmas Stories* by Charles Dickens ❄ *A Different Kind of Christmas* by Alex Haley ❄ *The Gift of the Magi: And Other Stories* by O. Henry ❄ *Carol of the Brown King: Nativity Poems* by Langston Hughes ❄ *Old Christmas* by Washington Irving ❄ *A Full House: An Austin Family Christmas* by Madeleine L' Engle ❄ *Circle of Wonder: A Native American Christmas Story* by N. Scott Momaday ❄ *The Night Before Christmas* by Clement Clarke Moore ❄ *Holidays on Ice* by David Sedaris ❄ *How The Grinch Stole Christmas* by Dr. Seuss ❄ *The First Christmas of New England* by Harriet Beecher Stowe ❄ *A Child's Christmas in Wales* by Dylan Thomas

Give the Gift of a Classic Children's Book

Little Women by Louisa May Alcott
The Book of Three by Lloyd Alexander
Tuck Everlasting by Natalie Babbitt
National Velvet by Enid Bagnold
Peter Pan by A. M. Barrie
The Wizard of Oz by Frank L. Baum
Madeline by Ludwig Bemelmans
Clifford the Big Red Dog by Norman Bridwell
Goodnight, Moon or *The Runaway Bunny*
by Margaret Wise Brown
The Story of Babar, the Little Elephant
by Jean De Brunhoff
A Little Princess or *The Secret Garden*
by Frances Hodgson Burnett
Alice in Wonderland by Lewis Carroll
Charlie and The Chocolate Factory
or *James & The Giant Peach* by Roald Dahl
Hardy Boy Mysteries by Franklin W. Dixon
The Black Stallion by Walter Farley
Harriet the Spy by Louise Fitzhugh
The Wind in the Willows by Kenneth Grahame
Harold and the Purple Crayon
by Crockett Johnson
Nancy Drew Mysteries by Carolyn Keene
The Jungle Book by Rudyard Kipling
From the Mixed-Up Files of Mrs. Basil E.
Frankweiler by E. L. Konigsburg
The Story of Ferdinand by Munro Leaf
A Wrinkle in Time by Madeleine L'Engle
The Lion, The Witch & The Wardrobe
by C. S. Lewis
Pippi Longstocking by Astrid Ericsson Lindgren
Winnie the Pooh by A. A. Milne
The Little Engine That Could by Watty Piper
The Tale of Peter Rabbit by Beatrix Potter

The Adventures of Curious George by H. A. Rey
The Little Prince by Antoine de Saint-Exupéry
Where the Wild Things Are! by Maurice Sendak
Black Beauty by Anna Sewell
The Giving Tree or *Where the Sidewalk Ends*
by Shel Silverstein
Encyclopedia Brown: Boy Detective
by Donald J. Sobol
Heidi by Johanna Spyri
Treasure Island by Robert Louis Stevenson
Cat in the Hat by Dr. Seuss
Eloise at the Plaza by Kay Thompson
The Hobbit by J. R. Tolkien
Mary Poppins by P. L. Travers
The Adventures of Tom Sawyer by Mark Twain
Charlotte's Web by T. H. White
The Sword in the Stone by T. H. White
Rebecca of Sunnybrook Farm
by Kate Douglas Wiggin
Little House on the Prairie
by Laura Ingalls Wilder
The Velveteen Rabbit by Margery Williams

Do give books—religious or otherwise—for Christmas. They're
never fattening, seldom sinful, and permanently personal.

—LENORE HERSHEY

Chocolates!

Want a presidential treat? Try Salt Caramels from **Fran's Chocolates** in Seattle: *franschocolates.com* or 800-422-FRAN. .

Lake Champlain Chocolates in Vermont is a holiday favorite: *lakechamplain-chocolate.com* or (800) 465-5909.

Let's not forget **Necco** American classics (Necco wafers, Mary Janes, Sweethearts, Sky Bar, Haviland Thin Mints, Mighty Malts) for nostalgia's sake: *necco.com.*

Simcha Sweets sells Kosher gourmet confections and chocolates: *SimchaSweets.com.*

La Maison du Chocolat is considered by many to be the best of the best: *lamaisondu-chocolat.com/en* or (800) 988-LMDC.

Li-Lac Chocolate's in New York's Greenwich Village, offers yummy confections (including chocolate tree ornaments, truffles, and 3-foot high chocolate santas) that can be made, wrapped, and shipped to order: (212) 242-7374. *li-lacchocolates.com*

West Coast confectioners **See's Candies** have earned their reputation for delicious holiday treats. Their "custom mix" box of chocolates is packed to your specifications: *sees.com* or (800) 895-7337.

Omanhene was listed in the *Consumers Digest* "Rating the World's Finest Chocolate." Omanhene uses cocoa beans from Ghana, and makes an all-natural hot cocoa mix: *oman-hene.com* or (414) 744-8780.

Try **Mrs. Williams Sugarfree Diabetic**

More diamonds are purchased at Christmastime (a third of the total) than during any other occasion.

Delights, "baked by a person with diabetes for people with or without diabetes: *mrs-williams.com* or (702) 362-2903.

The **Wessex Provender Deli** has the finest on-line foods available, including organic chocolate by **Green and Blacks and Duchy**: *provender.net.*

At **Gethsemani Farms** in Kentucky, monks make heavenly chocolate Bourbon walnut fudge: *gethsemanifarms.org* or (800) 549-0912.

Buy a **Best Chocolate of the Month Club** membership for your best friend at the "Sweetest Club on Earth:" *bestmonthlyclubs.com.*

Ghirardelli, the famous San Francisco chocolate manufacturer, has divine selections: *ghirardelli.com* or (800) 877-9338.

Godiva remains a favorite for fine chocolate; their hazelnut paste is highly lauded: *godiva.com* or call (800) 9-GODIVA.

Harry and David can't be beat for reliably delivered, beautifully gift-packaged holiday confections: *harryanddavid.com* or (877) 322-1200.

During a typical holiday season, about 1.76 billion candy canes are made.

Great Gifts for Your Boss

❧ Fancy Bean Coffee & Grinder ❧ Paperweight ❧ Cigars ❧ Briefcase ❧ Wine/Flower Club Membership ❧ Money Clip ❧ Spa Gift Certificate ❧ Coffee Table Book ❧ Sports/Concert ❧ Tickets ❧ Vintage Fountain Pen

Fruitcakes!

Although fruitcake definitely has an image problem, there *is* such a thing as a good one. Following is an invaluable fabulous fruitcake-finding resource.

Fudges brandy-soaked Empire cake, fruit-and-pecan cake, or Ginger Kringle fruitcake is available from **Wessex Provender Deli**: *provender.net.*

Monastery FruitCake is a fruitcake to convert fruitcake haters: An *Epinions* review calls it "sinful." Visit the monks, order a brandy fruitcake, and make a prayer request: *monasteryfruitcake.org.*

Sunshine Hollow Bakery ("For folks who don't like regular fruitcake") asserts that there are no "cheap fillers like raisins, citron, or bitter orange peel" in their delicious, pecan-filled fruitcakes: *sunshinehollow.com.*

Ranked as "best overall" in a *Wall Street Journal* taste test, **Gethsemani Farms** dark and spicy Kentucky Bourbon fruitcakes will never be used as substitute pigskin in the afternoon's touch football game. Trust the Trappists to make a good cake: *gethsemanifarms.org* or (800) 549-0912.

Harry and David have their own special fruitcake recipe: *harryanddavid.com* or (877) 347-7337.

About Christmas time there is a great plenty of good wishes sent about the kingdom.
—ALEXANDER POPE, 1736

Santa Claus is Coming to Town
The Legend of St. Nick

Santa Claus... His Life and Legacy

Most of us know Santa Claus as the jolly, red-cheeked gift bearer who shows up each Christmas season. During the past 1,700 years, however, he has taken many names and faces. One thing remains clear: the spirit of Father Christmas is so deeply ingrained in our culture, that he's bound to live on for millennia to come.

Before the days of Christianity, sailors prayed to the Greek god Poseidon for calm seas and safe journeys. But when the rise of Christianity brought the downfall of pagan gods, sailors still needed a hero . . . until news that a bishop in Asia Minor had all the powers of the Greek god and more.

That bishop's name was Nicholas, and he served in the late third and early fourth centuries in the town of Myra in what is now known as Turkey. Reportedly, Nicholas witnessed and performed several miracles throughout his lifetime. Even as a babe, he is said to have refused his mother's breast on fast days.

Tales spread of Nicholas' ability to control the storms at sea and lead seamen to their ports. After his death, he became the patron saint for sailors, fishermen, travelers, and many others.

St. Nicholas racked up so many purported miracles in his lifetime (and beyond) that he became a cult folk hero throughout the Middle Ages. He was perhaps most popular with children, for whom he left presents on the eve of his saint's day, December 5. But there was a time when Nicholas' status as miracle maker looked grim.

In the 1520s, at the beginning of the German Protestant Reformation, Martin Luther objected to the idea of a Catholic saint giving gifts to Protestant children. Luther and other reformers managed to rid the church of any saint-honoring customs around December 5th, but the legend of St. Nicholas stayed alive, quietly roaming German streets door-to-door in the name of *Christ-Kindlein*, the spirit of the Christ child who gave presents on Christmas Eve, December 24th.

By 1545, children in good Protestant homes throughout Germany were visited by Christ-Kindlein. This transference of traditions spread throughout Protestant Europe, and the idea of a wandering gift-giver became associated with the birth of Christ as well as pre-Christian winter solstice festivals. In English-speaking areas, Christ-Kindlein morphed into Kriss Kringle, an older secular Father Christmas figure—not surprisingly more like good old Saint Nicholas.

Hence, before the end of the Middle Ages, Saint Nicholas may have lost his sainthood, but he didn't lose his magic. He emerged unscathed and held a unique passport to virtually every European country. With a simple name change: *Père Noël* in France, *Nikolai Chudovorits* in Russia (there known as Father Frost), *Julesvenn* in Norway, *Julenisse* in Denmark, Nicholas allowed Protestants to have the best of both worlds. He could embody the sacred Christ

Child and the secular "Christmas Man."

The Santa Claus of Europe was a tall, skinny old man, dressed in furs or rags, who wandered the streets by foot or on horseback. Only after he arrived in New York did Jolly St. Nick gain weight, start traveling by reindeer, and establish a home base at the North Pole.

The Dutch settlers who established New Amsterdam (later called New York) in the early seventeenth century sailed in a ship with St. Nicholas as its figurehead; the patron saint of Amsterdam quickly became that of New York, as well. The Dutch erected their first church in his name and openly celebrated his feast day, a religious holiday that included food, festivity, and gifts. In less than one hundred years, the New York Historical Society was holding anniversary dinners for the city's favorite saint.

The writer Washington Irving, a member of the society, concocted *Diedrich Knickerbocker's History of New York* in 1809. It included rich details of *Sancte Claus*, the "jolly old elf" who traveled along rooftops and dropped down chimneys to deliver gifts to sleeping children. In 1822, Clement Clarke Moore used Irving's descriptions in "A Visit from St. Nicholas," a poem he wrote for his children. Moore gave us the names of Santa's eight reindeer, his telltale winks and nods, and his secret method for rising up chimneys (by "laying his finger aside of his nose"). By the 1860s, the illustrator Thomas Nast sealed Santa's image in people's minds across the nation, with his drawings in *Harper's Weekly*. Nast depicted Santa as a rotund figure with a workshop full of elves at the North Pole. The modern-day Santa was here to stay.

There is no telling if Santa would have survived the Dutch tradition in New York if it hadn't been for Irving, Moore, and Nast. Regardless of the century-old stories of Saint Nicholas that prevailed throughout Europe, today's Santa is distinctly American—a product of nineteenth-century New York.

Dear Editor:

I am 8 years old. Some of my friends say there is no Santa Claus. Papa says "If you see it in The Sun it's so." Please tell me the truth; is there a Santa Claus?   Virginia O'Hanlon

Yes, Virginia, There Is a Santa Claus
—Francis P. Church

Virginia, your little friends are wrong. They have been affected by the skepticism of a skeptical age. They do not believe except they see. They think that nothing can be which is not comprehensible by their little minds. All minds, Virginia, whether they be men's or children's, are little. In this great universe of ours man is a mere insect, an ant, in his intellect, as compared with the boundless world about him, as measured by the intelligence capable of grasping the whole of truth and knowledge.

Yes, Virginia, there is a Santa Claus. He exists as certainly as love and generosity and devotion exist, and you know that they abound and give to your life its highest beauty and joy. Alas! how dreary would be the world if there were no Santa Claus! It would be as dreary as if there were no Virginias. There would be no childlike faith then, no poetry, no romance to make tolerable this existence. We should have no enjoyment, except in sense and sight. The eternal light with which childhood fills the world would be extinguished.

Not believe in Santa Claus! You might as well not believe in fairies! You might get your papa to hire men to watch in all the chimneys on Christmas Eve to catch Santa Claus, but even if they did not see Santa Claus coming down, what would that prove? Nobody sees Santa Claus, but that is no sign that there is no Santa Claus. The most real things in the world are those that neither children nor men can see.

No Santa Claus! Thank God, he lives, and he lives forever. A thousand years from now, Virginia, nay, ten times ten thousand years from now, he will continue to make glad the heart of childhood.

—*THE NEW YORK SUN*, SEPTEMBER 21, 1897

Where to Send Santa's Letters

Mailing Santa Claus is as easy as putting your child's letter in an envelope addressed to "Santa Claus, North Pole." Make sure you put down the correct return address and enough postage for a standard first-class letter. Like all holiday mail, the letter can be given right to your mail carrier. Most of the letters are answered (with small gifts) by local volunteers working for the Operation Santa Claus program.

If you want to be sure of a response, you can write to Santa c/o Det. 2, 11th WS, Eilson AFB, Alaska, 99702. When you secretly enclose a "reply from Santa" with your child's letter, elves working part-time for the Air Force Weather Squadron will turn the mail around so that your child receives Santa's reply. Be sure to send the letter before December 10th for a response in time for Christmas.

To take it one step further, you can get an authentic North Pole postmark on Santa Claus' letter by sending a blank envelope with postage to Postmaster, Attn: Steve Cornelius, North Pole Branch U.S. Post Office, 325 Santa Claus Lane, North Pole, Alaska, 99705-9998. The turnaround time is around 7 to 8 days, anytime before December.

The idea of the Christmas stocking began in Great Britain, when Father Christmas supposedly once dropped some gold coins as he was coming down the chimney. Because someone had put their stockings out to dry over the fireplace, the coins were caught and saved. To this day, children hang their stockings on the mantlepiece in the hope that Santa will drop something inside.

Santa Hat Ornament

A perfect miniature of Santa's most recognizable feature to hang on your tree.

Half-circle of red felt with a 3" radius, fabric glue, ornament hanger, scissors, 2 cotton balls

1. Overlap the corners of the felt by about 1 $^1/_2$" to form a cone, and glue together.
2. Straighten the top of the ornament hanger, poke it through the hole at the cone's point, and then bend it back into a curve again.
3. Cut a small hole in the center of one cotton ball. Work your fingers into the hole, gently stretching the fibers into a narrow loop of cotton. Stop when the loop will fit around the bottom of the cone.
4. Glue the cotton to the bottom edge of the cone.
5. Form a gumball-size wad of cotton with the other cotton ball and glue it to the tip of the cone.

I stopped believing in Santa Claus when I was six. Mother took me to see him in a department store and he asked for my autograph.

—SHIRLEY TEMPLE BLACK

Santa Claus Is Coming To Town

You bet-ter watch out, you bet-ter not cry, Bet-ter not pout, I'm
mak-ing a list and check-ing it twice, Gon-na find out who's

tell - ing you why: San - ta Claus is com - in' to
naught-y and nice, San - ta Claus is com - in' to

town. He's
town. He

sees you when you're sleep - in', He knows when you're a - -

wake, He knows when you've been bad or good, so be

good for good-ness sake. Oh! You bet - ter watch out, you

bet - ter not cry, Bet - ter not pout, I'm tell - ing you why:

San - ta Claus is com - in' to town.

3. Little tin horns, Little toy drums,
Rudy-toot-toot, And rummy tum tums.
Santa Claus is coming to town.
Chorus

4. Little toy dolls, That cuddle and coo,
Elephants, boats, And kiddie cars too.

Santa Claus is coming to town.
Chorus

5. The kids in Girl and Boy Land.
Will have a jubilee.
They're gonna build a toyland town
All around the Christmas tree.
Chorus

One of Santa's most accomplished elves was Hermey, who traveled to the Island of Misfit Toys, tamed an abominable snowman, and became a dentist.

Scandinavian writers depicted gnomes in the 1800s as mischievous fairies—friends and helpers to Father Christmas.

In Sweden a gnome named Juletomten brings gifts in a sleigh pulled by goats.

A Short History of Elves

The belief in elves originated in the mythical tree spirits of northern Europe and Scandinavia. The Celts worshipped evergreens and the elfin spirits who lived in them. Also known as pixies, brownies, fairies, dryads, and huldefolk, these fairy-tale beings could either be benevolent or mischievous to people, depending upon whether or not the people had been on good behavior. Santa Clause himself is the "first elf" according to Clement Clarke Moore's 1822 poem, "A Visit from St. Nicholas." By 1850, Santa's elfin helpers appeared for the first time in the American picture book *Little Messenger Birds*, by Mrs. Caroline H. Butler. Around the same time, Scandinavian folktales as told by Finnish writer Zacharias Topelius and Swedish poet Victor Rydberg, revealed that the true purpose of elves was to help Father Christmas care for his reindeer, make toys in his workshop, and keep an eye on which children were naughty and which were nice.

Christmas This Year

Booth Tarkington

 omething more than a dozen years ago, at Princeton, I heard from one of the "Art Professors" that a painting by Mainardi, a fine example from the Floren tine Renaissance of the high period, could be bought in New York for far less than its worth. The great Depression was then upon us; the picture had been put through an auction sale and a dealer had bid it in for a fiftieth of what had once been paid for it.

I went to his galleries; he brought out the painting and I stood puzzled before it. The central figure was that of the blonde Virgin enthroned and holding the Christ child upon her lap. That was plain enough; but who were the two tall saints flanking the throne? One, holding a book, was a woman, probably identifiable as Ste. Justina; the other one was the problem—a long, thin, elderly man, bearded, ecclesiastically robed, red-gloved and carrying four loaves of bread in token of what function I couldn't guess.

One thing was certain: this ancient gentleman was immeasurably compassionate. That was markedly his expression. A deep world sadness underlay the look of pity; he was visibly a person who suffered less his own anguish and more that of others. You saw at once that he was profoundly sorry for all of humankind.

When I had the painting on my own wall at home, I found that a gentle melancholy pervaded the room and the old saint seemed to add a wistfulness. "Don't you really wish to know who I am?" he inquired to me whenever I looked his way.

I did indeed wish to know him and to understand his sorrow, which was one of the kind we call "haunting"—all the more so because it was universal. Of all the saints, he was the one who most mourned over the miseries of this tangled world. We got out our books, wrote to iconographical experts—and lo! we had our man. The sad old saint is—Santa Claus!

He is St. Nicholas of Bari and his four loaves of bread signify his giving, his generosity. In time, as the legend grew and changed, the most jocund and hearty of all symbolic figures emerged from this acutely sad and grieving one. St. Nicholas of Bari became "Old Saint Nick," "Kriss-kringle" (a most twisted alliterative) and Santa Claus.

He, the troubled and unhappy, now comes laughing down the chimney, fat and merry, to be the jovial inspiration of our jolliest season of the year. We say that time changed him, made this metamorphosis; but it was we— "we-the-people"—who did it. Time only let us forget that St. Nicholas was a sorrowful man.

Mainardi put a date on the painting. It is clear and neat upon a step of the Virgin's throne—1507. In the long march of mankind, the four hundred and thirty-eight years that have elapsed since the Tuscan painter finished his picture is but a breath. St. Nicholas as we know him now, our jolly, shouting friend, a frolic for the children, may become the saddest of all the saints again, someday. What made us brighten him into Santa Claus was our knowledge that the world was growing kinder than it was in 1507.

St. Nicholas of Bari knew only a cruel world. Christmas of this year needs the transfigured image of him—the jolly one who is merry because the world is wise—and kind.

Treats for Santa

Old-fashioned hot cocoa is the perfect treat on Christmas Eve. Leave a cup on the mantle for Santa when you go to bed; it's his favorite drink with chocolate chip cookies.

Hot Chocolate

3 tablespoons unsweetened cocoa
4 heaping tablespoons sugar
6 ounces boiling water
A few drops vanilla
12-ounce can evaporated milk
Whipped cream

1. Mix cocoa and sugar in a saucepan.
2. Add boiling water and simmer for 2 minutes, stirring frequently.
3. Add vanilla.
4. Add milk gradually, stirring with a whisk, and heat until bubbles appear around the sides of the pan.
5. Remove from the flame and continue to whisk for 2 more minutes.
6. Pour into mugs and top each with a dollop of whipped cream. Enjoy.

His eyes—how they twinkled! His dimples how merry!
His cheeks were like roses, his nose like a cherry!
His droll little mouth was drawn up like a bow,
And the beard of his chin was a s white as the snow;
The stump of a pipe he held tight in his teeth,
And the smoke it encircled his head like a wreath;
He had a broad face and little round belly,
That shook, when he laughed like a bowlful of jelly.

—CLEMENT CLARKE MOORE

Chocolate Chip Cookies

5 $1/3$ tablespoons butter at room temperature
$1/2$ cup sugar
$1/4$ cup packed brown sugar
1 egg
1 teaspoon vanilla extract
1 cup flour
$1/2$ teaspoon baking soda
$1/2$ teaspoon salt
1 cup semisweet chocolate chips

1. Preheat oven to 375° F.
2. In a large mixing bowl, cream together butter, white sugar, and brown sugar until light.
3. Add egg and vanilla. Mix well.
4. In a separate bowl, combine flour, baking soda, and salt, and gradually add to the above mixture. Mix well.
5. Add chocolate chips and mix well.
6. Drop mixture onto greased cookie sheet, one rounded tablespoon at a time, around 2" apart. Bake 8–10 minutes, until golden brown. Transfer cookies to wire racks and let cool.

Makes about 2 dozen cookies.

The Dutch Sinterklass arrives by boat on December 6th. Children leave a wooden shoe filled with hay and carrots for the donkey that carries his toys. If they're good, he leaves them a gift.

Up On The Housetop

1.

Up on the house-top rein-deer pause,

Out jumps good old San-ta Claus;

Down through the chim-ney with lots of toys,

All for the lit-tle ones, Christ-mas joys.

Ho, ho, ho! Who would-n't go!

Ho, ho, ho! Who would-n't go! _____

Up on the house top click, click, click,

Down through the chim-ney with good Saint Nick.

2. First comes the stocking of little Nell;
Oh, dear Santa, fit it well;
Give her a dollie that laughs and cries,
One that will open and shut her eyes.

Refrain

3. Next comes the stocking of little Will;
Oh, just see what a glorious fill;
Here is a hammer and lots of tacks,
Also a ball and a whip that cracks.

Refrain

163

THE BOY WHO LAUGHED
AT SANTA CLAUS   *Ogden Nash*

In Baltimore there lived a boy.
He wasn't anybody's joy.
Although his name was Jabez Dawes,
His character was full of flaws.
In school he never led his classes,
He hid old ladies' reading glasses,
His mouth was open when he chewed,
And elbows to the table glued.
He stole the milk of hungry kittens,
And walked through doors marked
NO ADMITTANCE.
He said he acted thus because
There wasn't any Santa Claus.
Another trick that tickled Jabez
Was crying "Boo!" at little babies.
He brushed his teeth, they said in town,
Sideways instead of up and down.

Yet people pardoned every sin,
And viewed his antics with a grin,
Till they were told by Jabez Dawes,
"There isn't any Santa Claus!"
Deploring how he did behave,
His parents swiftly sought their grave.
They hurried through the portals pearly,
And Jabez left the funeral early.

Like whooping cough, from child to child,
He sped to spread the rumor wild:
"Sure as my name is Jabez Dawes
There isn't any Santa Claus!"
Slunk like a weasel or a marten
Through nursery and kindergarten,
Whispering low to every tot,
"There isn't any, no there's not!"

The children wept all Christmas Eve
And Jabez chortled up his sleeve.

No infant dared hang up his stocking
For fear of Jabez' ribald mocking.
He sprawled on his untidy bed,
Fresh malice dancing in his head,
When presently with scalp a-tingling,
Jabez heard a distant jingling;
He heard the crunch of sleigh and hoof
Crisply alighting on the roof.

What good to rise and bar the door?
A shower of soot was on the floor.
What was beheld by Jabez Dawes?
The fireplace full of Santa Claus!
Then Jabez fell upon his knees
With cries of "Don't," and "Pretty please."
He howled, "I don't know where you read it,
But anyhow, I never said it!"

"Jabez," replied the angry saint,
"It isn't I, it's you that ain't.
Although there is a Santa Claus,
There isn't any Jabez Dawes!"
Said Jabez then with impudent vim,
"Oh, yes there is; and I am him!
Your magic don't scare me, it doesn't"—
And suddenly he found he wasn't!

From grimy feet to grimy socks,
Jabez became a Jack-in-the-box,
An ugly toy with springs unsprung,
Forever sticking out his tongue.
The neighbors heard his mournful squeal;
They searched for him, but not with zeal.
No trace was found of Jabez Dawes,
Which led to thunderous applause,
And people drank a loving cup
And went and hung their stockings up.

All you who sneer at Santa Claus,
Beware the fate of Jabez Dawes,
The saucy boy who mocked the saint.
Donder and Blitzen licked off his paint.

Santa by Any Other Name...

Whether it's "Father Christmas," "Père Noël," or "Sinterklas," the guy with the red suit and white beard is famous among children the world. Here are his aliases, by country:

Armenia...*Gaghant Baba*
Austria ....*Christkind*
Australia........................Kris Kringle, Saint Nick
Belgium, Netherlands.......................*Santakluse, Sankt Nickolaas*
Brazil, Spain...*Papa Noel*
Bulgaria..*Diado Coleda*
China ....*Sing Dan Lao Ren*
Czechoslovakia...............................*Svaty Miklas*
Denmark........................*Julenisse* or *Julemanden*
England....................................Father Christmas
Finland............Old Man Christmas, *Joulupukki*
France...........................*Père Noël* or *le Petit Noël*
Germany ....*St. Nikolaus, Weihnachtsmann*
Greece..*Nikolaos*
Hungary ....*Mikulas*
India...*Ganesha*
Indonesia ....*Sinterklas*
Italy ....*Babbo Natale, La Befana*
Japan............................*Santa Kurohsu, Hoteisho*
Poland.................................Star Man, *Gwiazdor*
Russia.................................*Nikolai Chudovorits*
Slovenia...*Bozicek*
Sweden ....*Jultomten*
Switzerland ....*Christkindl*
Yugoslavia ....*Deda Mraz*

North Pole Trivia

Illustrator Thomas Nast was the first to put Santa Clause's home on the map in 1882: his drawing showed Santa sitting on a box labeled, "Christmas Box 1882, St. Nicholas, North Pole."

Santa and his reindeer have a permanent home in Santa's Workshop at the North Pole Village in Wilmington, New York near Lake Placid.

In 1944, the Dahl and Gaske Development company purchased four square miles of private homestead near Fairbanks, Alaska to create the town North Pole in the hopes of luring toy companies to manufacture their wares there.

The post office there now handles as many as 60,000 letters each year addressed to Santa at the North Pole.

On the shortest day of the year, North Pole, Alaska gets three hours and forty-two minutes of sunshine.

In 1925, newspapers reported that reindeer would not be able to live at the North Pole because it actually exists on continually shifting floating sheets of ice, and that Santa's true home was in Finnish Lapland.

Geographically speaking, the North Pole is the point on Earth that is the true top of the planet where all lines of longitude converge. If you could actually plant your feet there, the rest of the world would be spinning beneath them.

The Geomagnetic North Pole is the point on Earth that marks the northern focus of the geomagnetic field that surrounds the globe. It lies in Greenland, 78°30' North, 69° West.

Compasses point to the Magnetic North Pole, which is about 1,000 miles south of the geographic North Pole, near Ellef Ringness Island in northern Canada.

A lesser-known North Pole, the Northern Pole of Inaccessibility, represents the furthest point in all directions from any coastline. About 700 miles from the nearest land, this pole is located north of Alaska at 84°03' North, 174°51' West.

Call for ye Jolly Jester

He's brimful of Fun.

His merry jokes make laughter

For Christmastide's begun.

Santa Suits for Sale

For serious Santas, **International Fun Shop** advertises complete head-to-toe velvet outfits for Santa, Mrs. Claus, and elves—including theatrical makeup, wigs and beards, realistic belly stuffers, Santa glasses, and toy bags. The Deluxe Majestic, Fun Shop's top-of-the-line Claus model, is extra plush: *fun-shop.com* or (800) 831-2597.

Nightmare Factory has very convincing elf ear tips, as well as their "standard" velour Santa Claus costume, which comes with beard and eyebrows. Get a load of the Grinch masks while visiting this unusually helpful website at *nightmarefactory.com*. You can e-mail *shop@nightmarefactory.com* or call (512) 858-5063 with questions.

The **Costume Salon's** easy-to-use website will take you through the rental process step by step, with special links for contacting them to give measurements, place your order, and return the costume. The Salon's costumes are spectacularly elaborate, so security deposits are hefty: *costumesalon.com* or (505) 988-7125.

The **Costumer's Manifesto** is a web source list for vendors that sell, rent, and custom-make suits for historical reenactments, parties, and theater: *costume.org*.

A visit to **CostumeZone.com's** Christmas Zone yields a variety of Santa and Mrs. Claus getups as well as elf ensembles, angel outfits, religious characters, accessories, and even child-size Santa clothes: *costumezone.com,* or email *info@costumezone.com* or by fax (888) 871-3622.

Costumes Galore has thousands of costumes for rent, with specific instructions for placing your order. Receive your Santa Claus outfit by good old UPS, or visit one of their Southern California stores: *costumesgalore.com* or email *info@costumesgalore.com* or (626) 683-8351.

Santa is even-tempered. Santa does not hit children over the head who kick him. Santa uses the term "folks" rather than "Mommy" and "Daddy" because of all the broken homes. Santa does not have a three-martini lunch. Santa does not borrow money from store employees. Santa wears a good deodorant.

—Jenny Zink (To employees of Western Temporary Services, the world's largest supplier of Santa Clauses)

Track Santa Online

Do you know you can harness the awesome capabilities of the North American Aerospace Defense Command (NORAD) to track nine flying reindeer and big red sleigh and they make their way around the world on Christmas Eve? Just click on over to *noradsanta.org* to follow Santa's Christmas route.

According to the Alaska Department of Fish and Game, male reindeer shed their antlers at the beginning of winter, while females keep theirs until after giving birth to their young the following spring, which means—if logic is to dictate truth—that all of Santa's reindeers must have been girls.

Rudolph with your nose so bright, won't you guide my sleigh tonight?

—JOHNNY MARKS

Dashing Through the Snow: Santa's Reindeer

Where did Santa get all those reindeer? Considering that he's a man who makes his home north of the 66th parallel, he likely picked up on customs from neighboring Lapps, Finns, Norwegians, Swedes, Russians, and indigenous Arctic peoples, for whom reindeer have been an important part of culture and lifestyle since the second century B.C.

Reindeer have long been part of Christmas celebrations. Renaissance writings from England describe the display of reindeer antlers at Christmas dances. Early depictions of reindeer pulling Santa's sleigh can be traced to the Finnish legend of Old Man Winter, who comes down from the mountains driving his reindeer and bringing the season's snow with him. In Russia as well, Father Frost arrives each winter driving a reindeer-pulled sled.

In the olden days, Santa may have been spotted with only one reindeer, but by 1823, he clearly had a posse. Clement C. Moore was the first to team Santa with eight of the antlered creatures in his quintessential Christmas poem, "A Visit from St. Nicholas." Now children know them by name: Dasher, Dancer, Prancer, Vixen, Comet, Cupid, Donder, and Blitzen.

The latecomer Rudolph didn't appear on the scene until 1939, when the Montgomery Ward company commissioned Robert L. May to write a Christmas story that the store could hand out to children as part of their Christmas promotions.

It took another decade before Rudolph became embedded in the hearts and minds of American audiences, with the popular Gene Autry song "Rudolph the Red-Nosed Reindeer" written by May's brother-in-law Johnny Marks. The chart-topping song has been sung at Christmastime ever since.

Reindeer Trivia

An Ice Age reindeer engraved on a cave wall in France is considered to be from 12,000 to 10,500 B.C. *There are about five million reindeer in the world.* Reindeer and caribou are actually two different names for the same species (*Rangifer tarandus*). *Among all deer species, reindeer are the only ones where both males and females sport antlers.* A reindeer's winter coat is made of three-inch long hollow hair that traps air inside in order to keep its body warm. *A reindeer can travel up to fifty miles a day while pulling a sled bearing twice its weight.* "Rudolph the Red Nosed Reindeer" sold two million copies in its first year and became the #2 best selling song of all time—after "White Christmas." *Reindeer are the most domesticated of all deer. For centuries, they've carried riders and pulled sleds for people who live in northern climates.* Santa's ninth reindeer was originally named Rollo—and then Reginald—before Robert L. May decided on Rudolph in his 1939 story.

A Christmas Moon

Mrs. Albert G. Latham

Little Lois had been to a charming Christmas party, and she was quite sorry when her big brother and sister came to take her home.

"Father Christmas has been to the party," she told them. "He gave me this funny paper thing, and says it will grow big and bright like a moon when it is lit up."

"I wish he would come and sweep those great clouds away from the real moon," said Roger. "It's so dark I can't see what path we are taking."

"And it's beginning to snow!" cried Cicely. "What fun! Three lost children out in the snow!"

"I'm dreffly frightened," said little Lois. "Carry me, Roger. I don't like being a lost child."

So Roger picked her up in his arms, and they wandered on in the darkness.

"Oh, dear Father Christmas, send us a moon!" cried Lois.

"Couldn't we light the one he gave you?" asked Cicely.

"Why, of course," said Roger, as he set Lois down, pulled out a box of matches, and lit the candle of the Chinese lantern.

In England, Father Christmas—who also brings gifts on Christmas eve—is a more stern version of Santa Claus.

"Oh, it's a lovely moon!" cried Lois, clapping her hands with delight. "It makes pretty colours all over you, Cicely."

I don't know whether Lois's lovely moon would have been quite bright enough to lead them to the right path, but it did something as good, for a voice came to them suddenly out of the darkness:

"Is that a will-o'-the-wisp that I see glimmering there, and will it help me to find three lost children?"

And of course it was Daddy come to look for them, and he declared he might never have found them, if the pretty paper moon had not led him to the very spot where they were.

ST. NICHOLAS   *Horatio Alger*

In the far-off Polar seas,
Far beyond the Hebrides,
Where the icebergs, towering high,
Seem to pierce the wintry sky,
And the fur-clad Esquimaux,
Glides in sledges o'er the snow,
Dwells St. Nick, the merry wight,
Patron saint of Christmas night.

Solid walls of massive ice,
Bearing many a quaint device,
Flanked by graceful turrets twain,
Clear as clearest porcelain,
Bearing at a lofty height
Christ's pure cross in simple white,
Carven with surpassing art
From an iceberg's crystal heart.

Here St. Nick, in royal state,
Dwells, until December late
Clips the days at either end,
And the nights at each extend;
Then, with his attendant sprites,
Scours the earth on wintry nights,
Bringing home, in well-filled hands,
Children's gifts from many lands.

Here are whistles, tops and toys,
Meant to gladden little boys;
Skates and sleds that soon will glide
O'er the ice or steep hill-side.
Here are dolls with flaxen curls,
Sure to charm the little girls;
Christmas books, with pictures gay,
For this welcome holiday.

In the court the reindeer wait;
Filled the sledge with costly freight.
As the first faint shadow falls,
Promptly from his icy halls
Steps St. Nick, and grasps the rein:
Straight his coursers scour the plain,
And afar, in measured time,
Sounds the sleigh-bells' silver chime.

Like an arrow from the bow
Speed the reindeer o'er the snow.
Onward! Now the loaded sleigh
Skirts the shores of Hudson's Bay.
Onward, till the stunted tree
Gains a loftier majesty,
And the curling smoke-wreaths rise
Under less inclement sides.

Built upon a hill-side steep
Lies a city wrapt in sleep.
Up and down the lonely street
Sleepy watchmen pace their beat.
Little heeds them Santa Claus;
Not for him are human laws.
With a leap he leaves the ground,
Scales the chimney at a bound.

Five small stockings hang below;
Five small stockings in a row.
From his pocket blithe St. Nick
Fills the waiting stockings quick;
Some with sweetmeats, some with toys,
Gifts for girls, and gifts for boys,
Mounts the chimney like a bird,
And the bells are once more heard.

Santa Claus! Good Christmas saint,
In whose heart no selfish taint
Findeth place, some homes there be
Where no stockings wait for thee,
Homes where sad young faces wear
Painful marks of Want and Care,
And the Christmas morning brings
No fair hope of better things.

Can you not some crumbs bestow
On these children steeped in woe;
Steal a single look of care
Which their sad young faces wear;
From your overflowing store
Give to them whose hearts are sore?
No sad eyes should greet the morn
When the infant Christ was born.

'Twas the Night Before Christmas

Christmas Eve

How Christmas is Celebrated Around the World

Throughout much of **Europe**, Christmas celebrations begin in early December and last more than a month, ending in mid-January. For children in the **Netherlands**, the season begins on December 5, *Sinterklaas* Eve, when they set out their wooden shoes to be filled with nuts, candy, and gifts from St. Nicholas. On December 6, St. Nicholas's Day, the patron saint of children can be found wandering the streets of **France**, **Holland**, and **Austria**, often with an ogre-like sidekick known as *Père Fouettard, Swarte Piet,* or *Knecht Ruprecht,* ready to punish children for their bad deeds. St. Nicholas carries a basket of treats and doles them out to boys and girls who promise to be good.

Christmas festivities begin on December 13 in **Denmark**, **Norway**, and **Sweden**, where Scandinavians celebrate St. Lucia's Day, in honor of a maiden who was martyred in A.D. 304 for being a Christian. Traditionally, the youngest girl of the house plays the part of Lucia, dressing in white robes and wearing an evergreen wreath on her head that's lit with a

halo of candles. She serves her parents coffee and freshly baked Lucia buns (marked with an "X" for Christ) in bed.

December 16 marks the first day of *Posadas* in **Mexico**, **Honduras**, and other **Latin American** countries. During the nine-day celebration of Mary and Joseph's pilgrimage to Bethlehem, people visit each other's homes, playing the part of weary travelers or stubborn innkeepers.

Little Christmas Eve begins in **Norway** and **Denmark** on December 23, when family and friends gather to sample the baked goodies and festive dishes prepared for the holiday. In **Germany**, the Christmas tree is revealed to children on December 24. *Christkinder*—children dressed as angels that symbolize the spirit of the Christ Child, travel door to door, helping to deliver presents on Christmas Eve. In **England**, parents decorate the tree on Christmas Eve after children have hung their stockings above the fireplace and gone to bed. At midnight, church bells ring in Christian

communities around the world celebrating the holy hour of Jesus' birth. After Midnight Mass services concludes in **France**, everyone returns home for *le reveillon,* a feast that often lasts until dawn, just before the children wake up to open Christmas presents.

In **Greece**, the exchange of Christmas presents doesn't take place until January 1, the feast day of St. Basil, who was one of the founding fathers of the Orthodox Church and is the patron saint of the poor. Others wait until Epiphany, or the Twelfth Day of Christmas, for exchanging gifts (as many Christians do in **Latin America**) to commemorate the day when the Wise Men brought their presents to the baby Jesus. On January 6, **Italian** boys and girls wait for the good Epiphany witch *Befana,* who enters homes through the chimney to fill the good children's shoes with treats and the misbehaving children's shoes with coal.

Every Christmas, Roman Catholic, Eastern Orthodox, Coptic, and Protestant Christians make a pilgrimage to the "little town" of **Bethlehem,** to kiss the sacred spot where Jesus was born. **Eastern Orthodox** and **Coptic Christians** observe dates according to the Julian calendar, and celebrate Christmas as late as January 7 and January 18 with midnight masses and a recreation of the Nativity.

CHRISTMAS EVE AT SEA

John Masefield

A wind is rustling "south and soft,"
   Cooing a quiet country tune,
The calm sea sighs, and far aloft
   The sails are ghostly in the moon.

Unquiet ripples lisp and purr,
   A block there pipes and chirps i' the sheave,
The wheel-ropes jar, the reef-points stir
   Faintly—and it is Christmas Eve.

The hushed sea seems to hold her breath,
   And o'er the giddy, swaying spars,
Silent and excellent as Death,
   The dim blue skies are bright with stars.

Dear God—they shone in Palestine
   Like this, and yon pale moon serene
Looked down among the lowing kine
   On Mary and the Nazarene.

The angels called from deep to deep,
   The burning heavens felt the thrill,
Startling the flocks of silly sheep
   And lonely shepherds on the hill.

To-night beneath the dripping bows,
   Where flashing bubbles burst and throng,
The bow-wash murmurs and sighs and soughs
   A message from the angels' song.

The moon goes nodding down the west,
   The drowsy helmsman strikes the bell;
Rex Judaeorum natus est,
   I charge you, brothers, sing *Nowell,*
Nowell,
Rex Judaeorum natus est.

Christmas Eve in the Blue Chamber

Jerome K. Jerome

 don't want to make you fellows nervous," began my uncle in a peculiarly impressive, not to say blood-curdling, tone of voice, "and if you would rather that I did not mention it, I won't; but, as a matter of fact, this very house, in which we are now sitting, is haunted."

"You don't say that!" exclaimed Mr. Coombes.

"What's the use of your saying I don't say it when I have just said it?" retorted my uncle somewhat annoyed. "You talk so foolishly. I tell you the house is haunted. Regularly on Christmas Eve the Blue Chamber" (they call the room next to the nursery the "Blue Chamber" at my uncle's) "is haunted by the ghost of a sinful man—a man who once killed a Christmas carol singer with a lump of coal."

"How did he do it?" asked Mr. Coombes, eagerly. "Was it difficult?"

"I do not know how he did it," replied my uncle; "he did not explain the process. The singer had taken up a position just inside the front gate, and was singing a ballad. It is presumed that, when he opened his mouth for B flat, the lump of coal was thrown by the sinful man from one of the windows, and that it went down the singer's throat and choked him."

"You want to be a good shot, but it is certainly worth trying," murmured Mr. Coombes thoughtfully.

"But that was not his only crime, alas!" added my uncle. "Prior to that he had killed a solo cornet player."

"No! Is that really a fact?" exclaimed Mr. Coombes.

"Of course it's a fact," answered my uncle testily. "At all events, as much a fact as you can expect to get in a case of this sort.

"The poor fellow, the cornet player, had been in the neighborhood barely a month. Old Mr. Bishop, who kept the 'Jolly Sand Boys' at the time, and from whom I had the story, said he had never known a more hard-working and energetic solo cornet player. He, the cornet player, only knew two tunes, but Mr. Bishop said that the man could not have played with more vigor, or for more hours a day, if he had known forty. The two tunes he did play were 'Annie Laurie' and 'Home, Sweet Home'; and as regarded his performance of the former melody, Mr. Bishop said that a mere child could have told what it was meant for.

"This musician—this poor, friendless artist—used to come regularly and play in this street just opposite for two hours every evening. One evening he was seen, evidently in response to an invitation, going into this

In France, children leave their shoes by the fireplace for *Père Noël* to fill on Christmas Eve.

very house, but was never seen coming out of it!"

"Did the townsfolk try offering any reward for his recovery?" asked Mr. Coombes.

"Not a penny," replied my uncle.

"Another summer," continued my uncle, "a German band visited here, intending—so they announced on their arrival—to stay till the autumn.

"On the second day after their arrival, the whole company, as fine and healthy a body of men as one would wish to see, were invited to dinner by this sinful man, and, after spending the whole of the next twenty-four hours in bed, left the town a broken and dyspeptic crew; the parish doctor, who had attended them, giving it as his opinion that it was doubtful if they would, any of them, be fit to play an air again."

"You—you don't know the recipe, do you?" asked Mr. Coombes.

"Unfortunately I do not," replied my uncle; "but the chief ingredient was said to have been railway dining-room hash.

"I forget the man's other crimes," my uncle went on; "I used to know them all at one time, but my memory is not what it was. I do not, however, believe I am doing his memory an injustice in believing that he was not entirely unconnected with the death, and subsequent burial, of a gentleman who used to play the harp with his toes; and that neither was he altogether unresponsible for the lonely grave of an unknown stranger who had once visited the neighbor-

hood, an Italian peasant lad, a performer upon the barrel-organ.

"Every Christmas Eve," said my uncle, cleaving with low impressive tones the strange awed silence that, like a shadow, seemed to have slowly stolen into and settled down upon the room, "the ghost of this sinful man haunts the Blue Chamber, in this very house. There, from midnight until cock-crow, amid wild muffled shrieks and groans and mocking laughter and the ghostly sound of horrid blows, it does fierce phantom fight with the spirits of the solo cornet player and the murdered carol singer, assisted at intervals by the shades of the German band; while the ghost of the strangled harpist plays mad ghostly melodies with ghostly toes on the ghost of a broken harp."

Uncle said the Blue Chamber was comparatively useless as a sleeping apartment on Christmas Eve.

"Hark!" said my uncle, raising a warning hand toward the ceiling, while we held our breath, and listened: "Hark! I believe they are at it now—in the Blue Chamber!"

I rose up and said that *I* would sleep in the Blue Chamber.

"Never!" cried my uncle, springing up. "You shall not put yourself in this deadly peril. Besides, the bed is not made."

"Never mind the bed," I replied. "I have lived in furnished apartments for gentlemen, and have been accustomed to sleep on beds that have never been made from one year's end to the other. I am young, and have had a clear conscience now for a month. The spirits will not harm me. I may even do them some little good, and induce them to be quiet and go away. Besides, I should like to see the show."

They tried to dissuade me from what they termed my foolhardy enterprise, but I remained firm and claimed my privilege. I was "the guest." "The guest" always sleeps in the haunted chamber on Christmas Eve; it is his right.

They said that if I put it on that footing they had, of course, no answer, and they lighted a candle for me and followed me upstairs in a body.

Whether elevated by the feeling that I was doing a noble action or animated by a mere general consciousness of rectitude is not for me to say, but I went upstairs that night with remarkable buoyancy. It was as much as I could do to stop at the landing when I came to it; I felt I wanted to go on up to the roof. But, with the help of the banisters, I restrained by ambition, wished them all good-night and went in and shut the door.

Things began to go wrong with me from the very first. The candle tumbled out of the candlestick before my hand was off the lock. It kept on tumbling out again; I never saw such a slippery candle. I gave up attempting to use the candlestick at last and carried the candle about in my hand, and even then it would not keep upright. So I got wild and threw it out the window, and undressed and went to bed in the dark.

I did not go to sleep; I did not feel sleepy at all; I lay on my back looking up at the ceiling and thinking of things. I wish I could remember some of the ideas that came to me as I lay there, because they were so amusing.

I had been lying like this for half an hour or so, and had forgotten all about the ghost, when, on casually casting my eyes round the room, I noticed for the first time a singularly contented-looking phantom sitting in the easy-chair by the fire smoking the ghost of a long clay pipe.

I fancied for the moment, as most people would under similar circumstances, that I must be dreaming. I sat up and rubbed by eyes. No! It was a ghost, clear enough. I could see the back of the chair through his body. He looked over toward me, took the shadowy pipe from his lips and nodded.

The most surprising part of the whole thing to me was that I did not feel in the least alarmed. If anything I was rather pleased to see him. It was company.

I said: "Good evening. It's been a cold day!"

He said he had not noticed it himself, but

dared say I was right.

We remained silent for a few seconds, and then, wishing to put it pleasantly, I said: "I believe I have the honor of addressing the ghost of the gentleman who had the accident with the carol singer?"

He smiled and said it was very good of me to remember it. One singer was not much to boast of, but still every little helped.

I was somewhat staggered at his answer. I had expected a groan of remorse. The ghost appeared, on the contrary, to be rather conceited

over the business. I thought that as he had taken my reference to the singer so quietly perhaps he would not be offended if I questioned him about the organ grinder. I felt curious about that poor boy.

"Is it true," I asked, "that you had a hand in the death of that Italian peasant lad who came to the town with a barrel-organ that played nothing but Scotch airs?"

He quite fired up. "Had a hand in it!" he exclaimed indignantly. "Who has dared to pretend that he assisted me? I murdered the youth myself. Nobody helped me. Alone I did it. Show me the man who says I didn't."

I calmed him. I assured him that I had never, in my own mind, doubted that he was the real and only assassin, and I went on and asked him what he had done with the body of the cornet player he had killed.

He said: "To which one may you be alluding?

"Oh, were there any more then?" I inquired.

He smiled and gave a little cough. He said he did not like to appear to be boasting, but that, counting trombones, there were seven.

"Dear me!" I replied, "you must have had quite a busy time of it, one way and another."

He said that perhaps he ought not to be the one to say so; but that really, speaking of ordinary middle-class society, he thought there were few ghosts who could look back upon a life of more sustained usefulness.

He puffed away in silence for a few seconds while I sat watching him. I had never seen a ghost smoking a pipe before, that I could remember, and it interested me.

I asked him what tobacco he used, and he replied: "The ghost of cut cavendish as a rule."

He explained that the ghost of all the tobacco that a man smoked in life belong to him when he became dead. He said he himself had smoked a good deal of cut cavendish when he was alive, so that he was well supplied with the ghost of it now.

I thought I would join him in a pipe, and he said, "Do, old man"; and I reached over and got out the necessary paraphernalia from my coat pocket and lit up.

We grew quite chummy after that, and he told me all his crimes. He said he had lived next door once to a young lady who was learning to play the guitar, while a gentleman who practiced on the bass-viol lived opposite. And he, with fiendish cunning, had introduced these two unsuspecting young people to one another, and had persuaded them to elope with each other against their parents' wishes, and take their musical instruments with them; and they had done so, and before the honeymoon was over, *she* had broken his head with the bass-viol, and *he* had tried to cram the guitar down her throat, and had injured her for life.

My friend said he used to lure muffin-men into the passage and then stuff them with their own wares till they burst. He said he had quieted eighteen that way.

Young men and women who recited long and dreary poems at evening parties, and callow youths who walked about the streets late at night, playing concertinas, he used to get together and poison in batches of ten, so as to save expenses; and park orators and temperance lecturers he used to shut up six in a small room with a glass of water and a collection-box apiece, and let them talk each other to death.

It did one good to listen to him.

I asked him when he expected the other ghosts—the ghosts of the singer and the cornet player, and the German band that Uncle John had mentioned. He smiled, and said they would never come again, any of them.

I said, "Why, isn't it true, then, that they meet you here every Christmas Eve for a row?"

He replied that it was true. Every Christmas Eve, for twenty-five years, had he and they fought in that room; but they would never trouble him or anybody else again. One by one had he laid them out, spoiled and made them utterly useless for all haunting purposes. He had finished off the last German band ghost that very evening, just before I came upstairs, and had thrown what was left of it out through the slit between the window sashes. He said it would never be worth calling a ghost again.

"I suppose you will still come yourself, as usual?" I said. "They would be sorry to miss you, I know."

"Oh, I don't know," he replied; "there's nothing much to come for now; unless," he added kindly, "you are going to be here. I'll come if you will sleep here next Christmas Eve."

"I have taken a liking to you," he continued; "you don't fly off, screeching, when you see a party, and your hair doesn't stand on end. You've no idea," he said, "how sick I am of seeing people's hair standing on end."

He said it irritated him.

Just then a slight noise reached us from the yard below, and he started and turned deathly black.

"You are ill," I cried, springing toward him; "tell me the best thing to do for you. Shall I drink some brandy, and give you the ghost of it?"

He remained silent, listening intently for a moment, and then he gave a sigh of relief, and the shade came back to his cheek.

"It's all right," he murmured; "I was afraid it was the cock."

"Oh, it's too early for that," I said. "Why, it's only the middle of the night."

"Oh, that doesn't make any difference to those cursed chickens," he replied bitterly. "They would just as soon crow in the middle of

In Germany families spend Christmas Eve at church. While at worship, the *Christkind*—or Christ Child—brings presents to their homes.

the night as at any other time—sooner, if they thought it would spoil a chap's evening out. I believe they do it on purpose."

He said a friend of his, the ghost of a man who had killed a tax collector, used to haunt a house in Long Acre, where they kept fowls in the cellar, and every time a policeman went by and flashed his searchlight down the grating, the old cock there would fancy it was the sun, and start crowing like mad, when, of course, the poor ghost had to dissolve, and it would, in consequence, get back home sometimes as early as one o'clock in the morning, furious because it had only been out for an hour.

I agreed that it seemed very unfair.

"Oh, it's an absurd arrangement altogether," he continued, quite angrily. "I can't imagine what our chief could have been thinking of when he made it. As I have said to him, over and over again, 'Have a fixed time, and let everybody stick to it—say four o'clock in summer, and six in winter. Then, one would know what one was about.'"

"How do you manage when there isn't any clock handy?" I inquired.

He was on the point of replying, when again he started and listened. This time I distinctly heard Mr. Bowles' cock, next door, crow twice.

"There you are," he said, rising and reaching for his hat; "that's the sort of thing we have to put up with. What *is* the time?"

I looked at my watch, and found it was half-past three.

"I thought as much," he muttered. "I'll wring that blessed bird's neck if I get hold of it." And he prepared to go.

"If you can wait half a minute," I said, getting out of bed, "I'll go a bit of the way with you."

"It's very good of you," he replied, pausing, "but it seems unkind to drag you out."

"Not at all," I replied; "I shall like a walk." And I partially dressed myself, and took my umbrella; and he put his arm through mine, and we went out together, the best of friends.

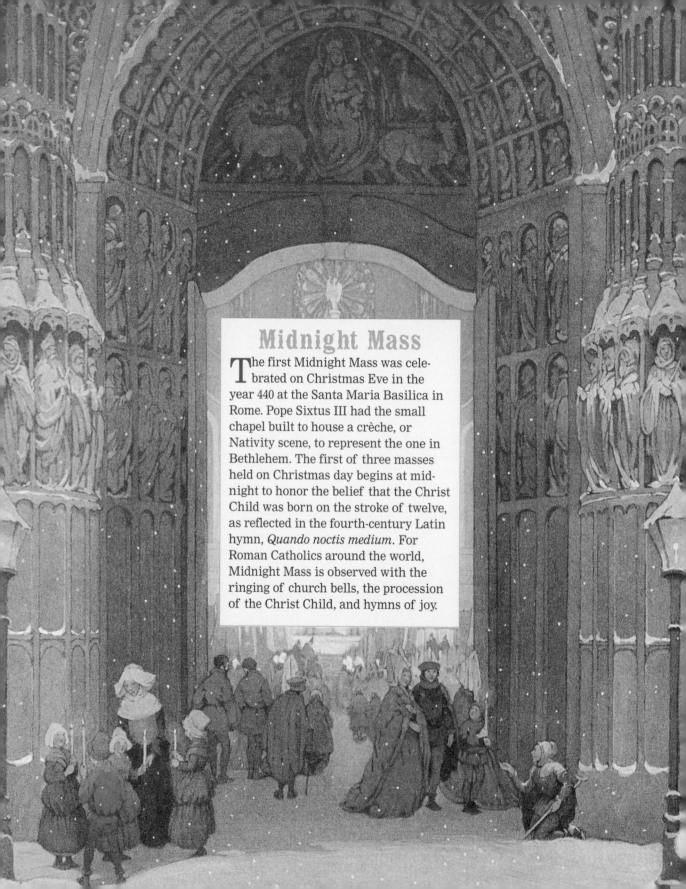

Midnight Mass

The first Midnight Mass was celebrated on Christmas Eve in the year 440 at the Santa Maria Basilica in Rome. Pope Sixtus III had the small chapel built to house a crèche, or Nativity scene, to represent the one in Bethlehem. The first of three masses held on Christmas day begins at midnight to honor the belief that the Christ Child was born on the stroke of twelve, as reflected in the fourth-century Latin hymn, *Quando noctis medium*. For Roman Catholics around the world, Midnight Mass is observed with the ringing of church bells, the procession of the Christ Child, and hymns of joy.

The Christmas Cracker

The Christmas Cracker was invented in France. It was originally a paper bag of bon bons that had to be pulled in different directions by two children in order to release its treats. In the 1860s, a British company created a "Christmas Cracker" which "exploded" like a firecracker when it was pulled apart. They were filled with miniature toys and were as long as three feet.

CHRISTMAS EVE

Lilian Holmes

It's Christmas, you know, Fiametta—
At least it's the night just before.
Father Christmas is due,
Let me whisper to you.
He doesn't come in at the door.

He doesn't come in through the window;
His way's a more wonderful way;
Over house-tops he glides,
Down the chimneys he slides,
And he's due, Fiametta, to-day!
Suppose he should mix up the stockings!
They're both the same colour and size;
It's really too bad,
It would be so sad
If I'd a wax doll with blue eyes.
If I go to sleep, Fiametta,
And you keep your eyes open wide,
You can just take a peep,
While I'm lying asleep,
To see what he's putting inside.

Oh, *do* keep awake, Fiametta!
My eyes are as heavy as lead,
 And if he should come
With a doll or a drum,
Just ask him for soldiers instead.

CAROL OF THE FIELD MICE

Kenneth Grahame

Villagers all, this frosty tide,
Let your doors swing open wide,
Though wind may follow, and snow beside,
Yet draw us in by your fire to bide;
    Joy shall be yours in the morning!

Here we stand in the cold and the sleet,
Blowing fingers and stamping feet,
Come from far away you to greet—
you by the fire and we in the street—
    Bidding you joy in the morning!

For ere one half of the night was gone,
Sudden a star has led us on,
Raining bliss and benison—
Bliss tomorrow and more anon,
    Joy for every morning!

Goodman Joseph toiled through the snow—
Saw the star o'er a stable low;
Mary she might not further go—
Welcome thatch, and litter below!
    Joy was hers in the morning!

And then they heard the angels tell
"Who were the first to cry Nowell?
Animals all, as it befell,
In the stable where they did dwell!
    Joy shall be theirs in the morning!"

I'm dreaming of a white Christmas.

—IRVING BERLIN

A VISIT FROM ST. NICHOLAS

Clement Clarke Moore

'Twas the night before Christmas, when all through the house
Not a creature was stirring, not even a mouse.
The stockings were hung by the chimney with care,
In hopes that St. Nicholas soon would be there.
The children were nestled all snug in their beds,
While visions of sugar-plums danced in their heads;
And mamma in her kerchief, and I in my cap,
Had just settled our brains for a long winter's nap—
When out on the lawn there arose such a clatter
I sprang from my bed to see what was the matter.
Away to the window I flew like a flash,
Tore open the shutter, and threw up the sash.
The moon on the breast of the new-fallen snow
Gave a lustre of midday to objects below;
When what to my wondering eye should appear
But a miniature sleigh and eight tiny reindeer,
With a little old driver, so lively and quick,
I knew in a moment it must be St. Nick!
More rapid than eagles his coursers they came,
And he whistled and shouted and called them by name.
"Now, Dasher! now, Dancer! now, Prancer and Vixen!
On, Comet! on, Cupid! on, Donder and Blitzen!—
To the top of the porch, to the top of the wall,
Now, dash away, dash away, dash away all!"
As dry leaves that before the wild hurricane fly,
When they meet with an obstacle mount to the sky,
So, up to the housetop the coursers they flew,
With a sleigh full of toys—and St. Nicholas, too.
And then, in a twinkling, I heard on the roof
The prancing and pawing of each little hoof.
As I drew in my head and was turning around,
Down the chimney St. Nicholas came with a bound:
He was dressed all in fur from his head to his foot,
And his clothes were all tarnished with ashes and soot:
A bundle of toys he had flung on his back,
And he looked like a peddler just opening his pack.
His eyes, how they twinkled! his dimples, how merry!

What Do Reindeer Eat?

Reindeer traditionally eat grasses, hay, moss, and tree bark. But at Christmastime, they expect to get treats just like the rest of us do. So when you're planning for Santa's visit Christmas Eve, don't forget Rudolph and his pals. Set out a plate of carrots, apple slices and sugar cubes, or try the recipe for Reindeer Mix below.

His cheeks were like roses, his nose like a cherry;
His droll little mouth was drawn up like a bow,
And the beard on his chin was as white as the snow.
The stump of a pipe he held tight in his teeth,
And the smoke, it encircled his head like a wreath.
He had a broad face and a little round belly
That shook, when he laughed, like a bowl full of jelly.
He was chubby and plump—a right jolly old elf;
And I laughed when I saw him, in spite of myself;
A wink of his eye, and a twist of his head,
Soon gave me to know I had nothing to dread.
He spoke not a word, but went straight to his work,
And filled all the stockings; then turned with a jerk,
And laying his finger aside of his nose,
And giving a nod, up the chimney he rose.
He sprang to his sleigh, to his team gave a whistle,
And away they all flew like the down of a thistle.
But I heard him exclaim, ere they drove out of sight,
"Happy Christmas to all, and to all a good-night!"

Reindeer Mix

1 cup granola
$2/3$ cup glitter
1 cup sugar cubes
1 cup dried cranberries

On Christmas Eve, combine ingredients in a sealed plastic bag. Shake vigorously to mix. Sprinkle on your lawn before bedtime or leave a bowl by the window.

The glitter will shine in the moonlight & lead the reindeer to your house.

Party Games for Grown-Ups

Liven up holiday parties and family Christmas gatherings with some time for fun and games. Let participants show off their keenness for obscure Christmas carols, or enjoy having the last "ho, ho, ho" during a "hats off" to Santa game. Reward winners (and losers) with a tin of Christmas cookies or small stocking stuffers.

Christmas Carol Charades

Assemble two or three groups equipped with a stopwatch. Each team thinks of a number of Christmas carols to pantomime to opposing teams. A member from one team acts out as many song titles as his or her teammates can guess in one minute. Each team takes turns until all participants have pantomimed. The team that guesses the most carols wins.

Holiday Draw!

Create a stack of index cards with yuletide words or phrases. Players assemble into two to four teams armed with pencil and paper. One member from each team takes a card from the stack and reads it. At the word "Go!" each player draws the word or phrase while the other team members guess. Try to get through as many cards as possible in one minute.

Santa Hat Game

This game is ideal during the course of an afternoon or evening, while other games or conversations are taking place. Outfit each guest with a Santa hat. The only rule is that no one can remove their hat until the host does. After some time has passed, the host slyly removes her hat. As participants slowly catch on, they, too, should discreetly remove their hats until one "Santa" is left.

Christmas Memory Box

How does Santa remember all those Christmas wishes? Practice! See how everyone stacks up to St. Nick in this recall challenge. Fill a large box or tray with a few dozen holiday items, such as a sprig of mistletoe, a shopping list, an ornament, nativity figures, a candy cane, and the like. Allow everyone to study the items for one minute, then remove the items from sight. Whoever can recall and write down the most items, wins.

Guess My Name

All players secretly write the name of a famous historical or fictional person somehow related to Christmas, such as "Irving Berlin," the angel "Gabriel," or "Ebenezer Scrooge" on index cards. Each person gets a name card taped to his or her back. Players must ask "yes" or "no" questions to decipher their names.

Party Games for Kids

Christmas gatherings are ideal times for spontaneous game-playing among cousins and friends who haven't seen each other in a while. Have fun with a host of games on hand that can be enjoyed by younger and older children alike.

The Cobweb Game

Before the game, string various pieces of yarn around the house. Tie candy canes or small stocking stuffers to the end of each string. Assign a color to each child. Participants must then follow the yarn of their color until they find the end and can collect their surprises.

Pin the Nose on Rudolph

Children can create their own rendition of Santa's eighth reindeer with colored markers on a large sheet of poster board (about 4' by 4'). Cut enough large circles out of shiny red wrapping paper or construction paper for each child, and affix pieces of double-stick tape to the backs. Then, let each participant take turns

wearing a blindfold while attempting to place Rudolph's nose in the right place. The winner will be judged . . . by a nose.

Christmas Charades

Divide players into two teams. Each team thinks of persons, places, or things related to Christmas, such as "shepherd," "Santa's Workshop," or "eggnog." One team member holds up the number of fingers representing the number of words to be guessed, then pantomimes the secret word or phrase to his or her teammates. The guessing team has one minute to answer correctly. After each person has had a chance to pantomime, the team with the most accurate guesses wins.

Caroling Musical Chairs

Arrange a circle of chairs in a room for each player but one. While a designated music leader plays Christmas music, participants walk around the chairs caroling until the music stops. At that point, everyone scrambles for a seat. The person left standing is "out." Another chair is removed from the circle, and the game continues in the same manner until only one person—the winner—is left seated.

Candy Cane Relay

Have players form two equal lines facing each other. Set up a bowl of candy canes at the head of each line, and an empty bowl at the end of each line. At the official "Go!" each team must pass the candy canes down the line one at a time until the empty bowl is filled. A dropped candy cane must go back to the beginning. The team that completes the relay first wins.

Christmas is Here
December 25

CHRISTMAS GREETING
FROM A FAIRY TO A CHILD

Lewis Carroll

Lady, dear, if Fairies may
    For a moment lay aside
Cunning tricks and elfish play,
    'Tis at happy Christmas-tide.

We have heard the children say—
    Gentle children, whom we love—
Long ago on Christmas Day,
    Came a message from above.

Still, as Christmas-tide comes round,
    They remember it again—
Echo still the joyful sound,
    "Peace on earth, good-will to men!"

Yet the hearts must childlike be
    Where such heavenly guests abide;
Unto children, in their glee,
    All the year is Christmas-tide!

Thus, forgetting tricks and play
    For a moment, Lady dear,
We would wish you, if we may,
    Merry Christmas, glad New Year!

Christmas History

Festivities with lights, feasting, gift giving, and merriment at the end of the year around the winter solstice have long been part of pre-Christian human history. Many people feared that the shortening days signaled the end of life, and developed rituals to bring back the sun and longer days. The conception of death and rebirth naturally became linked with the winter solstice, which is evident in many cultures and religious beliefs. Ancient Egyptians hallowed December 21 as the day the god Osiris died and was entombed. In ancient Greece, people celebrated the god Dionysus, who was reborn as a baby at this time. The ancient Mayans honored the "First Father," the deity One Hunahpu on this day. From December 17 through the 23, ancient Romans held the Feast of Saturnalia in honor of the god Saturn.

In the second century A.D., early Christians marked the first Nativity celebrations by observing Christ's birth with a reverent feast. It wasn't until A.D. 350, by decree of Pope Julius I, that Christians set aside December 25 as the official day to commemorate the birth of Jesus. As Christianity spread north from Rome and came into contact with Germanic and Nordic peoples who had their own winter solstice celebrations, the old fused with the new. Soon, pre-Christian elements such as the yule log, candles, light, evergreen, singing, feasting, giving of gifts, and tree decorating found new meaning and symbolism to hail the birth of the Son of God. The church attempted to ban pagan customs altogether, and supplanted pre-Christian holidays with religious ones in an effort to celebrate Christmas in a sacred rather than an earthly manner.

Legend has it that King Arthur celebrated the first Christmas in England in A.D. 521 with his Knights of the Round Table, upon their recapture of York. Certainly by the time of Pope Gregory I in the late sixth century, Christmas observances had become more commonplace. In medieval England, however, more pagan customs began to creep back into Christmas celebrations, turning the holiday into a raucous time of singing, dancing, feasting, plays, games, and carousing that lasted twelve days.

Eventually, Protestants spurned such "heathen" practices in favor of celebrating the Nativity with a more spiritual emphasis. Puritans, led by Oliver Cromwell in the mid-seventeenth century, successfully banned caroling and even locked church doors on Christmas. In the New World, Massachusetts Puritans forbade all Christmas festivities, deeming any celebration of the kind strictly illegal. As late as the 1870s in Boston, public schools remained open for classes on Christmas Day.

Meanwhile, the Germans had been keeping Christmas alive and well for centuries. The season began with St. Andrew's Night on November 30, and continued through January 13, the Octave of Epiphany—with sixteen other holidays in between. German-born Prince Albert introduced many of his homeland customs to Windsor Castle, which were then eagerly adopted by Victorian England. The European's infectious love for the holiday eventually spread to the United States as well, becoming a permanent fixture of American culture by the late nineteenth century.

Christmas Every Day

William Dean Howells

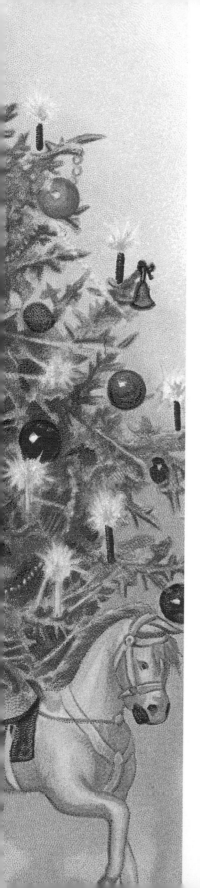

he little girl came into her papa's study, as she always did Saturday morning before breakfast, and asked for a story. He tried to beg off that morning, for he was very busy, but she would not let him. So he began:

"Well, once there was a little pig—"

She put her hand over his mouth and stopped him at the word. She said she had heard little pig stories till she was perfectly sick of them.

"Well, what kind of story *shall* I tell, then?"

"About Christmas. It's getting to be the season. It's past Thanksgiving already."

"It seems to me," argued her papa, "that I've told as often about Christmas as I have about little pigs."

"No difference! Christmas is more interesting."

"Well!" Her papa roused himself from his writing by a great effort. "Well, then, I'll tell you about the little girl that wanted it Christmas every day in the year. How would you like that?"

"First-rate!" said the little girl; and she nestled into comfortable shape in his lap, ready for listening.

"Very well, then, this little pig—Oh, what are you pounding me for?"

"Because you said little pig instead of little girl."

"I should like to know what's the difference between a little pig and a little girl that wanted it Christmas every day!"

"Papa," said the little girl, warningly, "if you don't go on, I'll *give* it to you!" And at this her papa darted off like lightning, and began to tell the story as fast as he could.

Well, once there was a little girl who liked Christmas so much that she wanted it to be Christmas every day in the year; and as soon as Thanksgiving was over she began to send postal cards to the old Christmas Fairy to ask if she mightn't have it. But the old Fairy never answered any of the postals; and, after a while, the little girl found out that the Fairy was pretty particular, and wouldn't even notice anything but letters, not even correspondence cards in envelopes; but real letters on sheets of paper, and sealed outside with a monogram—or your initial, any way. So, then, she began to send her letters; and in about three weeks—or just the day before Christmas, it was—she got a letter from the Fairy, saying she might have it Christmas every day for a year, and then they would see about having it longer.

The little girl was a good deal excited already, preparing for the old-fashioned, once-a-year Christmas that was coming the next day, and perhaps the Fairy's promise didn't make such an impression on her as it would have made at some other time. She just resolved to keep it to herself, and surprise everybody with it as it kept coming true; and then it slipped out of her mind altogether.

She had a splendid Christmas. She went to bed early, so as to let Santa Claus have a chance at the stockings, and in the morning she was up the first of anybody and went and felt them, and found hers all lumpy with packages of candy, and oranges and grapes, and pocket-books and rubber balls and all kinds of small presents, and her big brother's with nothing but the tongs in them, and her young lady sister's with a new silk umbrella, and her papa's and mamma's with potatoes and pieces of coal wrapped up in tissue paper, just as they always had every Christmas. Then she waited around till the rest of the family were up, and she was the first to burst into the library, when the doors were opened, and look at the large presents laid out on the library-table—books, and portfolios, and boxes of stationery, and breast-pins, and dolls, and little stoves, and dozens of handkerchiefs, and ink-stands, and skates, and snow-shovels, and photograph-frames, and little easels, and boxes of watercolors, and Turkish paste, and nougat, and candied cherries, and dolls' houses, and waterproofs—and the big Christmas-tree, lighted and standing in a waste-basket in the middle.

She had a splendid Christmas all day. She ate so much candy that she did not want any breakfast; and the whole forenoon the presents kept pouring in that the expressman had not had time to deliver the night before; and she went 'round giving the presents she had got for other people, and came home and ate turkey and cranberry for dinner, and plum-pudding and nuts and raisins and oranges and more candy, and then went out and coasted and came in with a stomach-ache, crying; and her papa said he would see if his

house was turned into that sort of fool's paradise another year; and they had a light supper, and pretty early everybody went to bed cross.

Here the little girl pounded her papa in the back, again.

"Well, what now? Did I say pigs?"

"You made them *act* like pigs."

"Well, didn't they?"

"No matter; you oughtn't to put it into a story."

"Very well, then, I'll take it all out."

Her father went on:

The little girl slept very heavily, and she slept very late, but she was wakened at last by the other children dancing 'round her bed with their stockings full of presents in their hands.

"What is it?" said the little girl, and she rubbed her eyes and tried to rise up in bed.

"Christmas! Christmas! Christmas!" they all shouted, and waved their stockings.

"Nonsense! It was Christmas yesterday."

Her brothers and sisters just laughed. "We don't know about that. It's Christmas to-day, any way. You come into the library and see."

Then all at once it flashed on the little girl that the Fairy was keeping her promise, and her year of Christmases was beginning. She was dreadfully sleepy, but she sprang up like a lark—a lark that had overeaten itself and gone to bed cross—and darted into the library. There it was again! Books, and portfolios, and boxes of stationery, and breast-pins—

"You needn't go over it all, Papa; I guess I can remember just what was there," said the little girl.

Well, and there was the Christmas-tree blazing away, and the family picking out their presents, but looking pretty sleepy, and her father perfectly puzzled, and her mother ready to cry. "I'm sure I don't see how I'm to dispose of all these things," said her mother, and her father said it seemed to him they had had something just like it the day before, but he supposed he must have dreamed it. This struck the little girl as the best kind of joke; and so she ate so much candy she didn't want any breakfast, and went 'round carrying presents, and had turkey and cranberry for dinner, and then went out and coasted, and came in with a—

"Papa!"

"Well, what now?"

"What did you promise, you forgetful thing?"

"Oh! oh, yes!"

Well, the next day, it was just the same thing over again, but everybody getting crosser; and at the end of a week's time so many people had lost their tempers that you could pick up lost tempers everywhere; they perfectly strewed the ground. Even when people tried to recover their tempers they usually got somebody else's, and it made the most dreadful mix.

The little girl began to get frightened, keeping the secret all to herself; she wanted to tell her mother, but she didn't dare to; and she was ashamed to ask the Fairy to take back her gift, it seemed ungrateful and ill-bred, and she thought she would try to stand it, but she hardly knew how she could, for a whole year. So it went on and on, and it was Christmas on St. Valentine's Day, and Washington's Birthday just the same as any day, and it didn't skip even the First of April, though everything was counterfeit that day, and that was some little relief.

After a while, coal and potatoes began to be awfully scarce, so many had been wrapped up in tissue paper to fool papas and mammas with. Turkeys got to be about a thousand dollars apiece—

"Papa!"

"Well, what?"

"You're beginning to fib."

"Well, *two* thousand, then."

And they got to passing off almost anything for turkeys—half-grown humming-birds, and even rocs out of the "Arabian Nights"—the real turkeys were so scarce. And cranberries—well, they asked a diamond apiece for cranberries. All the woods and orchards were cut down for Christmas-trees, and where the woods and orchards used to be, it looked just like a stubble-field, with the stumps. After a while they had to make Christmas-trees out of rags, and stuff them with bran, like old-fashioned dolls; but there were plenty of rags, because people got so poor, buying presents for one another, that they couldn't get any new clothes, and they just wore their old ones to tatters. They got so poor that everybody had to go to the poor-house, except the confectioners, and the fancy store-keepers, and the picture-booksellers, and the express-men; and *they* all got so rich and proud that they would hardly wait upon a person when he came to buy; it was perfectly shameful!

Well, after it had gone on about three or four months, the little girl, whenever she came into the room in the morning and saw those great ugly lumpy stockings dangling at the fire-place, and the disgusting presents around everywhere, used to just sit down and burst out crying. In six months she was perfectly exhausted; she couldn't even cry any more; she just lay on the lounge and rolled her eyes and panted. About the beginning of October she took to sitting down on dolls, wherever she found them—French dolls, or any kind—she hated the sight of them so; and by Thanksgiving she was crazy, and just slammed her presents across the room.

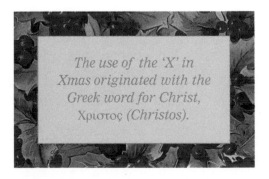

The use of the 'X' in Xmas originated with the Greek word for Christ, Χριστος (*Christos*).

By that time people didn't carry presents around nicely any more. They flung them over the fence, or through the window, or anything; and, instead of running their tongues out and taking great pains to write "For dear Papa," or "Mamma," or "Brother," or "Sister," or "Susie," or "Sammie," or "Billie," or "Bobby," or "Jimmie," or "Jennie," or whoever it was, and troubling to get the spelling right, and then signing their names, and "'Xmas, 188—," they used to write in the gift-books, "Take it, you horrid old thing!" and then go and bang it against the front door. Nearly everybody had built barns to hold their presents; but pretty soon the barns overflowed, and then they used to let them lie out in the rain, or anywhere. Sometimes the police used to come and tell them to shovel their presents off the sidewalk, or they would arrest them. "I thought you said everybody had gone to the poor-house," interrupted the little girl.

"They did go, at first," said her papa; "but after a while the poor-houses got so full that they had to send the people back to their own houses. They tried to cry, when they got back, but they couldn't make the least sound."

"Why couldn't they?"

"Because they had lost their voices, saying 'Merry Christmas' so much. Did I tell you how it was on the Fourth of July?"

"No; how was it?" And the little girl nestled closer, in expectation of something uncommon.

Well, the night before, the boys stayed up to celebrate, as they always do, and fell asleep before twelve o'clock, as usual, expecting to be wakened by the bells and cannon. But it was nearly eight o'clock before the first boy in the United States woke up, and then he found out what the trouble was. As soon as he could get his clothes on, he ran out of the house and smashed a big cannon-torpedo down on the pavement; but it didn't make any more noise than a damp wad of paper, and, after he tried about twenty or thirty more, he began to pick them up and look at them. Every single torpedo was a big raisin!

Then he just streaked it upstairs, and examined his firecrackers and toy-pistol and two-dollar collection of fireworks and found that they were nothing but sugar and candy painted up to look like fireworks! Before ten o'clock, every boy in the United States found out that his Fourth of July things had turned into Christmas things; and then they just sat down and cried—they were so mad. There are about twenty million boys in the United States, and so you can imagine what a noise they made. Some men got together before night, with a little powder that hadn't turned into purple sugar yet, and they said they would fire off *one* cannon, any way. But the cannon burst into a thousand pieces, for it was nothing but rock-candy, and some of the men nearly got killed. The Fourth of July orations all turned into Christmas carols, and when anybody tried to read the Declaration, instead of saying, "When in the course of human events it becomes necessary," he was sure to sing, "God rest you, merry gentlemen." It was perfectly awful.

The little girl drew a deep sigh of satisfaction. "And how was it at Thanksgiving?" she asked. Her papa hesitated. "Well, I'm almost afraid to tell you. I'm afraid you'll think it's wicked." "Well, tell, any way," said the little girl.

Well, before it came Thanksgiving, it had leaked out who had caused all these Christmases. The little girl had suffered so much that she had talked about it in her sleep; and after that, hardly anybody would play with her. People just perfectly despised her, because if it had not been for her greediness, it wouldn't have happened; and now, when it came Thanksgiving, and she wanted them to go to church, and have a squash-pie and turkey, and show their gratitude, they said that all the turkeys had been eaten up for her old Christmas dinners, and if she would stop the Christmases, they would see about the gratitude. Wasn't it dreadful? And the very next day the little girl began to send letters to the Christmas Fairy, and then telegrams, to stop it.

But it didn't do any good; and then she got to calling at the Fairy's house, but the girl that came to the door always said "Not at home," or "Engaged," or "At dinner," or something like that; and so it went on till it came to the old once-a-year Christmas Eve. The little girl fell asleep, and when she woke up in the morning—

"She found it was all nothing but a dream," suggested the little girl.

"No, indeed!" said her papa. "It was all every bit true!"

"Well, what *did* she find out then?"

"Why, that it wasn't Christmas at last, and wasn't ever going to be, any more. Now it's time for breakfast."

The little girl held her papa fast around the neck.

"You shan't go if you're going to leave it *so!*"

"How do you want it left?"

"Christmas once a year."

"All right," said her papa; and he went on again.

Well, there was the greatest rejoicing all over the country, and it extended clear up into Canada. The people met together everywhere, and kissed and cried for joy. The city carts went around and gathered up all the candy and raisins and nuts, and dumped them into the river; and it made the fish perfectly sick; and the whole United States, as far out as Alaska, was one blaze of bonfires, where the children were burning up their giftbooks and presents of all kinds. They had the greatest time!

The little girl went to thank the old Fairy because she had stopped it being Christmas, and she said she hoped she would keep her promise, and see that Christmas never, never came again. Then the Fairy frowned, and asked her if she was sure she knew what she meant; and the little girl asked her, why not? and the old Fairy said that now she was behaving just as greedily as ever, and she'd better look out. This made the little girl think it all over carefully again, and

she said she would be willing to have it Christmas about once in a thousand years; and then she said a hundred, and then she said ten, and at last she got down to one. Then the Fairy said that was the good old way that had pleased people ever since Christmas began, and she was agreed. Then the little girl said, "What're your shoes made of?" And the Fairy said, "Leather." And the little girl said, "Bargain's done forever," and skipped off, and hippity-hopped the whole way home, she was so glad.

"How will that do?" asked the papa.

"First-rate!" said the little girl; but she hated to have the story stop, and was rather sober. However, her mamma put her head in at the door, and asked her papa:

"Are you never coming to breakfast? What have you been telling that child?"

"Oh, just a moral tale."

The little girl caught him around the neck again.

"*We* know! Don't you tell *what*, Papa! Don't you tell *what!*"

BEFORE THE PALING OF THE STARS

Christina G. Rossetti

Before the paling of the stars,
　　Before the winter morn,
Before the earliest cock crow,
　　Jesus Christ was born;
Born in a stable,
　　Cradled in a manger,
In the world His hands had made
　　Born a stranger.

Priest and king lay fast asleep
　　In Jerusalem,
Young and old lay fast asleep
　　In crowded Bethlehem;
Saint and Angel, ox and ass,
　　Kept a watch together
Before the Christmas daybreak
　　In the winter weather.

Jesus on His mother's breast
　　In the stable cold,
Spotless Lamb of God was He,
　　Shepherd of the fold:
Let us kneel with Mary maid,
　　With Joseph bent and hoary,
With Saint and Angel, ox and ass,
　　To hail the King of Glory.

Dreaming of a White Christmas?

The residents of the following towns don't have to—for them, it's virtually guaranteed: Marquetta, Wisconsin, Sault Ste. Marie, Michigan, Hibbing and International Falls, Minnesota, Stampede Pass, Washington, most of Alaska—especially the town of Bettles, which can get 10 inches or more! In general, the north is a good bet for a white Christmas. Vermont's chance of snow on December 25 is a whopping 80 percent. Virginia's, however, is just 10 percent.

Carol of the Bells

Hark how the bells, sweet sil-ver bells, all seem to say throw cares a-way.

Christmas is here, bring-ing good cheer, to young and old, meek and the bold,

Dong ding dong ding, that is their song, with joy-ful ring, all ca-rol-ing.

One seems to hear words of good cheer from ev-'ry-where fill - ing the air.

Oh, how they pound, rais-ing the sound, o'er hill and dale, tell-ing their tale.

Gai - ly they ring _ while peo-ple sing _ songs of good cheer. Christ-mas is here.

Mer - ry, mer - ry, mer - ry, mer - ry Christ - mas. Mer-ry, mer-ry, mer-ry,

mer-ry Christ-mas. On, on they send, on with-out end, their joy-ful tone

to ev - 'ry home. Dong ding dong ding, dong Bong!

Christmas at Hyde Park

Eleanor Roosevelt

hen our children were young, we spent nearly every Christmas holiday at Hyde Park. We always had a party the afternoon of Christmas Eve for all the families who lived on the place. The presents were piled under the tree, and after everyone had been greeted, my husband would choose the children old enough to distribute gifts and send them around to the guests. My mother-in-law herself always gave out her envelopes with money, and I would give out ours. The cornucopias filled with old-fashioned sugar candies and the peppermint canes hanging on the trees were distributed, too, and then our guests would leave us and enjoy their ice cream, cake, and coffee or milk in another room. Later in the day, when the guests had departed, my husband would begin the reading of *A Christmas Carol*. He never read it through; but he would select parts he thought suitable for the youngest members of the family. Then, after supper, he would read other parts for the older ones.

On Christmas morning, I would get up and close the windows in our room, where all the stockings had been hung on the mantel. The little children would be put into our bed and given their stockings to open. The others would sit around the fire. I tried to see that they all had a glass of orange juice before the opening of stockings really began, but the excitement was so great I was not always successful.

Breakfast was late Christmas morning, and my husband resented having to go to church on Christmas Day and sometimes flatly refused to attend. But I would go with my mother-in-law and such children as she could persuade to accompany us. For the most part, however, the children stayed home. In later years, I went to midnight service on Christmas Eve, and we gave up going to church in the morning.

Christmas waves a magic wand over this world, and behold, everything is softer and more beautiful.
—Norman Vincent Peale

I remembered the excitement as each child grew old enough to have his own sled and would start out after breakfast to try it on the hill behind the stable. Franklin would go coasting with them, and until the children were nearly grown, he was the only one who ever piloted the bobsled down the hill. Everyone came in for a late lunch, and at dusk we would light the candles on the tree again. Only outdoor presents like sleds and skates were distributed in the morning. The rest were kept for the late-afternoon Christmas tree. Again they were piled

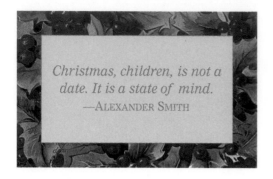

Christmas, children, is not a date. It is a state of mind.
—ALEXANDER SMITH

under the tree, and my husband and the children scrambled around it, and he called the names.

At first, my mother-in-law did a great deal of shopping and wrapping, and the Hyde Park Christmas always included her gifts. Later, she found shopping too difficult. Then she would give each person a check, though she managed very often to give her son the two things she knew he would not buy for himself—silk shirts and silk pajamas. These she bought in London, as a rule, and saved for his Christmas, which to her was always very special.

In the early years of our marriage, I did a great deal more sewing and embroidering than I've done since, so many of my gifts were things I had made. The family still has a few pieces of Italian cutwork embroidery and other kinds of my perfectly useless handwork. I look back, however, with some pleasure on the early Hyde Park days, when I would have a table filled with pieces of silk and make sachets of different scents. I would dry pine needles at Campobello Island and make them into sweet-smelling bags for Christmas. Now I rarely give a present I have made, and perhaps, it is just as well, for what one buys is likely to be better made!

Each of the children had a special preference in gifts. When Anna was a small child, her favorite present was a rocking horse, on which she spent many hours. Later, she was to spend even more hours training her own horse, which her great-uncle Mr. Warren Delano gave her. One of the nicest gifts we could possibly give her

as she grew older was something for her horse, Natomah. Jimmy loved boats from the very beginning, whether he floated them in the bathtub or later competed with his father in the regattas of toy boats on the Hudson River. Elliott was always trying to catch up with his older brother and sister; but because he was delicate as a child, I think he read more than the others. I remember that books and games were very acceptable gifts for him. Franklin, Jr., and John were a pair and had to have pretty much the same things, or they would quarrel over them. They had learned together to ride and to swim, so gifts for outdoor sports were always favorites of theirs.

My children teased me because their stockings inevitably contained toothbrushes, toothpaste, nail cleaners, soap, washcloths, etc. They said Mother never ceased to remind them that cleanliness was next to godliness—even on Christmas morning. In the toe of each stocking, I always put a purse, with a dollar bill for the young ones and a five-dollar bill for the older ones. These bills were hoarded to supplement the rather meager allowances they had. When I was able to buy sucre d'orge (barley sugar), I put that in their stockings, together with some old-fashioned peppermint sticks; but as they grew older, this confection seemed to vanish from the market, and I had to give it up and substitute chocolates. The stockings also contained families of little china pigs or rabbits or horses, which the children placed on their bookshelves.

The children themselves could probably tell much better than I can the things they remember most about these years. But I know that all of them have carried on many of the Hyde Park Christmas traditions with their children. Today, some of my grandchildren are establishing the same customs, and my great-grandchildren will one day remember the same kind of Christmas we started so many years ago.

I Saw Three Ships

I saw three ships come sail-ing in, On Christ-mas Day, On christ-mas Day; I Christ-mas Day in the morn-ing.

2. And what was in those ships all three,
On Christmas Day, on Christmas Day?
And what was in those ships all three?
On Christmas Day in the morning?

3. The Virgin Mary and Christ was there,
On Christmas Day, on Christmas Day.
The Virgin Mary and Christ was there,
On Christmas Day in the morning.

4. Then let us rejoice amain,
On Christmas Day, on Christmas Day,
Then let us rejoice amain,
On Christmas Day in the morning.

Christmas is the day that holds
all time together.
—ALEXANDER SMITH

Reliable religious statistics on exactly how many U.S. households celebrate Christmas are hard to come by, but data from the 2001 American Religious Identification Survey (ARIS) reveal that 76.5 percent (159 million) of Americans identify themselves as Christian; they would consider Christmas a holiday that has profound spiritual meaning for them. Among another 14 percent or so who say they do not identify with any religion are those who nevertheless celebrate Christmas, in a big way.

The Birth of Jesus

The story of the birth of Jesus is recounted in the Gospels of St. Matthew and St. Luke. According to St. Matthew, Joseph—the son of Jacob—was betrothed to Mary, who was great with child. To protect her from ridicule, or, according to Luke, to evade taxes, he traveled with her to Bethlehem where she could have the baby. An angel of the Lord visited Joseph in a dream and told him not to fear marriage, for the baby had been conceived by the Holy Ghost. The angel said to call the baby Jesus, for he would grow up to save his people from sin. St. Luke tells how Mary and Joseph had to place the newborn baby in a manger because they could find no room at the inn. Shepherds, who also heard the good tidings from an angel of the Lord, sought out the baby. Wise men from the east who claimed to see the star of the King of the Jews arrived, too, celebrating the birth of Jesus with gifts of gold, frankincense, and myrrh.

Scholars place the date of Jesus' actual birth sometime around the year 3 or 4 B.C. Based on the likelihood of when shepherds would have been tending sheep at night, Jesus was probably born in the spring during the lambing season, or in the fall when shepherds typically collected their flocks.

The Angel that presided o'er my birth
Said, "Little creature, formed of joy and mirth,
Go love without the help of anything on earth."
—WILLIAM BLAKE

BORN IN BETHLEHEM (St. Luke 2:1-16)

And it came to pass in those days, that there went out a decree from Caesar Augustus, that all the world should be taxed.

(*And* this taxing was first made when Cyrenius was governor of Syria.)

And all went to be taxed, every one into his own city.

And Joseph also went up from Galilee, out of the city of Nazareth, into Judæa, unto the city of David, which is called Bethlehem; (because he was of the house and lineage of David:)

To be taxed with Mary his espoused wife, being great with child.

And so it was, that, while they were there, the days were accomplished that she should be delivered.

And she brought forth her firstborn son, and wrapped him in swaddling clothes, and laid him in a manger; because there was no room for them in the inn.

And there were in the same country shepherds abiding in the field, keeping watch over their flock by night.

And, lo, the angel of the Lord came upon them, and the glory of the Lord shone round about them: and they were sore afraid.

And the angel said unto them, Fear not: for, behold, I bring you good tidings of great joy, which shall be to all people.

For unto you is born this day in the city of David a Saviour, which is Christ the Lord.

And this *shall* be a sign unto you; Ye shall find the babe wrapped in swaddling clothes, lying in a manger.

And suddenly there was with the angel a multitude of the heavenly host praising God, and saying,

Glory to god in the highest, and on earth peace, good will toward men.

And it came to pass, as the angels were gone away from them into heaven, the shepherds said one to another, Let us now go even unto Bethlehem, and see this thing which is come to pass, which the Lord hath made known unto us.

And they came with haste, and found Mary, and Joseph, and the babe lying in a manger.

WELL, SO THAT IS THAT

W. H. Auden

Well, so that is that. Now we must dismantle the tree,
Putting the decorations back into their cardboard boxes—
Some have got broken—and carrying them up to the attic.
The holly and mistletoe must be taken down and burnt,
And the children got ready for school. There are enough
Left-overs to do, warmed up, for the rest of the week—
Not that we have much appetite, having drunk such a lot,
Stayed up so late, attempted—quite unsuccessfully—
To love all our relatives, and in general
Grossly overestimated our powers. Once again
As in previous years we have seen the actual Vision and failed
To do more than entertain it as an agreeable
Possibility, once again we have sent Him away
Begging though to remain His disobedient servant,
The promising child who cannot keep His word for long.

Legalized Recognition of Christmas Day

1836	Alabama
1838	Arkansas, Louisiana
1845	Connecticut
1848	Pennsylvania
1849	New York, Virginia
1850	Georgia, Vermont
1851	California
1852	Rhode Island
1854	New Jersey
1855	Delaware, Massachusetts
1856	Minnesota
1857	Ohio, Tennessee
1858	Maine
1861	Colorado, Illinois Nevada, New Hampshire, Wisconsin
1862	Iowa, Maryland, Oregon
1863	Idaho, North Dakota
1864	Kentucky
1865	Michigan, Montana
1868	Kansas
1870	District of Columbia, West Virginia
1873	Nebraska
1875	Indiana, South Carolina
1876	New Mexico
1877	Missouri, South Dakota
1879	Texas
1880	Mississippi
1881	Arizona, Florida, North Carolina
1882	Utah
1886	Wyoming
1888	Washington
1890	Oklahoma

A CHRISTMAS CAROL

Martin Luther

Ah! dearest Jesus. Holy Child.
Make Thee a bed, soft, undefil'd
Within my heart, that it may be
A quiet chamber kept for Thee.
My heart for very joy doth leap,
My lips no more can silence keep.
I too must sing, with joyful tongue.
That sweetest ancient cradle song.

 Glory to God in highest Heaven,
 Who unto man His Son hath given.
While angels sing, with pious mirth.
A glad New Year to all the earth.

> A lovely thing about Christmas is that it's compulsory, like a thunderstorm, and we all go through it together.
>
> —GARRISON KEILLOR

Christmas Travel

Out of the 280 or so million people in the United States, roughly 60 million hit the road during December, according to the Bureau of Transportation Statistics. That means the great majority—about 220 million people—stay home for the holidays.

"Merry Christmas" in Many Languages

Afrikaans ....*Geseënde Kersfees*
Aleut ....*Kamgan Ukudigaa*
Czech ....*Velike Vanoce*
Danish ....*Glaedelig Jul!* (Glad Yule!)
Dutch ....*Hartelijke Kerstgroeten!*
Esperanto ....*Gojan Kristnaskon*
Finnish ....*Hauskaa Joulua!*
French ....*Joyeux Noël!*
German ....*Froehliche Weinachten!*
Greek ....*Kala Christouyenna*
Hawaiian ....*Mele Kalikimaka*
Italian ....*Bono Natale!*
Japanese ....*Meri Kurisumasu*
Polish .....*Wesolych Swiat Bozego Narodzenia*
Portuguese ....*Boas Festas!*
Spanish...........................*¡Feliz Navidad!*
Swahili ....*Kuwa Na Krismasi Njema*
Swedish...........................*God Jul!*
Tagalog ....*Maligayang Pasko*
Vietnamese.................*Chuc Mung Gian Sinh*
Welsh ....*Nadolig Llawen*

What Can I Give Him?
Charity at Christmastime

A Merry Christmas

from *Little Women*

Louisa May Alcott

Jo was the first to wake in the gray dawn of Christmas morning. No stockings hung at the fireplace, and for a moment she felt as much disappointed as she did long ago, when her little sock fell down because it was so crammed with goodies. Then she remembered her mother's promise and, slipping her hand under her pillow, drew out a little crimson-covered book. She knew it very well, for it was that beautiful old story of the best life ever lived, and Jo felt that it was a true guidebook for any pilgrim going the long journey. She woke Meg with a "Merry Christmas," and bade her see what was under her pillow. A green-covered book appeared, with the same picture inside, and a few words written by their mother, which made their one present very precious in their eyes. Presently Beth and Amy woke to rummage and find their little books also—one dove-colored, the other blue—and all sat looking at and talking about them, while the east grew rosy with the coming day.

In spite of her small vanities, Margaret had a sweet and pious nature, which unconsciously influenced her sisters, especially Jo, who loved her very tenderly, and obeyed her because her advice was so gently given.

"Girls," said Meg seriously, looking from the tumbled head beside her to the two little nightcapped ones in the room beyond, "Mother wants us to read and love and mind these books, and we must begin at once. We used to be faithful about it, but since Father went away and all this war trouble unsettled us, we have neglected many things. You can do as you please, but I shall keep my book on the table here and read a little every morning as soon as I wake, for I know it will do me good and help me through the day."

Then she opened her new book and began to read. Jo put her arm round her and, leaning cheek to cheek, read also, with the quiet expression so seldom seen on her restless face.

The word angel comes from the Greek term *angelos,* meaning "messenger."

"How good Meg is! Come, Amy, let's do as they do. I'll help you with the hard words, and they'll explain things if we don't understand," whispered Beth, very much impressed by the pretty books and her sisters' example.

"I'm glad mine is blue," said Amy. And then the rooms were very still while the pages were softly turned, and the winter sunshine crept in to touch the bright heads and serious faces with a Christmas greeting.

"Where is Mother?" asked Meg, as she and Jo ran down to thank her for their gifts, half an hour later.

"Goodness only knows. Some poor creeter come a-beggin', and your ma went straight off to see what was needed. There never *was* such a woman for givin' away vittles and drink, clothes and firin'," replied Hannah, who had lived with the family since Meg was born, and was considered by them all more as a friend than a servant.

"She will be back soon, I think, so fry your cakes, and have everything ready," said Meg, looking over the presents which were collected in a basket and kept under the sofa, ready to be produced at the proper time. "Why, where is Amy's bottle of cologne?" she added, as the little flask did not appear.

"She took it out a minute ago, and went off with it to put a ribbon on it, or some such notion," replied Jo, dancing about the room to take the first stiffness off the new army slippers.

"How nice my handkerchiefs look, don't they? Hannah washed and ironed them for me, and I marked them all myself," said Beth, looking proudly at the somewhat uneven letters which had cost her such labor.

"Bless the child! She's gone and put 'Mother' on them instead of 'M. march.' How funny!" cried Jo, taking up one.

"Isn't it right? I thought it was better to do it so, because Meg's initials are M. M., and I don't want anyone to use these but Marmee," said Beth, looking troubled.

"It's all right, dear, and a very pretty idea— quite sensible, too, for no one can ever mistake now. It will please her very much, I know," said Meg, with a frown for Jo and a smile for Beth.

"There's Mother. Hide the basket, quick!" cried Jo, as a door slammed and steps sounded in the hall.

Amy came in hastily, and looked rather abashed when she saw her sisters all waiting for her.

"Where have you been, and what are you hiding behind you?" asked Meg, surprised to see, by her hood and cloak, that lazy Amy had been out so early.

"Don't laugh at me, Jo! I didn't mean anyone should know till the time came. I only meant to change the little bottle for a big one, and I gave *all* my money to get it, and I'm truly trying not to be selfish any more."

As she spoke, Amy showed the handsome flask which replaced the cheap one, and looked so earnest and humble in her little effort to forget herself that Meg hugged her on the spot, and Jo pronounced her "a trump," while Beth ran to the window, and picked her finest rose to ornament the stately bottle.

"You see I felt ashamed of my present, after reading and talking about being good this morning, so I ran round the corner and changed it the minute I was up: and I'm so glad, for mine is the handsomest now."

Another bang of the street door sent the basket under the sofa, and the girls to the table, eager for breakfast.

> Somehow not only for Christmas
> But all the long year through,
> The joy that you give to others
> Is the joy that comes back to you.
> And the more you spend in blessing
> The poor and lonely and sad,
> The more of your heart's possessing
> Returns to make you glad.
> —John Greenleaf Whittier

"Merry Christmas, Marmee! Many of them! Thank you for our books; we read some, and mean to every day," they cried, in chorus.

"Merry Christmas, little daughters! I'm glad you began at once, and hope you will keep on. But I want to say one word before we sit down. Not far away from here lies a poor woman with a little newborn baby. Six children are huddled into one bed to keep from freezing, for they have no fire. There is nothing to eat over there, and the oldest boy came to tell me they were suffering hunger and cold. My girls, will you give them your breakfast as a Christmas present?"

> If you have much, give of your wealth;
> If you have little, give of your heart.
> —ARAB PROVERB

They were all unusually hungry, having waited nearly an hour, and for a minute no one spoke—only a minute, for Jo exclaimed impetuously, "I'm so glad you came before we began!"

"May I go and help carry the things to the poor little children?" asked Beth eagerly.

"I shall take the cream and the muffins," added Amy, heroically giving up the articles she most liked.

Meg was already covering the buckwheats, and piling the bread into one big plate.

"I thought you'd do it," said Mrs. March, smiling as if satisfied. "You shall all go and help me, and when we come back we will have bread and milk for breakfast, and make it up at dinnertime."

They were soon ready, and the procession set out. Fortunately it was early, and they went through back streets, so few people saw them, and no one laughed at the queer party.

A poor, bare, miserable room it was, with broken windows, no fire, ragged bedclothes, a sick mother, wailing baby, and a group of pale, hungry children cuddled under one old quilt, trying to keep warm.

How the big eyes stared and the blue lips smiled as the girls went in!

"Ach, mein Gott! It is good angels come to us!" said the poor woman, crying for joy.

"Funny angels in hoods and mittens," said Jo, and set them laughing.

In a few minutes it really did seem as if kind spirits had been at work there. Hannah, who had carried wood, made a fire, and stopped up the broken panes with old hats and her own cloak. Mrs. March gave the mother tea and gruel, and comforted her with promises of help, while she dressed the little baby as tenderly as if it had been her own. The girls meantime spread the table, set the children round the fire, and fed them like so many hungry birds—laughing, talking, and trying to understand the funny broken English.

"Das ist gut!" "Die Engel-kinder!" cried the poor things as they ate and warmed their purple hands at the comfortable blaze.

The girls had never been called angel children before, and thought it very agreeable, especially Jo, who had been considered a "Sancho" ever since she was born. That was a very happy breakfast, though they didn't get any of it; and when they went away, leaving comfort behind, I think there were not in all the city four merrier people than the hungry little girls who gave away their breakfasts and contented themselves with bread and milk on Christmas morning.

"That's loving our neighbor better than ourselves, and I like it," said Meg, as they set out their presents while their mother was upstairs collecting clothes for the poor Hummels.

Not a very splendid show, but there was a great deal of love done up in the few little bundles, and the tall vase of red roses, white chrysanthemums, and trailing vines, which stood in the middle, gave quite an elegant air to the table.

"She's coming! Strike up, Beth! Open the door, Amy! Three cheers for Marmee!" cried Jo, prancing about while Meg went to conduct Mother to the seat of honor.

Beth played her gayest march, Amy threw open the door, and Meg enacted escort with great dignity. Mrs. March was both surprised and touched, and smiled with her eyes full as she examined her presents and read the little notes which accompanied them. The slippers went on at once, a new handkerchief was slipped into her pocket, well scented with Amy's cologne, the rose was fastened in her bosom, and the nice gloves were pronounced a "perfect fit."

There was a good deal of laughing and kissing and explaining, in the simple, loving fashion which makes these home festivals so pleasant at the time, so sweet to remember long afterward, and then all fell to work.

The morning charities and ceremonies took so much time that the rest of the day was devoted to preparations for the evening festivities. Being still too young to go often to the the-

> Love came down at Christmas,
> Love all lovely, Love Divine;
> Love was born at Christmas,
> Stars and Angels gave the sign.
>
> —CHRISTINA ROSSETTI

ater, and not rich enough to afford any great outlay for private performances, the girls put their wits to work, and—necessity being the mother of invention—made whatever they needed. Very clever were some of their productions—pasteboard guitars, antique lamps made of old-fashioned butter boats covered with silver paper, gorgeous robes of old cotton, glittering with tin spangles from a pickle factory, and armor covered with the same useful diamond-shaped bits left in sheets when the lids of tin preserve pots were cut out. The furniture was used to being turned topsy-turvy, and the big chamber was the scene of many innocent revels.

No gentlemen were admitted, so Jo played male parts to her heart's content and took immense satisfaction in a pair of russet-leather boots given her by a friend, who knew a lady who knew an actor. These boots, in old foil, and a slashed doublet once used by an artist for some picture, were Jo's chief treasures and appeared on all occasions. The smallness of the company made it necessary for the two principal actors to take several parts apiece, and they certainly deserved some credit for the hard work they did in learning three or four different parts, whisking in and out of various costumes, and managing the stage besides. It was excellent drill for their memories, a harmless amusement, and employed many hours which otherwise would have been idle, lonely, or spent in less profitable society.

On Christmas night, a dozen girls piled onto the bed which was the dress circle, and sat before the blue and yellow chintz curtains in a most flattering state of expectancy. There was a good deal of rustling and whispering behind the curtain, a trifle of lamp smoke, and an occasional giggle from Amy, who was apt to get hysterical in the excitement of the moment. Presently a bell sounded, the curtains flew apart, and the Operatic Tragedy began.

"A gloomy wood," according to the one playbill, was represented by a few scrubs in pots, green baize on the floor, and a cave in the distance. This cave was made with a clotheshorse for a roof, bureaus for walls, and in it was a small furnace in full blast, with a black pot on it and an old witch bending over it. The stage was dark and the glow of the furnace had a fine effect, especially as real steam issued from the kettle when the witch took off the cover. A moment was allowed for the first thrill to subside, then Hugo, the villain, stalked in with a clanking sword at his side, a slouched hat, black beard, mysterious cloak, and the boots. After pacing to and fro in much agitation, he struck his forehead, and burst out in a wild strain, singing of his hatred of Roderigo, his love for Zara, and his pleasing resolution to kill the one and win the other. The gruff tones of Hugo's voice, with an occasional shout when his feelings overcame him, were very impressive, and the audience applauded the moment he paused for breath. Bowing with the air of one accustomed to public praise, he stole to the cavern and

ordered Hagar to come forth with a command-ing, "What ho, minion! I need thee!"

Out came Meg, with gray horsehair hanging about her face, a red and black robe, a staff, and cabalistic signs upon her cloak. Hugo demanded a potion to make Zara adore him, and one to destroy Roderigo. Hagar, in a fine dramatic melody, promised both, and proceeded to call up the spirit who would bring the love philter:

> Hither, hither, from thy home,
> Airy sprite, I bid thee come!
> Born of roses, fed on dew,
> Charms and potions canst thou brew?
> Bring me here, with elfin speed,
> The fragrant philter which I need;
> Make it sweet and swift and strong,
> Spirit, answer now my song!

A soft strain of music sounded, and then at the back of the cave appeared a little figure in cloudy white, with glittering wings, golden hair, and a garland of roses on its head. Waving a wand, it sang,

> Higher I come,
> From my airy home,
> Afar in the silver moon.
> Take the magic spell,
> And use it well,
> Or its power will vanish soon!

And dropping a small, gilded bottle at the witch's feet, the spirit vanished. Another chant from Hagar produced another apparition—not a lovely one, for with a bang an ugly black imp appeared and, having croaked a reply, tossed a dark bottle at Hugo and disappeared with a mocking laugh. Having warbled his thanks and put the potions in his boots, Hugo departed, and Hagar informed the audience that, as he had killed a few of her friends in times past, she has cursed him, and intends to thwart his plans, and be revenged on him. Then the curtain fell, and

the audience reposed and ate candy while discussing the merits of the play.

A good deal of hammering went on before the curtain rose again, but when it became evident what a masterpiece of stage carpentering had been got up, no one murmured at the delay. It was truly superb! A tower rose to the ceiling; halfway up appeared a window with a lamp burning at it, and behind the white curtain appeared Zara in a lovely blue and silver dress, waiting for Roderigo. He came in gorgeous array, with plumed cap, red cloak, chestnut love-locks, a guitar, and the boots, of course. Kneeling at the foot of the tower, he sang a serenade in melting tones. Zara replied and, after a musical dialogue, consented to fly. Then came the grand effect of the play. Roderigo produced a rope ladder, with five steps to it, threw up one end, and invited Zara to descend. Timidly she crept from her lattice, put her hand on Roderigo's shoulder, and was about to leap gracefully down when "Alas! alas for Zara!" she forgot her train—it caught in the window, the tower tottered, leaned forward, fell with a crash, and buried the unhappy lovers in the ruins!

A universal shriek arose as the russet boots waved wildly from the wreck and a golden head emerged, exclaiming, "I told you so! I told you so!" With wonderful presence of mind, Don Pedro, the cruel sire, rushed in, dragged out his daughter, with a hasty aside—

"Don't laugh! Act as if it was all right!"—and, ordering Roderigo up, banished him from the kingdom with wrath and scorn. Though decidedly shaken by the fall of the tower upon him, Roderigo defied the old gentleman and refused to stir. This dauntless example fired Zara: she also defied her sire, and he ordered them both to the deepest dungeons of the castle. A stout little retainer came in with chains and led them away, looking very much frightened and evidently forgetting the speech he ought to have made.

Act third was the castle hall, and here Hagar appeared, having come to free the lovers and finish Hugo. She hears him coming and hides, sees him put the potions into two cups of wine and bid the timid little servant, "Bear them to the captives in their cells, and tell them I shall come anon." The servant takes Hugo aside to tell him something, and Hagar changes the cups for two others which are harmless. Ferdinando, the "Minion," carries them away, and Hagar puts back the cup which holds the poison meant for Roderigo. Hugo, getting thirsty after a long warble, drinks it, loses his sits, and after a good deal of clutching and stamping, falls flat and dies, while Hagar informs him what she has done in a

song of exquisite power and melody.

This was a truly thrilling scene, though some persons might have thought that the sudden tumbling down of a quantity of long hair rather marred the effect of the villain's death. He was called before the curtain, and with great propriety appeared, leading Hagar, whose singing was considered more wonderful than all the rest of the performance put together.

Act fourth displayed the despairing Roderigo on the point of stabbing himself because he has been told that Zara has deserted him. Just as the dagger is at his heart, a lovely song is sung under his window, informing him that Zara is true but in danger, and he can save her if he will. A key is thrown in, which unlocks the door, and in a spasm of rapture he tears off his chains and rushes away to find and rescue his lady-love.

Act fifth opened with a stormy scene between Zara and Don Pedro. He wishes her to go into a convent, but she won't hear of it and, after a touching appeal, is about to faint when Roderigo dashes in and demands her hand. Don Pedro refuses, because he is not rich. They shout and gesticulate tremendously but cannot agree, and Roderigo is about to bear away the exhausted Zara, when the timid servant enters with a letter and a bag from Hagar, who has mysteriously disappeared. The latter informs the party that she bequeaths untold wealth to the young pair and an awful doom to Don Pedro, if he doesn't make them happy. The bag is opened, and several quarts of tin money shower down upon the stage till it is quite glorified with the glitter. This entirely softens the "stern sire." He consents without a murmur, all join in a joyful chorus, and the curtain falls upon the lovers kneeling to receive Don Pedro's blessing in attitudes of the most romantic grace.

Tumultuous applause followed but received an unexpected check, for the cot bed, on which the "dress circle" was built, suddenly shut up and extinguished the enthusiastic audience. Roderigo and Don Pedro flew to the rescue, and all were taken out unhurt, though many were speechless with laughter. The excitement had hardly subsided when Hannah appeared, with "Mrs. March's compliments, and would the ladies walk down to supper."

This was a surprise even to the actors, and when they saw the table, they looked at one another in rapturous amazement. It was like Marmee to get up a little treat for them, but anything so fine as this was unheard of since the departed days of plenty. There was ice cream—actually two dishes of it, pink and white—and cake and fruit and distracting French bonbons and, in the middle of the table, four great bouquets of hothouse flowers!

It quite took their breath away; and they

stared first at the table and then at their mother, who looked as if she enjoyed it immensely.

"Is it fairies?" asked Amy.

"It's Santa Claus," said Beth.

"Mother did it." And Meg smiled her sweetest, in spite of her gray beard and white eyebrows.

"Aunt March had a good fit and sent the supper," cried Jo, with a sudden inspiration.

"All wrong. Old Mr. Laurence sent it," replied Mrs. March.

"The Laurence boy's grandfather! What in the world put such a thing into his head? We don't know him!" exclaimed Meg.

"Hannah told one of his servants about your breakfast party. He is an odd old gentleman, but that pleased him. He knew my father years ago, and he sent me a polite note this afternoon, saying he hoped I would allow him to express his friendly feeling toward my children by sending them a few trifles in honor of the day. I could not refuse, and so you have a little feast at night to make up for the bread-and-milk breakfast."

"That boy put it into his head, I know he did! He's a capital fellow, and I wish we could get acquainted. He looks as if he'd like to know us but he's bashful, and Meg is so prim she won't let me speak to him when we pass," said Jo, as the plates went round, and the ice began to melt out of sight, with ohs and ahs of satisfaction.

"You mean the people who live in the big house next door, don't you?" asked one of the girls. "My mother knows old Mr. Laurence, but says he's very proud and doesn't like to mix with his neighbors. He keeps his grandson shut up, when he isn't riding or walking with his tutor, and makes him study very hard. We invited him to our party, but he didn't come. Mother says he's very nice, though he never speaks to us girls."

"Our cat ran away once, and he brought her back, and we talked over the fence, and were getting on capitally—all about cricket, and so on— when he saw Meg coming, and walked off. I

August 22 is "Be an Angel Day." Celebrate by committing acts of kindness.

mean to know him some day, for he needs fun, I'm sure he does," said Jo decidedly.

"I like his manners, and he looks like a little gentleman; so I've no objection to your knowing him, if a proper opportunity comes. He brought the flowers himself, and I should have asked him in, if I had been sure what was going on upstairs. He looked so wistful as he went away, hearing the frolic and evidently having none of his own."

"It's a mercy you didn't, Mother!" laughed Jo, looking at her boots. "But we'll have another play sometime that he can see. Perhaps he'll help act. Wouldn't that be jolly?"

"I never had such a fine bouquet before! How pretty it is!" And Meg examined her flowers with great interest.

"They are lovely! But Beth's roses are sweeter to me," said Mrs. March, smelling the half-dead posy in her belt.

Beth nestled up to her, and whispered softly, "I wish I could send my bunch to Father. I'm afraid he isn't having such a merry Christmas as we are."

> "God bless us every one!" Said Tiny Tim, the last of all.
>
> —CHARLES DICKENS
> *A CHRISTMAS CAROL*

Gifts and Cards That Give Back

Want to make a statement with your Christmas gifts this year, while helping the hungry, protecting animals and children, and promoting peace and human rights? Here's a sampling of organizations that have on-line catalogs of gift items featuring clothing, mugs, greeting cards, e-cards, artwork, calendars, edible treats, and special holiday items. All proceeds go to charity.

Choose **God's Love We Deliver** gifts to help those living with HIV: *godslovewedeliver.org.*

Purchases from the **ASPCA store** help prevent cruelty, fear and suffering in animals: *aspcaonlinestore.com* or call (888) 277-2210.

UNICEF offers a beautiful array of greeting cards, e-cards, and gifts: *unicefusa.org.*

Sierra Club campaigns for a clean environment and human rights and offers, cards, books, and other gifts: *sierraclub.org/store.*

Promote peaceful and creative activism through the **Greenpeace Store**: *cafepress.com/greenpeace.*

Support the Drew Bledsoe Foundation's **Parenting With Dignity™** by shopping on-line via their links. Merchandise, books, music, and videos for kids and parents: *shopanddonate.info/main_menu.htm*

Fifty to eighty percent of the purchase price of all products sold by the **Susan G. Komen Foundation** benefits the foundation and its fight against breast cancer: *komen.org* or (877) 465-6636.

RING OUT WILD BELLS

Alfred Lord Tennyson

Ring out wild bells to the wild sky,
The flying cloud, the frosty light;
The year is dying in the night;
Ring out, wild bells, and let him die.

Ring out the old, ring in the new,
Ring, happy bells, across the snow;
The year is going, let him go;
Ring out the false, ring in the true,

Ring out the grief that saps the wind,
For those that here we see no more;
Ring out the feud of rich and poor,
Ring in redress to all mankind.

Ring out the want, the care, the sin,
The faithless coldness of the times;
Ring out, ring out my mournful rhymes,
But ring the fuller minstrel in.

Ring out old shapes of foul disease,
Ring out the narrowing lust of gold;
Ring out the thousand wars of old,
Ring in the thousand years of peace.

Ring in the valiant man and free,
The larger heart, the kindlier hand;
Ring out the darkness of the land,
Ring in the Christ that is to be.

> Christmas is not a time nor a season, but a state of mind. To cherish peace and goodwill, to be plenteous in mercy, is to have the real spirit of Christmas.
>
> —CALVIN COOLIDGE

Some say ...
William Shakespeare

Some say that ever 'gainst that season comes
Wherein our Saviour's birth is celebrated,
The bird of dawning singeth all night long:
And then, they say, no spirit dare stir abroad,
The nights are wholesome, then no planets strike,
No fairy takes nor witch hath power to charm,
So hallow'd and so gracious is the time.

—HAMLET, ACT 1, SCENE 1

In The Bleak Midwinter

In the bleak mid - win - ter, fros - ty winds made moan,

earth stood hard as i - ron, wa - ter like a stone.

Snow was fall - ing, snow on snow, snow ___ on ___ snow,

in the bleak mid - win - ter long _____ a - go.

2. Our God, heaven cannot hold Him, nor earth sustain;
   Heaven and earth shall flee away when He comes to reign.
   In the bleak midwinter a stable place sufficed
   The Lord God Almighty, Jesus Christ.

3. Enough for Him, Whom cherubim, worship night and day,
   Breastful of milk, and a mangerful of hay;
   Enough for Him, Whom angels fall before,
   The ox and ass and camel which adore.

4. Angels and archangels may have gathered there,
   Cherubim and seraphim thronged the air;
   But His mother only, in her maiden bliss,
   Worshipped the beloved with a kiss.

5. What can I give Him, poor as I am?
   If I were a shepherd, I would bring a lamb;
   If I were a Wise Man, I would do my part;
   Yet what I can I give Him: give my heart.

I'll bring you Prosperity

The largest Christmas tip on record was given in 1876, by publisher James Gordon Bennett, Jr to a waiter at Delmonico's restaurant in New York City following Christmas breakfast. The tip was $6000, which would be worth approximately $100,000 today.

The first cash Christmas bonuses were paid out by New York financial institutions in the 1870s.

Tipping Guidelines

The tradition of giving a Christmas tip took root in England centuries ago when, the day after Christmas, on Boxing Day, the English merchant class made a point of giving boxed food and gifts to tradespeople as well as members of the servant and service class. This holiday tradition continues as an opportunity to express gratitude to those who make our lives easier through the services they render throughout the year. Tipping can be in the form of cash or a gift, and can vary depending upon how regularly you rely on a particular service. Here are some general guidelines:

Apartment building superintendent: $40–$100
Babysitter: 1–3 nights' pay
Cleaning person: 1 day's pay–1 weeks' pay
Day care worker: $15–$25
Dog walker/pet sitter: 1 day's pay
Doorman: $20–$80
Gardener: $10–$50
Hairdresser: cost of one visit
Mail carrier: up to $20
Maintenance worker: $20–$100
Manicurist: cost of one visit
Nanny/Au pair: 1–2 weeks' pay
Newspaper carrier: $10–$25
Private garbage collector: $15–$20
Private parking attendant: $10–$30
Professional fitness trainer: cost of one session

A CAROL FOR CHILDREN

Ogden Nash

God rest you merry, Innocents,
Let nothing you dismay,
Let nothing wound an eager heart
Upon this Christmas day.

Yours be the genial holly wreaths,
The stockings and the tree;
An aged world to you bequeaths
Its own forgotten glee.

Soon, soon enough come crueler gifts,
The anger and the tears;
Between you now there sparsely drifts
A handful yet of years.

Oh, dimly, dimly glows the star
Through the electric throng;
The bidding in temple and bazaar
Drowns out the silver song.

The ancient altars smoke afresh,
The ancient idols stir;
Faint in the reek of burning flesh
Sink frankincense and myrrh.

Gaspar, Balthazar, Melchior!
Where are your offerings now?
What greetings to the Prince of War,
His darkly branded brow?

Two ultimate laws alone we know,
The ledger and the sword—
So far away, so long ago,
We lost the infant Lord.

Only the children clasp His hand;
His voice speaks low to them,
And still for them the shining band
Wings over Bethlehem.

God rest you merry, Innocents,
While Innocence endures.
A sweeter Christmas than we to ours
May you bequeath to yours.

Christmas Angels

The word angel comes from the Greek word *angelos*, which means "messenger." Before the birth of Christ, these heavenly messengers proclaimed his coming and were the first to announce the arrival of the Messiah. According to the Gospel of St. Luke, the angel Gabriel visited a young virgin named Mary, who was betrothed to Joseph of the house of David, and told her that she was considered blessed among women. When Mary didn't know how to respond, the angel assured her not to fear, for she had found favor with God. Gabriel said she would conceive a child that would be called Jesus. The angel spoke great words about this holy child, telling Mary that he would reign over a kingdom that knows no end. Mary, a virgin, asked the angel how this could

come to pass. The angel told Mary that the Holy Ghost would visit her, and the blessed babe that would be born of her would be known as the Son of God.

Gabriel's news came true, and when the virgin Mary gave birth to the baby Jesus, St. Luke tells of another angel that appeared

According to a recent survey, 77 percent of Americans believe in the existence of angels.

before some shepherds tending their flocks at night. The shepherds, having never seen an angel, were clearly afraid. But the angel said, "Fear not: for, behold, I bring you good tidings of great joy, which shall be to all people." The angel told them about the birth of the savior, who they would find "wrapped in swaddling clothes, lying in a manger." At that moment, a multitude of the heavenly beings appeared exclaiming praises to God, peace on earth, and goodwill toward men. The shepherds hurried to Bethlehem, where they found Mary, Joseph, and the Christ child lying in a manger.

From this Gospel story, many legends about Christmas angels have arisen. One particular tale, found among manuscripts in an old Sicilian monastery, tells of all the creatures on earth that sought out the baby Jesus to present him with gifts. Even trees went to Bethlehem to see the holy child. The fruit-bearing trees had plenty to give, but the poor fir tree, with only evergreen needles, had nothing to offer. When an angel saw that the other trees had pushed the little fir tree away, the heavenly being invited some stars to come and sit on the fir tree's branches. Upon seeing the twinkling tree, the baby Jesus blessed it, and so began the tradition of decorating the Christmas tree to celebrate Jesus' birth.

The Miraculous Staircase

Arthur Gordon

n that cool December morning in 1878, sunlight lay like an amber rug across the dusty streets and adobe houses of Santa Fe. It glinted on the bright tile roof of the almost completed Chapel of Our Lady of *light* and on the nearby windows of the convent school run by the Sisters of Loretto. Inside the convent, the Mother Superior looked up from her packing as a tap came on her door.

"It's *another* carpenter, Reverend Mother," said Sister Francis Louise, her round face apologetic. "I told him that you're leaving right away, that you haven't time to see him, but he says. . . ."

"I know what he says," Mother Magdalene said, going on resolutely with her packing. "That he's heard about our problem with the new chapel. That he's the best carpenter in all of New Mexico. That he can build us a staircase to the choir loft despite the fact that the brilliant architect in Paris who drew the plans failed to leave any space for one. And despite the fact that five master carpenters have already tried and failed. You're quite right, Sister; I don't have time to listen to that story again."

"But he seems such a nice man," said Sister Francis Louise wistfully, "and he's out there with his burro, and. . . ."

"I'm sure," said Mother Magdalene with a smile, "that he's a charming man, and that his burro is a charming donkey. But there's sickness down at the Santo Domingo pueblo, and it may be cholera. Sister Mary Helen and I are the only ones here who've had cholera. So we have to go. And you have to stay and run the school. And that's that!" Then she called, "Manuela!"

A young Indian girl of 12 or 13, black-haired and smiling, came in quietly on moccasined feet. She was a mute. She could hear and understand, but the Sisters had been unable to teach her to speak. The Mother Superior spoke to her gently: "Take my things down to the wagon, child. I'll be right there." And to sister Francis Louise: "You'd better tell your carpenter friend to come back in two or three weeks. I'll see him then."

"Two or three weeks! Surely you'll be home for Christmas?"

"If it's the Lord's will, Sister. I hope so."

In the street, beyond the waiting wagon, Mother Magdalene could see the carpenter, a bearded man, strongly built and taller than most Mexicans, with dark eyes and a smiling, wind-burned face. Beside him,

laden with tools and scraps of lumber, a small gray burro stood patiently. Manuela was stroking its nose, glancing shyly at its owner. "You'd better explain," said the Mother Superior, "that the child can hear him, but she can't speak."

Goodbyes were quick—the best kind when you leave a place you love. Southwest, then, along the dusty trail, the mountains purple with shadow, the Rio Grande a ribbon of green far off to the right. The pace was slow, but Mother Magdalene and Sister Mary Helen amused themselves by singing songs and telling Christmas stories as the sun marched up and down the sky. And their leathery driver listened and nodded.

Two days of this brought them to Santo Domingo Pueblo, where the sickness was not cholera after all, but measles, almost as deadly in an Indian village. And so they stayed, helping the harassed Father Sebastian, visiting the dark adobe hovels where feverish brown children tossed and fierce Indian dogs showed their teeth.

At night they were bone-weary, but sometimes Mother Magdalene found time to talk to Father Sebastian about her plans for the dedication of the new chapel. It was to be in April; the Archbishop himself would be there. And it might have been dedicated sooner, were it not for this incredible business of a choir loft with no means of access—unless it were a ladder.

"I told the Bishop," said Mother Magdalene, "that it would be a mistake to have the plans drawn in Paris. If something went wrong, what could we do? But he wanted our chapel in Santa Fe patterned after the Sainte Chapelle in Paris, and who am I to argue with Bishop Lamy? So the talented Monsieur Mouly designs a beautiful choir loft high up under the rose window, and no way to get to it."

"Perhaps," sighed Father Sebastian, "he had in mind a heavenly choir. The kind with wings."

"It's not funny," said Mother Magdalene a bit sharply. "I've prayed and prayed, but apparently there's no solution at all. There just isn't room on the chapel floor for the supports such a staircase needs."

The days passed, and with each passing day Christmas drew closer. Twice, horsemen on their way from Santa Fe to Albuquerque brought letters from Sister Francis Louise. All was well at the convent, but Mother Magdalene frowned over certain paragraphs. "The children are getting ready for Christmas," Sister Francis Louise wrote in her first letter. "Our little Manuela and the carpenter have become great friends. It's amazing how much he seems to know about us all. . . ."

And what, thought Mother Magdalene, is the carpenter still doing there?

The second letter also mentioned the carpenter. "Early every morning he comes with another load of lumber, and every night he goes away. When we ask him by what authority he does these things, he smiles and says nothing. We have tried to pay him for his work, but he will accept no pay. . . ."

Work? What work? Mother Magdalene wrinkled up her nose in exasperation. Had that soft-hearted Sister Francis Louise given the man permission to putter around in the new chapel? With firm and disapproving hand, the Mother Superior wrote a note ordering an end to all such unauthorized activities. She gave it to an Indian pottery-maker on his way to Santa Fe.

But that night the first snow fell, so thick and heavy that the Indian turned back. Next day at noon the sun shone again on a world glittering with diamonds. But Mother Magdalene knew that another snowfall might make it impossible for her to be home for Christmas. By now the sickness at Santo Domingo was subsiding. And so that afternoon they began the long ride back.

The snow did come again, making their slow progress even slower. It was late on Christmas Eve, close to midnight, when the tired horses plodded up to the convent door. But lamps still burned. Manuela flew down the steps, Sister Francis Louise close behind her. And chilled and weary though she was, Mother Magdalene sensed instantly an excitement, an electricity in the air that she could not understand.

Nor did she understand it when they led her, still in her heavy wraps, down the corridor, into the new, as-yet-unused chapel where a few candles burned. "Look, Reverend Mother," breathed Sister Francis Louise. "Look!"

Like a curl of smoke the staircase rose before them, as insubstantial as a dream. Its top rested against the choir loft. Nothing else supported it; it seemed to float on air. There were no banisters. Two complete spirals it made, the polished wood gleaming softly in the candlelight. "Thirty-three steps," whispered Sister Francis Louise. "One for each year in the life of Our Lord."

Mother Magdalene moved forward like a woman in a trance. She put her foot on the first step, then the second, then the third. There was not a tremor. She looked down, bewildered, at Manuela's ecstatic, upturned face. "But it's impossible! There wasn't time!"

"He finished yesterday," the Sister said. "He didn't come today. No one has seen him anywhere in Santa Fe. He's gone."

"But *who* was he? Don't you even know his *name*?"

The Sister shook her head, but now Manuela pushed forward, nodding emphatically. Her mouth opened; she took a deep, shuddering breath; she made a sound that was like a gasp in the stillness. The nuns stared at her, transfixed. She tried again. This time it was a syllable, followed by another. "Jo-sé." She clutched the Mother Superior's arm and repeated the first word she had ever spoken. "José!"

Sister Francis Louise crossed herself. Mother Magdalene felt her heart contract. José—the Spanish word for Joseph. Joseph the Carpenter. Joseph the Master Woodworker of....

"José!" Manuela's dark eyes were full of tears. "José!"

Silence, then, in the shadowy chapel. No one moved. Far away across the snow-silvered town Mother Magdalene heard a bell tolling midnight. She came down the stairs and took Manuela's hand. She felt uplifted by a great surge of wonder and gratitude and compassion and love. And she knew what it was. It was the spirit of Christmas. And it was upon them all.

Author's Note. You may see the inexplicable staircase itself in Santa Fe today. It stands just as it stood when the chapel was dedicated almost a hundred years ago—except for the banister, which was added later. Tourists stare and marvel. Architects shake their heads and murmur, "Impossible." No one knows the identity of the designer-builder. All the Sisters know is that the problem existed, a stranger came, solved it and left.

The 33 steps make two complete turns without central support. There are no nails in the staircase; only wooden pegs. The curved stringers are put together with exquisite precision; the wood is spliced in seven places on the inside and nice on the outside. The wood is said to be a hard-fir variety, nonexistent in New Mexico. School records show that no payment for the staircase was ever made. ▧

> The devil, that rascal also known as Satan, was once an angel himself. He may have even been chief of the seraphim or cherubim order that is, until he sinned against God and was expelled from heaven.

How to Help at Christmastime and All the Year

We have provided a list below, complete with contact information, for some of the nation's largest volunteer and charitable organizations, as well as some local organizations in the larger metropolitan areas. If your area is not covered below, keep in mind you can always contact your local, hospital, community center, church, or Mayor's office for local volunteer opportunities.

United Way of America has helped create **Volunteer Solutions**, an online volunteer matching tool. Visit the site to create a profile and begin finding ways to help locally: *volunteersolutions.org*.

The National Coalition for the Homeless web site maintains an exhaustive list of shelters by state: *nationalhomeless.org*.

Many churches sponsor or take part in feeding programs and other community outreach projects. Funders of soup kitchens and shelter programs run by local churches include cities, states, corporations, institutions, and individuals. Included is a short listing of contacts. Churches often have difficulty finding overnight volunteers for their shelter programs. Unlike city-run shelters, churches usually fill their small number of beds with clients who are referred by organizations that vouch for them.

United Methodist Committee on Relief: (800) 554-8583.

For a list of volunteer opportunities at Methodist churches across the country: *new.gbgm-umc.org*.

Marble Collegiate Church (Reformed Church in America): *marblechurch.org*.

Catholic Charities USA: *catholiccharitiesusa.org* or (703) 549-1390.

Not to be overlooked is **Points of Light & Hands On Network**, which boasts more than 370 "Cares" or "Hands On" affiliates in cities across the United States. See individual cities' listings for opportunities to work at coat drives, holiday parties, and shelters. Want to host an event in your area or find your local affiliate? City Cares will help you: *handsonnetwork.org* or (404) 979-2900.

Founded in 1987, **New York Cares** is something of a volunteer clearinghouse in the Big Apple, matching volunteers with projects administered by schools, social service agen-

cies, and environmental groups to help those disenfranchised by age, illness, or poverty. At Christmastime, consider working for the large-scale New York Cares Secret Santa Program or the New York Cares Coat Drive. New York Cares partners with churches, nonprofits, and community volunteer groups to run soup kitchens and a host of other programs. Tutor a child, visit the elderly, feed the hungry—even help revitalize city gardens: *nycares.org* or (212) 228-5000.

God's Love We Deliver in New York is committed to improving the health and well-being of adults and children living with HIV, AIDS, and other serious illnesses. They are famous for their daily deliveries of highly nutritious home-cooked meals to those unable to cook or buy fresh ingredients. Special holiday meals and toys for clients are the order of the day. Their spectacular web site has a volunteer newsletter and lots of photos. Check out their special on-line catalog of gift items and delectables: *godslovewedeliver.org* or (212) 294-8100.

In the San Francisco Bay area, **Project Open Hand** runs a similar program: *openhand.org* or (415) 447-2300.

Meals on Wheels makes and delivers home-cooked nutritious meals to the needy. There are chapters all over the country. To find the one nearest you, check out the web site for the Meals on Wheels Association of America: *mowaa.org* or (703) 548-5558.

Chicago Cares has parties for recipients and get-togethers for its volunteers: *chicagocares.org* or (312) 780-0800.

The annual **Chicago Bears Coat Drive** has had twenty successful years. Drop off gently used coats at all Illinois Salvation Army locations: *chicagobears.com/community* or (773) 725-1100 (for Salvation Army locations).

Dozens of schools, churches and businesses serve as collectors for the **Philadelphia Cares Coat Drive** each year: *philacares.com* or (215) 564-4544.

Community Impact, serving the San Francisco Bay Area, organizes "done-in-a-day" volunteer projects of all sorts to make it easy for anyone to lend a hand. Each winter, they put out the call for help with end-of-year fund-

> I will honor Christmas in my heart, and try to keep it all the year.
>
> —CHARLES DICKENS,
> *A CHRISTMAS CAROL*

raising and holiday parties that CI coordinates for Bay Area youth and their families: *communityImpact.org* or (415) 541-9616.

Boston Cares started their affiliate with only two service projects; now they have over 150 projects each month. According to the web site: "Volunteers are able to return to the same project week after week if they choose or they can build a home one Saturday, read to kids the next Tuesday evening and serve meals to the homeless the following Wednesday night": *bostoncares.org* or (617) 422-0910.

The Salvation Army's web site features a guide to help you value items you plan to drop off at any of the organization's many thrift stores, and a link to their "Salvationists" web site. The Army emphasizes "the advancement of the Christian religion...of education, the relief of poverty, and other charitable objects beneficial to society or the community of mankind as a whole." Each winter, bell ringers

man "Christmas Kettles" to collect cash to provide free Christmas dinner to needy families at home and for the homeless at area centers. Volunteer at your local division through your territory's web site:

National: *salvationarmyusa.org.*
Eastern: *use.salvationarmy.org.*
Central: *usc.salvationarmy.org.*
Southern: *uss.salvationarmy.org.*
Western: *usw.salvationarmy.org.*

Every October, November, and December, the **Marine Corps Reserve Toys for Tots Program**, supported by the **Marine Toys for Tots Foundation**, collects new, un-wrapped toys in communities with Marine Corps

Reserve Units and in others through affiliated community groups. The Marines rely on local welfare agencies, church groups and other local community agencies to assist in distributing the toys to needy children. Local businesses provide drop-off locations and warehouse space. The TFT web site makes it easy to volunteer: simply scroll down the listing of states at the bottom of the home page. Click on the contact for your community, fill out the e-mail form, and a coordinator will contact you: *toysfortots.org* or (703) 640-9433.

Write a letter to Santa . . . or answer one. **Global Schoolhouse**, which focuses on collaborative learning, runs a Letters to Santa Project in which primary school students write letters on-line, and secondary students answer them as Santa: *globalschoolnet.org/ programs/santa.*

According to the **United States Postal Service** web site, "Post offices and Santa continue to work together, as they've been doing for years." In 1912, Postmaster General Frank J. Hitchcock authorized local postmasters to allow letters addressed simply "Santa Claus." To help Santa fulfill children's wish lists, contact your local post office and ask about Letters to Santa. USPS asks that you use only letter-size paper, refrain from inserting bulky items such as candy, and print your return address clearly on the envelope: *usps.com* or (800) ASK-USPS.

New York's United Hospital Fund, which hosts forums, committees, task forces, and grant programs to better the health care of New Yorkers, estimates that there now 50,000 active volunteers in New York's hospital system: *uhfnyc.org* or (212) 494-0700.

Boston's prestigious health-care institutions benefit from the volunteerism of the many college students in the area. **Partners HealthCare**, founded by **Massachusetts General Hospital** and **Brigham and Women's Hospital**, provides a good Internet starting point: *partners.org*; *massgeneral.org* or (617) 726-2000.

The **University of Texas at Houston** operates an informative web site listing their hospital affiliations: *med.uth.tmc.edu.*

Founded in 1878, **Los Angeles County+USC Medical Center (LAC+USC)** is the largest academic institution in the United States: *ladhs.org* or (323) 226-2622.

God Rest You Merry, Gentlemen

1. God rest you merry, gentlemen, let nothing you dismay, Remember Christ our Savior was born on Christmas day, To save us all from Satan's pow'r, When we were gone astray.

Refrain

O, tidings of comfort and joy, comfort and joy, O, tidings of comfort and joy.

2. "Fear not, then," said the angel,
Let nothing you affright,
This day is born a Saviour
Of a pure Virgin bright,
To free all those who trust in Him
From Satan's power and might."
Chorus

3. Now to the Lord sing praises,
All you within this place,
And with true love and brotherhood
Each other now embrace;
This holy tide of Christmas
All others doth deface.
Chorus

The **United Hospital Foundation** in Minnesota features on-line volunteer applications for adults and juniors: *unitedhospital.com/ahs/united.nsf* or (651) 241-8644.

National Public Radio provides renowned coverage of domestic and international news as well as such diverse programming as "Car Talk," "The DNA Files," and "World of Opera." Donations can be sent to NPR, 635 Massachusetts Ave, NW, Washington, D.C., 20001.

Located in East Harlem, NYC, **The Edwin Gould Academy** is a co-educational residential facility for at risk adolescents and teens. Most students are placed there by foster care or the juvenile justice system to receive guidance not previously offered to them: *edwingouldacademy.org* or (212) 828-2173.

Special Olympics is an international organization dedicated to empowering individuals with mental retardation to become physically fit, productive and respected members of society through sports training and competition: *specialolympics.org* or (800) 700-8585.

Mothers Against Drunk Driving (MADD). Considering the number of parties that take place during this season, it's important to support MADD's mission to stop drunk driving, support the victims of this violent crime, and prevent underage drinking: *madd.org* or (800) 438-6233.

Doctors Without Borders delivers emergency aid to victims of armed conflict, epidemics, and natural and man-made disasters, and to others who lack care due to social or geographical isolation: *doctorswithoutborders.org* or (888) 392-0392.

Partnership for Caring is a national, nonprofit organization devoted to raising expectations for excellent end-of-life care and increasing demand for such care: *partnershipforcaring.org* or (800) 658-8896.

Since its founding in 1976 by Millard and Linda Fuller, **Habitat for Humanity International**, a nonprofit housing organization, has built and rehabilitated over 300,000 houses with families in need. Homeowner families are chosen according to their need, their ability to repay the no-interest mortgage, and their willingness to work in partnership with Habitat. To donate money or materials, or to volunteer: *habitat.org* or (800) 422-4828.

The **Leukemia & Lymphoma Society** is the world's largest voluntary health organization dedicated to funding blood cancer research, education and patient services: *leukemia.org* or (800) 955-4572.

Known worldwide by its panda logo, **World Wildlife Fund (WWF)** is dedicated to protecting the world's wildlife and wildlands: *worldwildlife.org* or (800) 960-0993.

PBS is a private, non-profit media enterprise owned and operated by the nation's 356 public television stations. Individual donations represent the single largest source of support for public television stations around the country. Become a member: *pbs.org* or (703) 739-5000.

The International Campaign for Tibet (ICT) is dedicated to help protect and preserve the identity of the Tibetan people both within Tibet and in exile. ICT works to promote human rights and self-determination for Tibetans and to protect their culture and environment: *savetibet.org* or (202) 785-1515.

The list of organizations provided represent a small portion of all non-profits out there. We also encourage you to seek out other organizations in your area that provide services to your local community.

INDEX